TRUE
ADVENTURE
STORIES

First published in 2007 by Usborne Publishing Ltd,
Usborne House, 83-85 Saffron Hill, London
EC1N 8RT, England.
www.usborne.com

A catalogue record for this title is available from
the British Library

Printed in Great Britain

Edited by Jane Chisholm and Rosie Dickins
Designed by Mary Cartwright and Brian Voakes
Cover photograph © Digital Vision/Getty Images
Illustrations by Jeremy Gower, Gary Cross and Peter Ross

CONTENTS

TRUE SURVIVAL STORIES

Paul Dowswell

CONTENTS

Dive to disaster

Just off the coast of New Hampshire, USA, the submarine *Squalus* (pronounced Skway-lus) sailed briskly along the surface of the Atlantic Ocean. It was 8:40am, on May 23, 1939. Brand new, *Squalus* was undergoing sea-trials before she was delivered to the US Navy.

As she cut through the choppy sea, her captain, 35-year-old Lieutenant Oliver Naquin, stood face to the wind and spray on the conning tower. The previous 19 test dives he had carried out with his ship had all gone to plan, but the next procedure would test both the 56 men in his crew, and their vessel, to the limit. *Squalus* was about to carry out a practice crash-dive, an emergency procedure where a submarine under attack on the surface submerges as quickly as possible.

Naquin called down to his radio operator, ordering him to report their position to the submarine's home port of Portsmouth, New Hampshire. When he was satisfied all was well, he took one final breath of salty sea air then hit a button on the bridge which sounded the crash dive alarm. As a klaxon reverberated around the narrow ship, he hurried below to the control room, closing the upper and lower tower hatches as he climbed down into the depths of the submarine.

Inside the control room, men stood alert by dials and instruments, immersed in the intricate sequence of events that would take his submarine smoothly under the water.

Naquin called out a series of well-rehearsed commands:
"Secure all vents."
"Rig sub for diving."
"Flood main ballast tanks one and two."
"Open valves – bow buoyancy tanks."
"Main tanks three to seven – stand by."

Everything was going like clockwork. Standing next to Naquin was his chief officer Lieutenant Walter Doyle. His eyes were glued to an instrument panel known as the "Christmas tree". As all outside vents and hatches were closed, a set of indicator lights changed from red to green to show that the ship was sealed against the sea.

Naquin caught Doyle's eye and smiled briskly. The ship's ballast tanks rapidly filled with water, and *Squalus* swiftly sank to 15m (50ft). On the surface, less than a minute after Naquin had sounded the alarm, all was calm. It was as if the submarine had never been there.

Squalus settled underwater and Naquin and Doyle congratulated themselves on a successful operation. But then a strange fluttering in Naquin's ears made him startle, and he realized immediately that something terrible was happening to his ship.

An instant later, a terrified sailor looked up from an intercom and shouted, "The engine room is flooding!" Naquin gave the order to surface immediately. Compressed air hissed into the flooded ballast tanks and the stricken submarine began to rise. Her bow broke the surface, but tons of water were now cascading into the rear of the ship. The weight in her stern dragged her sharply down, and *Squalus* was swallowed by the sea.

Inside was mayhem. In flickering light, tools, fittings, even torpedoes, unhinged by the steep angle of the dive, rained down on hapless sailors. Those who had not anchored themselves in a secure perch, tumbled along the ship and into bulkheads that separated each compartment. In the flooding rear section of the submarine, soaking men struggled to escape before heavy, steel, watertight doors were slammed shut to block off the rising torrent.

Sea water now rushed into the network of interconnecting pipes that ran throughout the submarine, and jets of water spurted over men and equipment from bow to stern. Along the length of the ship, the crew struggled desperately to seal air and communication pipes.

As *Squalus* sank, another catastrophe threatened to destroy the ship before it even hit the bottom. In the forward battery room, ranks of batteries, which powered the vessel when she was underwater, were threatening to explode and blow the submarine to fragments.

Acrid blue sheets of flame flashed across the room, and spitting white arcs of electricity crackled from terminal to terminal. With extraordinary courage, chief electrician Lawrence Gainor thrust his arm into the guts of the submarine's electrical machinery and shut off the power supply. One disaster at least had been averted, but now *Squalus* had been plunged into complete darkness.

With the lights off and the contents of the submarine beginning to settle, *Squalus* continued to drift to the sea bottom in eerie silence. Inside, each man, alone in his black topsy-turvy world, waited dumbfounded for the impact to come. Every one of the crew, from Naquin downward, could only pray that when their ship hit the ocean floor it would not split open like a bursting balloon.

Squalus sinking toward the ocean floor

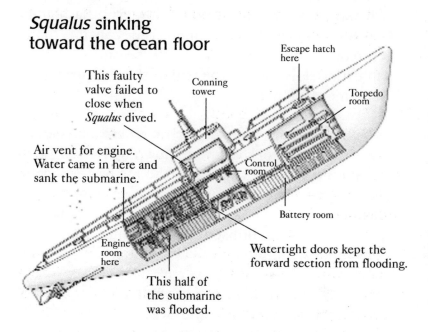

Escape hatch here

This faulty valve failed to close when *Squalus* dived.

Conning tower

Torpedo room

Air vent for engine. Water came in here and sank the submarine.

Control room

Battery room

Watertight doors kept the forward section from flooding.

Engine room here

This half of the submarine was flooded.

Four minutes passed before *Squalus* hit the bottom with a jarring thud. But the hull held firm. This much they had survived. When the ship had settled, several flashlights were brought out, and small cones of light pierced the pitch dark. Naquin and Doyle began to take stock of the situation. Water had entered via an open air vent to the engine room. Their "Christmas tree" had indicated that all vents were closed to the sea, so a fault must have developed in both the vent's closing mechanism, and the indicator light.

That much was obvious. But who of the crew was still left alive? In the ghostly glow of a flashlight, Charles Kuney, who manned the control room intercom, tried to contact all sections of the submarine. His calls to the rear of the ship met with an ominous silence.

It gradually became clear that all compartments behind the control room were now flooded, and the 26 men normally stationed in the aft battery room and both engine rooms must have been trapped and drowned. In the forward section, 33 men remained alive. Some were bruised and bleeding, but none were seriously injured.

Things could be worse, thought Naquin to himself. But one thought was bothering him immensely. He knew the only thing they could do was wait to be rescued. But the control room depth gauge showed that they were 73m (240ft) below the surface. No submarine crew had ever before been rescued from this far beneath the sea.

Naquin tried to dismiss such thoughts, and immediately instructed his crew to release emergency flares, which floated to the surface and then launched themselves into the air. A marker

buoy was also sent up from the submarine, with a telephone link to enable any rescuers to communicate with the crew. It carried a sign saying:
   "Submarine sunk here.
   Telephone inside."
If the marker buoy or flares were not spotted, the navy authorities would soon know something was wrong. *Squalus* was due to report back to base at her next scheduled call in at 9:40 that morning.

The most immediate problem the crew faced was suffocation. Not only did they need a supply of air to breathe, but there was also the danger of asphyxiation by poisonous carbon dioxide gas, which each man produced with every exhaled breath.

The ship's batteries presented another lethal danger. Chemicals inside them could react with sea water to produce deadly chlorine gas, and water inside the hull was slowly rising all the time.

To conserve their air supply, Naquin ordered his men to remain as still and as quiet as possible, with no talking or moving around unless absolutely necessary. Soda lime, a powder which absorbs carbon dioxide, was sprinkled around the ship. All hands were issued with a "Momsen Lung". This was a crude form of aqualung, shaped like a rubber hot-water bottle attached to a breathing mask. It was designed to give a sailor enough air to breathe while he tried to swim from a submarine escape hatch up to the surface. *Squalus* was almost certainly too deep for such a device to be effective, but the "Lungs" could be used by the crew for a refreshing blast of fresh air, when the air inside the hull became too foul to breathe.

In the dim haze of the emergency lights that now lit the submarine's interior, the surviving members of the crew curled up in corners. There was nothing to do now but wait.

Back at Portsmouth, the *Squalus*'s failure to contact her home base had been noted, and a rescue operation was now being mounted. By 1:00 that afternoon, a team of divers – including underwater rescue expert Charles "Swede" Momsen, inventor of the Momsen Lung – had been summoned from Washington, and were flying in by seaplane. *Squalus*'s sister ship, *Sculpin*, and several tugs were dispatched to her last reported position to assist in any rescue.

In New London, 320km (200 miles) south of Portsmouth, the US Navy rescue vessel *Falcon* also set sail to join them. *Falcon* carried a McCann Rescue Chamber – a newly invented diving bell based on an idea of Momsen's. But it had never been used in a real-life rescue before, and training exercises had been in much shallower water.

Aboard the *Squalus*, at noon, a meal of canned fruit was handed out. Sugar in the food would warm the chilly crew. Then soon after lunch something else happened to lift their spirits – they heard the dull drubbing of propeller blades above the ship. Five hours after their catastrophic dive, *Sculpin* had arrived. The surface submarine swiftly located the marker buoy sent up earlier that day, and her captain quickly made contact with Naquin via the telephone in the buoy.

But no sooner had Naquin reeled off the depth and location of his sunken submarine than the telephone line snapped, cutting *Squalus* off from the outside world. It was 7:30 that evening before rescuers located her again, after the tug *Penacook* had trawled for four hours and finally hooked an anchor onto a railing on *Squalus*'s deck.

Inside the sunken submarine the temperature was now falling rapidly to that of the sea outside – a near freezing 4°C (39°F). Dank, dripping condensation filled the already water-logged interior, and flood water inside the hull was still slowly rising. Naquin ordered a meal of beans, tomatoes and fruit to be given out. Now it was much colder, he also had blankets distributed to his weary crew. The stale air had made them drowsy and, despite their fear and the cold, many whiled away the waiting hours in an uneasy sleep.

On the surface another tug, *Wandank*, had arrived, and disturbed the dozing crew with the noise of an onboard oscillator. This device sent a high-pitched tone underwater and could be used to transmit Morse code – a form of signalling in which a series of short or longer bleeps stands for each letter of the alphabet.

When he heard the piercing ping of the oscillator, Naquin immediately ordered two of his men to the conning tower to reply. Using a small sledgehammer, they hammered out a response on the thin metal cover of the tower. Slowly and carefully, they passed on the news that only 33 of the submarine's crew remained alive.

It was not until 4:20 the next morning that *Falcon* and its rescue chamber arrived. Aboard the ship was Allen McCann, the chamber's chief designer, who was anxious to know how his invention would work at such a depth. But Momsen, who was in overall charge of the rescue operation, was still unsure of what to do. Maybe water could be pumped out of the flooded rear section, and the submarine would rise to the surface?

But no one on the surface knew why *Squalus* had sunk, so this idea was rejected. Momsen also wondered whether the men could use his "Momsen Lungs" to escape. But the submarine was too deep to be sure they had enough air to reach the top. Untried though it was, the McCann Rescue Chamber looked like the best option available.

So, by 9:30 that morning, *Falcon* had anchored herself directly above *Squalus*, and a diver was lowered down into the ocean to attach a thick guide cable to the submarine's escape hatch. The small flotilla of rescue ships on the surface had now been joined by another boat full of journalists, who had made a choppy 15-hour journey out to the scene of the accident.

The diver succeeded in placing the cable on *Squalus*, and crew in the hull cheered when they heard his footsteps on the deck. Everything was now in place, and the McCann's Rescue Chamber was about to be used for its first real rescue. Momsen picked his two best divers to go down with it. Then the chamber was carefully winched over the side of *Falcon*.

The journey from the surface down to the stricken submarine took 15 minutes. Eventually, the chamber made contact with *Squalus*'s bow, and then steel bolts anchored it in position over the

Lowering the Rescue Chamber

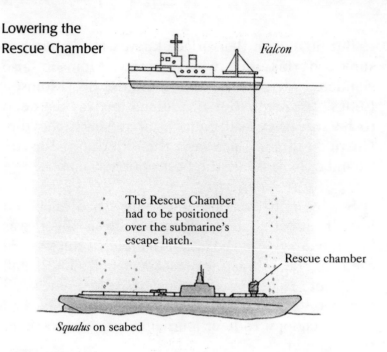

Falcon

The Rescue Chamber had to be positioned over the submarine's escape hatch.

Rescue chamber

Squalus on seabed

escape hatch. As water drained away, a sailor in *Squalus* rapidly began to turn the wheel that secured the hatch in place.

It soon swung open and a blast of foul and freezing air rushed into the chamber. The men inside looked down the hatch to see a collection of dull, drawn faces looking up at them. The divers had expected at least a cheer or welcome, and were stunned by the silence that greeted them. One of them, rather lost for words, said at last, "Well, we're here!"

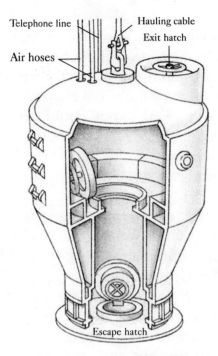

Telephone line

Air hoses

Hauling cable

Exit hatch

Escape hatch

McCann Rescue Chamber

Perhaps the survivors on the *Squalus* did not realize that the arrival of the chamber meant that their lives had been saved? Perhaps they suspected that there was still a great deal of danger to endure before they would return safely to the surface?

As soon as the hatch opened, the divers in the chamber began to pass down soup, coffee and sandwiches. Then clean air was pumped down from the surface, filling the *Squalus* with wonderful, fresh, life-giving oxygen.

21

After an hour, it was time to return to the top. Seven men climbed into the chamber. After a slow ascent, it broke surface and was hauled aboard the *Falcon*. Momsen and McCann were delighted. Their invention had worked. They could see no reason why the remaining 26 men on board the *Squalus* should not be rescued, and so the chamber was readied for another dive.

But inside the submarine all was far from well. Thick, choking clouds of chlorine gas were rising from batteries contaminated by sea water. As soon as he realized the danger, Naquin acted quickly. Before anyone could be poisoned by the gas, he led his remaining crew through to the forward torpedo room. The bulkhead door to the battery room was then sealed, to prevent any more of the gas from reaching them.

Now the survivors were crammed into an even smaller space. There was nothing to do but huddle down, as they had done before, and wait for rescue. As they waited, Naquin reflected that his crew had acted with great courage. Despite their terrible predicament, and the death of half their shipmates, no one had panicked, or disobeyed orders.

On the surface, the diving chamber was readied for its next descent. But, as soon as it was lowered into the water, the cable jammed and the chamber had to be hoisted up to the surface again. This time, the descent was made without further problems, and nine men were rescued. Another trip followed without incident, and now only eight men remained inside the stricken submarine.

By the time the divers were ready for their final descent, dusk had fallen over the ocean, and searchlights lit the chamber as it entered the water. Once again the docking with *Squalus* went smoothly, and the final eight men, including Naquin and Doyle, climbed aboard. They could hardly believe their lives were to be spared from the disaster that had overtaken their submarine. But the sea was reluctant to give up its victims and the next three hours would be quietly terrifying.

The ascent began at 8:40pm. But, halfway up, the cable hauling the chamber to the surface jammed. The two divers operating it hit the motor with their fists, then kicked it in a rage. Nothing moved. There was only one thing left to do – the chamber would have to return to the submarine, and a diver would have to be sent down to free the cable.

The 10 men waited patiently. At least there was light and air in the chamber, and they were in radio contact with the surface. But everyone knew how dangerous their situation was. Who could say for sure they would not be trapped here, as they had been aboard the *Squalus*?

Eventually, a tapping on the side of the chamber told them a diver had arrived. He quickly freed the jammed reel, and the chamber began to climb up to the *Falcon* at a steady 1.5m (5ft) a minute.

But there was more trouble in store. On the surface, in the stark light of the searchlights, men on board the *Falcon* noticed strands in the cable had begun to snap and unravel. These strands must have been damaged when the cable had jammed.

Momsen again ordered the chamber to return to the bottom of the ocean. The men inside could not believe how fate was taunting them. Again, they sat through another slow descent until a dull clang told them they had reached the submarine. Once again they endured another terrible wait until the chamber moved again. Staring down at the hatch at the bottom of the chamber Naquin could imagine his dead crew members floating in the hull, silently beckoning him to join them.

On board the *Falcon* there was feverish activity. Another diver was sent down to fasten a new cable to the chamber, but he was swiftly overcome with exhaustion and had to be pulled back to the surface.

Yet another diver entered the chilly water and descended to the sea bottom, but he too failed to attach the new cable. Divers in the 1930s wore heavy, clumsy outfits and needed to be exceptionally strong. Working in deep water was highly dangerous, and a diver could stay underwater for only a few minutes at a time. At night, such underwater work was even more difficult.

Momson was defeated. There was nothing left to do but haul the chamber to the surface with its fraying cable. Fearful that the steam pulley which usually hauled it in would pull too hard and snap the cable, Momsen and McCann decided their men would have to pull the chamber up by hand.

So, in a freezing wind, and after an exhausting day, a team of men began the laborious task of dragging the chamber to the surface, hauling and relaxing the cable with the swell of the sea.

After 10 minutes, the threadbare section of cable emerged from the sea. Momsen could see that it was as thin as a piece of string. Watching with wide-eyed trepidation, he found himself bathed in sweat, despite the cold.

With incredible delicacy, a clamp was attached to the cable below the break. Once this was done, the crew on the *Falcon* knew they had saved the men in the chamber. If the cable broke now, they had another one attached to it, to reel it in.

The chamber was eventually winched aboard at 12:38am, and the final survivors of *Squalus* staggered out on to the deck of the *Falcon*. After their 40-hour ordeal, the chill night air and stinging sea spray had never felt so wonderful.

After the ordeal

Squalus was salvaged (brought back from the sea bottom) six months after its disastrous dive. Pumped full of air, it rose to the surface with such force that its bow shot 9m (30ft) out of the water. When shown a photograph of this, American president Franklin Roosevelt joked that it looked like a sailfish leaping out of the water. Navies traditionally rename all salvaged ships, so *Squalus* became known as *Sailfish*.

Although all its electronic equipment was ruined by sea water and had to be replaced, much of the submarine was undamaged. With four of the original *Squalus* crew on board, *Sailfish* went on to fight in World War Two against the Japanese in the Pacific. *Sailfish* survived the war, and was then broken up for scrap. On Veteran's Day 1946, sections of *Sailfish*, including the bridge, conning tower and part of the deck, were unveiled as a memorial in Portsmouth Harbor, to those who had died in the submarine service. This memorial can still be seen today.

Sculpin, which had helped in the rescue operation, was less lucky in the war. In November 1943 she was sunk by Japanese Navy ships, and 21 of the crew were taken prisoner. They were placed on board a Japanese aircraft carrier, *Chuyo*, which was attacked and sunk a month later by *Sailfish*. Only one of *Sculpin*'s crew survived.

Hindenburg's hydrogen inferno

Perhaps the *Hindenburg* was the most amazing flying machine ever built. Its size alone was extraordinary. At 245m (804ft) long, it was as big as an ocean liner – a mere 23m (78ft) shorter than the Titanic.

Most of the airship was made up of 16 huge bags (called cells) of hydrogen gas. This was what lifted the craft into the sky, as hydrogen is lighter than air. Once airborne, the airship was driven along at 125kmph (78mph) by four powerful 1,100 horsepower diesel engines.

The skin of the *Hindenburg* was painted a silky, elegant grey, but on its tail were two black and red swastikas – the symbol of Germany's ruling Nazi party. Partly built with the help of state aid from the Nazis, right from the start of its life in 1936 the *Hindenburg* was seen as a symbol of German might and prestige. No sooner had it made its first few test flights than Nazi propaganda minister Joseph Goebbels ordered it to fly over every German city with a population larger than 100,000. It would arrive blaring patriotic music from loudspeakers and dropping Nazi Party propaganda leaflets on the astounded citizens below.

Barely two months after its maiden voyage, the *Hindenburg* began to fly across the Atlantic, taking passengers between Frankfurt, Germany and Lakehurst, New Jersey, an airport just outside New York City. The service was a fantastic success, despite the fact that the cost – $810 there and back – was astronomical. (In 1936 this would have been enough money to buy a new family car.)

Expensive it may have been, but the rich of Europe and America flocked to use the service. At the time, it was the only airborne crossing of the Atlantic (aircraft flights did not begin until 1939), and the journey could be done in a breathtaking two and a half days. In the 1930s the quickest transatlantic crossing by sea was at least five days.

The opulent interior of the *Hindenburg* was designed to make any passenger feel that their money was being well spent. Behind the control gondola below the nose were two decks fitted into the vast steel frame structure of the airship. On the upper deck was the passenger accommodation. Passengers slept in 25 cabins, each lined with pearly-grey linen and furnished with two bunk-style berths and hot and cold running water.

Inside the *Hindenburg*

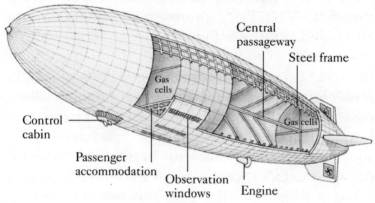

As with any exclusive hotel, shoes could be left outside the doors to be cleaned overnight by staff. There was a promenade and lounge each side of the craft, with huge observation windows which could be opened. Inside the lounge were lightweight but elegant tables and chairs, and even a grand piano made of ultralight metal covered in yellow pigskin. The dining room offered such German culinary delights as Bavarian-style fattened duckling and roast gosling, which could be washed down with the best available German wines.

The lower deck contained the crew's quarters and galley (kitchen) which used electric stoves. There was also a passenger bar with a smoking room, which contained one electric lighter. Connected to the rest of the airship via an airlock, it was designed to allow passengers to drink and smoke without any danger of igniting the hydrogen gas which kept the *Hindenburg* airborne. Everything was designed to be both lightweight and luxurious, although some corners were cut in order to keep down the weight. The cabins, for example, were separated only by foam-covered fabric, and there was only one shower between 50 or so passengers.

The first year's transatlantic service in 1936 had been a great success, and each of the *Hindenburg*'s 10 flights had been fully booked. Airships were notoriously vulnerable to bad weather, so the service only ran in the spring and summer months, and began again the following year in May.

The first Atlantic crossing of 1937 began on the evening of May 3, at Rhein-Main World Airport, Frankfurt. Aboard were 42 passengers and 55 members of the crew. This first flight was not a sell-out, but the Deutsche Zeppelin-Reederei company that operated the *Hindenburg* was confident their service would still bring in a profitable supply of rich and famous passengers throughout the summer.

With all his passengers and luggage aboard, Captain Max Pruss ordered: "*Schiff hoch!*" ("Up Ship!") and the ground crew released the mooring ropes that kept the *Hindenburg* anchored to the ground. To mark the first flight of the year, a brass band in blue and yellow uniforms stood on the runway playing the German national anthem, and other patriotic tunes.

Free to float upward, the airship's seven million cubic feet of hydrogen gas lifted the craft into the air. It rose so gently the passengers on board only realized they were taking off because the waving figures on the ground were gradually getting smaller. One journalist who had taken an earlier flight was so impressed by the smoothness of the airship's flight, he wrote: "You feel as though you were carried in the arms of angels". Sometimes passengers who boarded the evening flight and retired to their cabins did not even realize the airship had taken off. With good reason, the Zeppelin company boasted that no passenger had ever suffered from air sickness.

When the airship reached 90m (300ft), huge wooden propellers began to turn on the four diesel engines, drowning out the band below. With a thunderous drone the *Hindenburg* vanished into the night. On that evening in May the weather was perfect, and passengers spent a thrilling hour before supper watching the gleaming beacons of small towns and huge pools of city lights roll leisurely past beneath them.

Captain Max Pruss sat confidently in the forward control gondola. A veteran World War One zeppelin commander, he had spent many years flying these huge airships. Among his responsibilities was ensuring the *Hindenburg* remained stable in its flight. A roll of more than two degrees from the horizontal could send wine bottles crashing from tables and play havoc with food preparation in the galley.

With Pruss in the dimly lit cabin was Ernst Lehmann, director of the Zeppelin company. Both men had every faith in their magnificent craft, but were all too well aware that the safety record of huge airships over the previous few years had been unsettling. In 1930, Britain's R101 had crashed in flames, and almost all on board had been killed. The USA had had no more success mastering these aerial giants. Two similarly huge craft had both crashed within two years of their maiden flights.

Still, despite the problems other nations faced, Germany had built themselves an enviable reputation as the only country capable of flying airships without disaster. For six years now, there had been a successful passenger service. Germany had been the first to invent and make widespread use of these craft, so perhaps their experience gave them the edge.

But even the *Hindenburg* had potentially fatal flaws, not least the lighter-than-air gas that German airships used to lift themselves into the sky. Hydrogen is the same element that burns so fiercely on the Sun. If a gas cell leaked, a mere spark could cause an inferno.

The *Hindenburg* flew confidently on, over the Atlantic. When the airship reached Newfoundland, Pruss took her down low to give his passengers a closer look at the beautiful icebergs lining their way.

The flight reached New York on May 6 – three days after leaving Frankfurt. Strong winds had delayed their arrival time at Lakehurst by several hours. Crossing over Manhattan, the *Hindenburg* flew so low over the Empire State Building that passengers could clearly see photographers on top of the skyscraper snapping away.

It was early afternoon when the *Hindenburg* approached Lakehurst Airfield. But storms were brewing, and Captain Pruss decided that the winds were too strong and that the *Hindenburg* should wait a while before she landed. Below, family and friends who had turned up to meet passengers at Lakehurst at the scheduled arrival time of 6:00am, faced an even more frustrating wait.

Among them were scores of newspaper, newsreel and radio journalists, eager to record the arrival of this modern-day wonder. The *Hindenburg* was still a tremendous novelty, and a large crowd of onlookers had gathered to watch her land.

Eventually the decision was made to bring the *Hindenburg* in. At 5:00pm a siren at the airfield sounded, to summon the 92 navy and 139 civilian airfield personnel needed to handle the mooring lines that would hold the *Hindenburg* to the ground. At 7:10pm the airship began its final descent. Aboard, the passengers gathered with their luggage in the ship's lounge, ready to disembark down the airship's main stairway.

Watching the scene was radio reporter Herb Morrison, broadcasting live for a Chicago radio station. His report began peacefully enough. As the airship loomed out of the evening sky and drifted down to her mooring mast, he told his listeners:

"Here it comes, ladies and gentlemen, and what a sight it is. . . a thrilling one, a magnificent sight. The mighty diesel engines roar."

But death was waiting for the *Hindenburg* at Lakehurst. At 7:25pm, just forward of the mighty tail fins, two crewmen inside the ship noticed a sight that turned their blood to ice. Lurking in the middle of the number four gas cell was a bright blue and yellow ball of curling fire.

On the ground, observers could see a faint pink glow inside the ship, which gave it a curiously transparent quality. One witness likened it to a Japanese lantern. Then, within a second, the entire cell exploded with a muffled WHUUMP, and fierce flames burst out of the silver canvas covering. A huge, orange fireball erupted into a gigantic mushroom of smoke and flames, and began to devour the still airborne vessel.

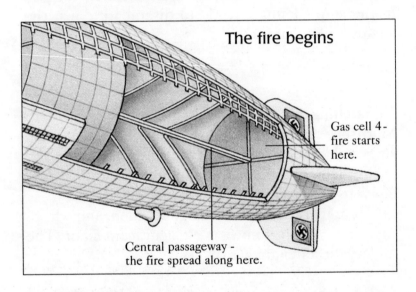

The fire begins

Gas cell 4 - fire starts here.

Central passageway - the fire spread along here.

Herb Morrison watched aghast, his voice turning from awed appreciation to hysteria.

"It's burst into flame! Get out of the way! Get out of the way, please!" he begged the aircrew on the ground. "This is terrible. This is one of the worst catastrophes in the world! The flames are 500 feet into the sky."

Most of the passengers and crew were in the front section of the *Hindenburg*. Their first inkling of the disaster was seeing figures below scatter in panic over the wet ground, which had suddenly taken on a garish red glow. Within seconds the ship was lurching wildly, and flames engulfed the passenger decks.

In the control cabin, the initial explosion was so muffled one officer just thought a landing rope had broken. But then frenzied shouts of "FIRE" alerted the crew to the true situation. As hydrogen gas at the rear of the *Hindenburg* burned away, the airship sank, bottom down. As the stern fell, the bow rose, and passengers preparing to jump from the open observation windows saw the ground, and their hopes of survival, reel rapidly away from them.

The sharp angle of the *Hindenburg* turned the central passageway that ran from its tip to its tail into a chimney, and a huge tongue of flame shot out from its nose – "like fire from a volcano," said one witness. Crewmen in the forward section clung hopelessly to metal girders but, scorched by the heat, they lost their grip and fell into the swirling inferno below. But as the fire from the rear spread throughout the body of the *Hindenburg*, and gas burned off more evenly, the ship began to level off, and settled on the ground with a ghastly hiss.

Herb Morrison could not bear to watch.

"Oh, the humanity! Those passengers. I can't talk, ladies and gentlemen. . . Honest, it is a mass of smoking wreckage. . . I am going to step inside where I can't see it. Listen folks, I am going to have to stop for a minute because I have lost my voice."

Then, to the amazement of onlookers, people began to stumble and crawl from the raging conflagration. With extraordinary bravery, ground crew, who seconds before had been running for their lives, turned around and plunged into the burning wreck, "like dogs after rabbits," said one eyewitness.

Those who survived generally owed their lives to where they were on the ship. The crewmen in the tail, who had seen the fire start, dashed to safety when the stern hit the ground. Flames and heat always rise upward, so those under the explosion were in the best position to make a successful escape.

Some passengers used their wits to save themselves. One, a professional acrobat, hung from a window sill as the ship rose and fell, only jumping when he knew he could survive the fall. Another, finding himself lying on the ground surrounded by burning rubble, burrowed under the wet sand to safety.

Others were just lucky. One dazed, elderly woman simply walked down the ship's retractable steps, which had been broken open by the violent landing. One crew member survived the flames when a water tank burst open above him, momentarily dousing a clear path away from the blaze.

One passenger, Leonhard Adelt, realized the airship was ablaze when it was 37m (120ft) from the ground. As he contemplated jumping, the ship suddenly hit the ground with a tremendous impact which threw him and his wife against the floor. Tables and chairs piled up and blocked their exit, so they leapt 6m (20ft) from the open window onto the soft sand below. Then everything went black as the airship crashed down on top of them.

Surrounded by burning oily clouds, they clawed through the white-hot metal struts and wires. Too numb with shock to feel pain, they struggled to find a route to safety. Adelt remembered, "It was like a dream. Our bodies had no weight. They floated like stars through space."

Another passenger on the *Hindenburg*, Margaret Mather, remembered that when the ship stood sharply on its stern, she was thrown into a corner and several other people landed on top of her. Then flames, "bright red and very beautiful," blew into the passenger area. Mather watched others jump from the windows, but she was too stunned to move, imagining she was in "a medieval picture of an inferno". Then a loud cry brought her quickly to her senses. "Aren't you coming?" shouted one of the ground crew who had dived into the flames, and out she ran.

In the control cabin beneath the ship, 12 officers and men were the last to leave. As white-hot metal crashed around them, they forged a path through the flames. Captain Pruss attempted to rescue a trapped crewman, and burned his face badly. Ernst Lehmann had more severe injuries. He emerged from the wreckage a human torch. Onlookers beat the flames from his burning clothes as he mumbled, "I don't understand it." The future of his company had gone up in smoke. He died early the next morning.

The whole airship had been engulfed by fire in a mere 32 seconds. Because the *Hindenburg* was a world-famous phenomenon, and because journalists had been present at Lakehurst in such great numbers, pictures and stories of the catastrophe quickly flashed around the world. People everywhere were stunned by the tragedy, much as they had been by the sinking of the Titanic, 25 years earlier.

The flames died down leaving only a burning hot skeleton of twisted metal. Altogether 35 people on board the *Hindenburg* died. One man on the ground was also killed. But perhaps the most extraordinary aspect of the disaster was that 62 passengers and crew were able to walk out of the wreckage and live to tell the tale.

After the ordeal

Herb Morrison's radio report had been recorded, and was broadcast all around the world. His horrified account can still be heard today whenever newsreel footage of the disaster is shown in television documentaries.

In Germany, members of the ruling Nazi party saw the *Hindenburg* as a symbol of the power and prestige of the Third Reich. They were quick to blame the disaster on sabotage, but could produce no serious evidence to back this up. A board of inquiry set up to investigate the fire concluded it was caused by a hydrogen gas leak ignited by a spark of static electricity.

Hugo Eckener, chairman of the Zeppelin company, described the airship's fire as "the hopeless end of a great dream". The notion of huge airships carrying passengers across the ocean died in the flames at Lakehurst. To this day, airships remain an airborne gimmick, suitable mainly for advertising slogans.

The cause of the fire is still controversial. Some scientists are convinced that it was not hydrogen that caught fire, but the fabric skin of the *Hindenburg*. There are several compelling reasons why this might be the case. Hydrogen burns with a blue or neutral flame, whereas witnesses compared the *Hindenburg* fire with "a fireworks display", with bright red and orange flames. The *Hindenburg* did not drop to the ground immediately, which also suggests that it was something else burning, rather than hydrogen.

The skin of the *Hindenburg* was coated with a mixture of ground metals and other chemicals, to ensure it was taut and durable. This chemical combination was highly inflammable, and has recently been described by one scientist as "a respectable rocket propellant".

Despite their insistence that sabotage was the cause of the disaster, the Nazis quietly changed the skin coating of the *Graf Zeppelin*, the sister ship of the *Hindenburg*, to a less combustible mixture. This airship, which was also lifted into the air by hydrogen gas, went on to fly over a million miles without incident.

Some aeronautical scientists think that the use of hydrogen, both as a fuel and as a way of lifting aircraft, has been unfairly overlooked in the development of aerial transportation because of the *Hindenburg* disaster. They point out that hydrogen is no more inflammable and dangerous than petrol (gasoline) which is used all the time.

Captain Bligh's boatload of trouble

William Bligh, captain of Royal Navy vessel *Bounty*, began the morning of April 28, 1789, tied to a mast on the deck of his ship. He was surrounded by his mutinous crew, who even now were wondering whether or not to kill him.

The leader of the mutineers was Bligh's own second in command, Fletcher Christian. The two men had once been close friends and perhaps it was this that had saved Bligh's life. Christian had argued fiercely with his fellow mutineers to stop them from killing their hated captain on the spot.

The man tied to the mast was a curious mixture of qualities. He was honest, and had a strong sense of duty, but he also had an arrogant manner and terrible temper. He often subjected the ship's officers, especially Christian, to public and withering contempt.

The mutiny had been a long time coming, and a more sensitive man than Bligh would have taken steps to avoid it. The *Bounty* was on an around-the-world trip to deliver breadfruit plants from the Pacific to slave plantations in the West Indies, where slave owners thought it would provide cheap food for their slaves. After a harsh and difficult voyage the *Bounty* had recently spent a lengthy stopover in Tahiti. Here the crew had enjoyed the beautiful island, and the company of its friendly inhabitants.

They found it difficult to adjust to life back at sea. Bligh, in turn, felt his crew were slacking, and that harsh discipline was called for to lick them back into shape. In the days before the mutiny his unthinking persecution of Christian had intensified, and he continued to humiliate him in front of the crew. Christian resented this intensely, and his loyalty to Bligh withered away. The Captain's bullying manner also lost him the respect of the crew he once addressed as "a parcel of lubberly rascals".

Now, Christian and the mutineers intended to sail back to Tahiti and the life they had enjoyed there, but first there were two serious problems to resolve. Firstly, what would they do with Captain Bligh? Secondly, not all the crew had mutinied – 18 men had remained loyal to their captain, and they were currently under guard, elsewhere on the ship.

Despite all the resentment he felt toward him, Christian could not bring himself to kill Bligh.

Neither could he kill those of the crew still loyal to their captain. These were fellow shipmates for whom he bore no ill-will at all. So a compromise was reached. Bligh, and all those loyal to him, would be placed in a small boat loaded with supplies, and set adrift.

So, on that April morning, Bligh and 18 of his crew were ushered off the *Bounty* at bayonet point and crammed into the ship's launch, so tightly there was no room to lie down. On the boat were five days' food and drink, and a handful of navigation instruments.

The sailors on the launch pulled away from the *Bounty*, with the catcalls and jeers of the mutineers ringing in their ears. Ahead lay a very uncertain future. Christian had given them a fighting chance, at least, although he had also put their lives in very grave danger.

Gradually the *Bounty* grew smaller and smaller, until it became a small speck and drifted over the horizon. Aboard the tiny launch Bligh and his loyal crew felt terribly alone in the huge ocean. Their boat had oars and sails, but it was designed for short journeys between ship and shore, and was in no way suitable for the kind of voyage they would have to undertake in order to survive. For now, the weather was calm, but these were often stormy seas.

Overcrowding on the boat also made a bad situation worse. Bligh's men were cold, wet and very hungry, they could not sleep and were constantly having to bail out water in order to keep the launch afloat. As well as this, some of the men felt deep resentment towards Bligh, and thought he was to blame for the mutiny. For many on the boat, their loyalty to him was based not on respect but fear of the law. They knew that being part of the mutiny meant they could never return home. At best they would face a lifetime in exile, and at worst a military execution in the form of slow strangulation at the end of a rope and yard-arm.

Bligh knew, more than any of them, the dangers ahead. He had sailed these waters some years previously with Captain Cook, the famous Pacific explorer, who had been killed by hostile islanders. He also knew that their nearest safe haven was a Dutch trading colony at Kupang, on the island of Timor. Here they could rejoin a British ship and make their way home. But Timor was 6,300km (3,900 miles) away. A journey like that could take 50 days.

Bligh decided their first priority would be to find food for the journey, so he directed the launch toward Tofua Island, which the *Bounty* had passed on the night before the mutiny. He knew nothing of the islanders there, and had to trust to luck that they would be friendly.

The launch landed on a sandy cove on the island. The men waded ashore, grateful to be away from their cramped little boat. They rested as best they could, and looked for food, but all they could find was a handful of coconuts. On the next day, islanders came to visit them. At first these people were friendly, and traded food for the men's uniform buttons and beads. But when they realized Bligh's crew were castaways, and not a party from an armed ship, their attitude changed, and they became more aggressive.

Bligh realized too late that a kind of hostile standoff had developed. He and his men needed to leave the island as soon as possible, but they all knew their leaving might provoke an all-out attack. The longer they stayed, the worse the situation became. More islanders were arriving at the beach. They gathered together in groups and began to knock stones together in a sinister, intimidating manner. Bligh had seen islanders behave like this shortly before Captain Cook had been killed.

Beckoning his crew to gather around, Bligh spoke to them in a low voice.

"I fear these savages mean to kill us," he told them bluntly, "and will do so as soon as we intend to leave. I propose that we wait until nightfall, and slowly fill our boat. Then we will tell our friends here we shall sleep at sea and trade with them again in the morning."

Bligh's crew were all too aware of the danger they were in, and looked to their captain to save them. All agreed that this was the best thing to do.

As dusk fell over the beach, the launch was duly loaded. But, as the men inched toward their boat, the islanders all stood up and again began to knock stones together. When Bligh's men reached the water's edge the stones rained down on them, and the islanders charged toward them.

The ship's quartermaster, John Norton, was closest to the shore, and he bravely turned to face their attackers. He was immediately struck down and savagely clubbed to death, but his great courage saved his crewmates. The rest of them reached the launch, and cast off to sea. As the islanders followed through the shallow surf, Bligh and others distracted them by throwing clothes overboard. This ruse worked successfully. The islanders stopped to pick the clothes up, and the boat sailed out of reach to the safety of the open sea.

Bruised and terrified by their encounter, the crew sailed on in grim silence. They passed other lush, green islands along their route back to Timor, but no one dared even suggest they land there.

The food on board the launch was pitifully inadequate for such a long journey. There were a few coconuts brought from the Tofuans, a supply of ship's biscuits, which were rapidly going rotten, a few pieces of salted pork, 12 bottles of rum, and several barrels of fresh water. Bligh realized that to have any chance of survival they would have to ration their provisions very carefully.

He stood on the stern of the launch and addressed his weary crew.

"God willing, if we complete our journey successfully, we shall be at sea at least 50 days. Our provisions must last this amount of time. We have but a miserable ration, and I can give each man here no more than one ounce of biscuit, and one quarter pint of water a day. I ask each of you to swear before the others that he will accept the ration I give him, and not ask for more."

Something in Bligh's manner must have reassured the crew. They all agreed that this is what they would do, and sailed away from Tofua in good spirits. Two days passed and the launch made good progress, but on the third morning away from Tofua, the sun rose red and fiery – a sure sign that a storm would soon be upon them. But that morning brought more ill luck. As they passed the island of Waia, two large sailing canoes set out after them, causing great alarm in the launch. The men were sure that if the canoes caught up with them, they would be killed and eaten.

Bligh took firm command, ordering six of his strongest men to the oars, and they rowed for their very lives. For three terrible hours the canoes gave chase, only to abandon their quarry in the early afternoon. But no sooner had the crew recovered from that harrowing chase, than the weather came to torment them. The wind began to howl and torrential rain tore into the fragile boat.

That night was the worst one yet. Bligh noted in his log: "We bore away across the sea where the navigation is but little known (and) not a star could be seen to steer by." Everyone was too cold and miserable to sleep, and when dawn finally came the storm showed no sign at all of receding. But it was now that Bligh showed the kind of leadership and humanity that would have saved him from his mutiny had he the sense to realize it before. He cheerfully instructed his crew to remove their clammy, sodden clothes and dip them in the sea, which was warmer than the rain. When they had done this, he gave each man a spoonful of rum, which also warmed them up.

Bligh knew that sailors cast away in open boats often become listless and apathetic. They curl up motionless, as static as their changeless circumstances. He was determined to prevent this from happening, and knew the only way to survive would be to keep the crew alert and in good spirits. To do this he divided the men into two groups. While one group sailed the boat, the others lay in the bottom and rested. The two groups switched every four hours. This routine gave shape to what would have been an otherwise endless, shapeless day.

To fill the long hours Bligh turned the highlight of each day – the handing out of rations at 8:00 in the morning, noon and sunset – into a lengthy ritual. The daily amount for each man was weighed out on a scale made from two coconut halves. A couple of pistol bullets served as weights and the whole process of preparing each portion kept the entire crew entranced.

Biscuits were always on the menu, but Bligh kept his small supply of salted pork as an occasional surprise, delighting the boat by handing out tiny strips. Bligh invited his men to make their paltry rations last as long as any ordinary meal. He always broke his food into tiny morsels, and ate it very slowly.

Occasionally someone on the boat caught a seabird that was unlucky enough to land on the side of the boat. This was swiftly killed and then shared out in a naval custom called "Who shall have this?" Firstly, the bird was cut into small sections. Then, one man pointed to a piece and called out, "Who shall have this?" Another man, who had his back to them all, called out a name at random, and the piece went to that man. In this way arguments about who ate which part of the bird were avoided. In his log, Bligh wryly noted the "great amusement" in the boat, when he was given such unappetizing parts as the beak or feet to eat.

Between meals, Bligh would often entertain his men with stories about earlier voyages, and encourage them to share their own adventures. He was a brilliant navigator and seaman, and drew maps to show them where they were going, and how far they had gone. Each night he led his crew in pitiful prayers, saying, "Bless our miserable morsel of bread, and may it be sufficient for our undertaking."

When spirits sagged he would try to lift them with cheerful sailors' songs. He also had the shrewd idea of getting the crew to sew together a patchwork Union Jack flag from bundles of signal flags that had been thrown into the boat when they had left the *Bounty*. Bligh told them they would use this flag to identify themselves when they sailed into Kupang port, in

Timor. But making the flag also kept the men occupied, and was a symbol of hope for the end of their ordeal.

For 15 days the tiny boat pushed on through an unbroken spell of bad weather, and the men were constantly drenched and freezing. In his log book, which Bligh diligently continued to fill in, he recorded:

"We were so covered with rain and salt we could scarcely see. Our appearances were horrible. I could look no way, but I caught the eye of someone in distress. Extreme hunger was now too evident. The little sleep we got was in the midst of water, and we constantly awoke with cramps and pains in our bones."

Worse was to come. 21 days into the voyage, Bligh realized their biscuits were not going to last. The ration would have to be cut from three to two portions a day. Although the men took the news without protest, the decision, he wrote in his log, was like robbing them of life.

Then, at last, on May 24 he was able to write: "For the first time, during the last fifteen days, we experienced comfort and warmth from the sun." They sailed on for another week, and although Bligh's well thought out routine kept them going, the crew were visibly fading before his eyes. Then, nearly a month into the journey, they began to notice signs of land. Not island land, which they had avoided for fear of their lives, but the huge continent of Australia, then known as New Holland.

At first they saw a broken branch float by. Then many birds began to wheel around the launch. Best of all, there were clouds, which always form around the coast, which could be constantly seen on the western horizon. When the sound of the sea roaring against rocks was carried toward them by the wind, the men knew they would soon be standing on solid ground.

On May 28, their small boat passed carefully through the Great Barrier Reef, just off the Australian coast. The continent was still almost entirely unknown and almost certainly hostile territory. At the time, there was only one European settlement there, far to the south at Port Jackson (now called Sydney). Despite their fear of what might await them, Bligh's crew were euphoric at the prospect of reaching dry land. Later that day, they made landfall at a deserted, offshore island that Bligh christened Restoration Island. Many of the men were so weak they could hardly stand, but others tore at oysters on the rocks, guzzling down as much as they could eat.

Later that day, in a copper pot taken from the *Bounty*, they cooked a delicious stew with oysters and pork. Each man had a whole 500ml (one pint) to himself. As they ate, Bligh cautioned his men not to eat the fruits and berries that surrounded them. All were unknown to Europeans, and some were bound to be poisonous. But many of the men chose to ignore his warning. On board the boat Bligh's expert seamanship and gallant attempts to keep the crew in good spirits commanded a grudging respect, but on land old resentments boiled up, and the good relationship he had built up with his crew evaporated.

Bitter quarrels broke out as Bligh tried to keep discipline among his men. He felt it was his duty to return everyone safely to England, and the only way to do this was to share everything they had between them. The sicker members of the party, especially, needed to be looked after. But other men, starved and exhausted after so long at sea, felt that everyone should look after themselves. They wanted to eat what they found, rather than contributing to a common share.

Bligh sensed his command was rapidly slipping from him, and took desperate measures, drawing his cutlass on one seaman who had spoken to him rebelliously. "I determined (decided) either to preserve my command or die in the attempt." he wrote in his log.

Order was restored, but it was a miserable, quarrelsome party that set sail again, on the second leg of their journey to Timor. Despite the stopover, their health and morale soon plummeted. By the time land was sighted again, after another 10 days at sea, most of the men were too weak even to cheer.

So, on June 14, 1789, 47 days after the mutiny, the Union Jack was unfurled and Bligh's launch sailed into the port of Kupang. Bligh's log entry for that day is full of justifiable pride in his achievement, but he also wrote:

"Our bodies were nothing but skin and bones, our limbs were full of sores, and we were clothed in rags. In this condition, the people of Timor beheld us with a mixture of horror, surprise and pity."

From Kupang they were taken to Java, and then homeward on a Dutch merchant ship. The journey to England took nine months. Several of Bligh's men, weakened by their ordeal, died on the way. The arguing continued too. Bligh had two of his crew imprisoned aboard the ship for daring to suggest he had falsified expenses forms.

Yet, despite his obvious faults, the irascible Captain William Bligh had taken his men on an extraordinary 6,300km (3,900 miles) journey to safety, and so ensured that 11 of them would live to see their families again.

After the ordeal

Bligh returned to England to discover he was the father of twin girls, and to write a best-selling account of the *Bounty* mutiny. In the summer of 1790, he faced a court-martial for the loss of his ship, but was acquitted.

The following year he was given a new ship, *HMS Providence*, in which he returned to Tahiti and successfully transported breadfruit plants to the West Indies, where they still grow today. From this period onwards, his nickname among fellow officers was "Breadfruit" Bligh.

In 1808 he was appointed governor of New South Wales in Australia. His attempt to restrict the import of alcohol to the territory led to an army mutiny against him, and he was imprisoned by his own troops for 26 months. This did not harm his navy career, and by the time he retired he had reached the rank of rear admiral. He died, aged 63, in 1817.

Fletcher Christian, who led the *Bounty* mutiny, fled with nine other mutineers and 18 Tahitians to remote and uninhabited Pitcairn Island, in the South Pacific. Here, Christian and most of his companions met violent deaths, squabbling among themselves or with the Tahitians. Today Pitcairn Island is inhabited by 18 families. Between them they have only four surnames, three of which – Christian, Young and Brown – belong to the original mutineers.

Other members of the mutineers, who decided to stay in Tahiti, were eventually arrested when Royal Navy ships visited the island. Several of them were hung from the yard-arm of a ship – the traditional navy punishment for mutiny.

The story of the mutiny on the *Bounty* continues to fascinate, and books on the subject have been in print for the last two hundred years. At least three films have been made of the episode, most recently in 1984 as *The Bounty*, starring Anthony Hopkins as Captain Bligh and Mel Gibson as Fletcher Christian.

Bligh and Christian's different approaches to leadership and their men is now a common case study in management training courses, and the events of the mutiny are available as a computer game.

Adrift in the desert

A small plane cut a lonely path through the pitch black sky. The drone of its single propeller engine was the only sound for miles around. Below, in the impenetrable darkness, lay the vast Sahara Desert. Inside the tiny cockpit were French pilot Antoine de Saint-Exupéry and his co-pilot André Prévot. It was the day before New Year's Eve, 1935.

The two men had been flying in the dark since leaving Benghazi, Libya, four hours before. They were attempting to fly from Paris to Saigon faster than anyone before them. If they broke the record before the end of the year, they would win a prize of 150,000 francs.

Their immediate destination was Cairo, Egypt, but they should have arrived there by now. Blinking back exhaustion Saint-Exupéry, known to all as Saint-Ex, offered Prévot another cigarette. Both men strained their eyes trying to find some landmark to tell them where they might be. But beyond the wing-lights there was nothing to be seen. Surely, below, there was a river or a city that would give them a clue to their whereabouts?

They flew on, but as every minute passed, it became more and more obvious that they were completely, hopelessly lost. The fuel indicator on the aircraft instrument panel was now worryingly low, and a night-time landing in the desert would almost certainly be fatal.

Then, all at once, both men spotted a lighthouse blinking in the darkness.

"Thank Heavens! We must be near to the coast. Let's go down to have a closer look," said Saint-Ex.

"Once we get a view of the coastline, I'll soon find us on the map," said Prévot, "and if I can't, then we'll just have to land next to the lighthouse and ask for directions."

The engine strained as Saint-Ex dived, but an instant later the plane smashed quite unexpectedly into the ground, shuddering violently as it plunged across the desert. Inside the cockpit the two men braced themselves for a violent, fiery death. But no explosion came, and the plane rapidly screeched to a grinding halt.

"What the devil happened there?" yelled Prévot, angrily.

"Never mind that," said Saint-Ex, "Let's get out of here before this thing blows up."

The two men scrambled out into the cool night

air and ran for their lives. When they had put a safe distance between them and the plane, they stopped to catch their breath.

"Any broken bones?" asked Saint-Ex. "No? Me neither. You're shaking like a leaf. . ."

"Just bruises by the feel of it," said Prévot. "Anyway, as I said, what the devil happened there?"

Saint-Ex looked embarrassed.

"We must have been a lot closer to the ground than I thought. But here we are. Frankly, I can't believe we're still alive, and the plane didn't go up in a fireball. Maybe there's just no fuel left in the tank?"

Prévot smiled. He too was beginning to realize how lucky they were to have survived.

"You're right, let's be grateful for that! Look at all these black pebbles on the ground. They're just like ball bearings. We must have rolled along on them. Now, where's that lighthouse?"

But all around, as far as their eyes could see in the darkness, there was only desert. They listened for the comforting crash of waves lapping on a beach, but there was nothing to hear but the sound of their own breathing.

Prévot spoke first.

"That lighthouse we both saw wasn't really there, was it?"

"Doesn't look like it," said Saint-Ex, who was beginning to feel quite worried. "Probably a reflection from the instrument panel on the cockpit window. We're in serious trouble aren't we?"

The two men wandered back to the plane to check their supplies. Their water container had burst when they crashed, its contents instantly soaked up by the arid ground. Between them they had a small flask of coffee, half a bottle of wine, a slice of cake, a handful of grapes and an orange.

As the excitement of the crash wore off, they both began to feel cold.

"Pretty chilly for a desert," said Prévot.

"Pretty bad place for a crash, my friend," said Saint-Ex. "Boiling hot by day. Freezing cold by night, and not a soul for miles around. We'll be better off inside the plane for the moment."

They crawled into the wreckage and waited for dawn. Neither man could sleep, for each was too well aware of their desperate situation. If they had crashed on a recognized flight path, they might be rescued within a week. But they were completely lost – specks in a huge, sprawling desert. A search party could spend six months looking, and still not find them. In the heat of the day, their supplies might last five hours.

"Here's a comforting thought," said Saint-Ex wryly. "I've been told that out in the desert a man can live less than a day without water. I'm beginning to wonder if we'd have been better off dying in the plane when it hit the ground."

A slow dawn broke over the desert. As the darkness receded, Saint-Ex and Prévot were able to see exactly what sort of landscape they had landed in. All around, rising and falling in dunes and hillocks, black pebbles stretched to the horizon. Not a single blade of grass grew from the ground. Their surroundings looked as lifeless as the moon.

The two men studied their map forlornly. Even if they knew where they had landed, it would have offered little comfort. The vast emptiness of the desert was punctuated by the occasional symbol for a well or religious institution, but these map markings were few, and far apart.

"It looks pretty hopeless," said Prévot, "but maybe there's an oasis nearby?"

Saint-Ex nodded encouragingly. "Let's head off east before it gets too hot – we were supposed to be going that way anyway – and see what we can find."

The two wrote their plan for the day in huge 10m

(30ft) letters in the ground, in case anyone should find their plane when they were gone. Then they headed off, scraping their boots behind them to leave a trail away from the plane.

They soon forgot to mark their route, and after five hours of aimless wandering, they began to worry that they would not be able to find their way back. The day wore on and the sun rose higher in the sky. The fierce desert heat grew more intense and drained the strength from their bones.

In the shimmering light, mirages too began to torment them. A faint shape on the horizon could be a fort or a town. A dark shadow to the west could be vegetation. Lakes glistened in the distance, but all vanished when Saint-Ex and Prévot approached.

After six hours, both men were terribly thirsty, and had begun to despair. Then Prévot shouted with glee, "Look! Tracks!"

"They're ours," said Saint-Ex glumly, "I just know they are. Let's follow them anyway, they'll lead us back to the plane."

Sure enough, after another hour stumbling along the path the tracks made, they returned to the wreckage of their aircraft. Here they had left the last of their supplies, and they both drank down the coffee and wine with no thought for the next day.

"Let's make a fire," said Saint-Ex. "It'll keep us warm at night, and someone may even spot it."

They dragged a piece of wing away from the plane, and doused it with left-over fuel. It burned with a thick, black smoke, which stood out starkly against the cloudless sky. Staring into the flames, Saint-Ex imagined he could see his wife's face looking up at him sadly from under the rim of her hat. Prévot too thought of his family and the grief his death would cause them.

"I do have some good news," said Saint-Ex, breaking the silence between them. "I've found some animal burrows nearby. Something is managing to live in this wilderness, so perhaps we can too. Let's set some traps before we go to bed, and maybe we'll have something to eat for breakfast."

Next morning they emerged from the plane feeling full of hope. Both men had slept better and now they were determined to beat the desert. They began by wiping dew off the wings of the plane with a rag. But when they wrung out the rag, it yielded only a spoonful of liquid – a sickening mixture of water, paint and oil.

Prévot had a plan.
"They'll definitely have noticed we're missing by

now, so I'm going to stay with the plane today. It's too hot to go walking about, and I want to be here to light a fire in case a search plane goes by."

"Good idea," said Saint-Ex. "You do that and I'll go out foraging."

So that was what they did.

Saint-Ex's traps were empty, but he did notice tracks nearby. Saint-Ex thought the three-toed imprint was probably a desert fox's footprint. He followed the tracks until he came to the animal's feeding ground – a few miserable shrubs, with tiny golden snails among the branches. Saint-Ex was not desperate enough to try the snails – anyway they were probably poisonous, and there was no water to be had from the shrubs, so he pressed on.

As he trudged through the desert, thirst began to torment him terribly. The mirages began as well, although in his weakening state Saint-Ex wondered if these were actually hallucinations instead. First there was a man standing on a nearby ridge. That turned out to be a rock. Then he saw a sleeping Bedouin – a desert tribesman. Saint-Ex rushed over to wake him, but that turned out to be a tree trunk. It was so ancient it had turned into smooth black charcoal.

Then Saint-Ex saw a desert convoy of Bedouins and their camels moving along the horizon, and called out to an empty desert. A monastery, a city, the sound of the sea, all followed in succession. But Saint-Ex was a philosophical character. Rather than be tormented by these illusions, he allowed himself to be amused. In his dazed state, he staggered around laughing at his circumstances.

The mirages faded with the dwindling light. As night fell despair swept over him again, and Saint-Ex cried out in anguish. But his voice was no more than a hoarse whisper. He returned empty-handed to Prévot, who had lit a fire to guide him back.

In the flickering light, Saint-Ex saw something that made his heart leap. Prévot was talking to two Bedouins – they had been saved! These men would give them food and water, and guide them out of the wasteland. But as Saint-Ex approached, the two strangers vanished. There was only Prévot after all.

That night they tore a parachute into six sections and laid it on the ground, covered with stones to stop the wind from blowing it away. This, they hoped, would catch the morning dew and provide them with much-needed water. They shared their final orange and sank into an exhausted sleep.

❖

At dawn the next morning, Saint-Ex and Prévot wrung out nearly two litres (four pints) of water from the parachute fabric into the only container they had – an empty fuel tank. Unfortunately their pitiful supply of life-saving water was horribly contaminated, both by the lining of the tank and by the chemicals used to treat the parachute. It was a queasy yellow-green and tasted utterly revolting. After trying to force down a couple of mouthfuls, both men spent the next fifteen minutes retching into the sand.

After the spasms subsided they sat together feeling terribly ill.

"There's no chance of a search party finding us here, is there?" said Saint-Ex. "Let's head into the unknown. I know we're probably walking to our deaths, but at least there's a chance we'll find something or someone to save us. If we stay here, we're just submissively accepting our fate. And while I'm strong enough to walk I don't want to do that."

Prévot shrugged. "You're right. What can I say? Let's go."

They headed east, for no particular reason, trudging slowly through the sand, saying nothing to save their parched throats. Baked by the scorching sun, his head held down to avoid the tormenting mirages, Saint-Ex felt as if he were pursued by a wild beast, and even imagined he could feel its breath on his face.

The day dragged by in a mildly delirious way, and by dusk they were so thirsty they could not swallow, and a thin crust of sand covered their lips. But, as the sun set, Prévot saw a lake glistening on the horizon. Saint-Ex knew this was an hallucination, but his friend was so sure what he could see was real he went staggering off to investigate.

How a mirage works

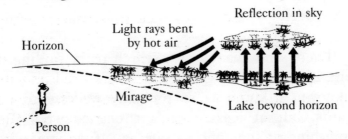

Mirages happen when light rays from objects beyond the horizon are reflected in the sky and bent by layers of warm air. This makes things look closer than they are.

Saint-Ex did not have the strength to stop him, and lay down in the sand and stones and began to daydream about the sea. He fell into a strange dream-like state and stared half-awake at the moon, which seemed to loom unnaturally large above him. Then he saw lights bobbing in the darkness – a search party come to rescue them. A figure loomed out of the dark. It was Prévot. The lights had been another hallucination. The two men began to bicker at each other's stupidity, their patience with each other and their terrible situation finally boiling over. Then they stopped.

"I guess we're in a bad way," said Prévot, his voice a hoarse rasp.

"I'm desperate for a drink," Saint-Ex whispered through cracked lips. "There must be something we can slake our thirst on."

The two had taken a medicine box with them, and now they eyed the small bottles of liquid inside it. There was alcohol, ether and iodine – all extremely poisonous ointments. Saint-Ex tried the ether, but it stung his mouth sharply. The alcohol made his throat tighten alarmingly, and one whiff of the brown iodine was enough to convince him he could not drink it.

Darkness fell, and the two men faced their first night away from the shelter of the plane. Deserts are very hot during the day, but at night they can become extremely cold, and a fierce wind swept over the two men.

"Would you believe it. I'm freezing to death!" said Saint-Ex, his teeth chattering with the cold.

Lacking any other shelter, he dug himself a shallow trough and covered his body with sand and pebbles, until only his head stuck out. As long as he stayed still, the cold did not cut into him.

Prévot tried to keep warm by walking around and stamping his feet. For him, a hole in the ground reminded him too much of a grave. He also built a feeble fire with a few twigs, but this soon went out in the fierce wind.

That night seemed to last forever, and when dawn finally came it brought no dew. But at least they could still speak.

"We're OK," Saint-Ex reasoned. "When people are dying from thirst and exhaustion, their throats close up and a bright light fills their eyes. Neither of us is in that state. Let's hurry off, and travel as far as we can before the sun gets too hot."

Prévot nodded weakly. By now both men were so dehydrated they had ceased to sweat. As the sun rose in the sky, they became weaker and started to see flashes of light before their eyes. A French folksong *Aux marches du palais* (*To the steps of the palace*) played constantly in Saint-Ex's head, but he could not remember the words.

They struggled on but their legs began to buckle beneath them. The black pebbles that surrounded their plane had now given way to soft sand, which was even more difficult and exhausting to walk through. The horrible taste in their parched mouths was a constant torment. The urge to lie down in the warm sand and sink into an endless sleep was overwhelming.

But, as they stopped to rest, a sixth sense told Saint-Ex that life was nearby. A ripple of hope passed between him and Prévot, "like a faint breeze on the surface of a lake", as he recalled. Ahead were footprints. Then they heard noises. Saint-Ex saw three dogs chasing each other. But Prévot did not see them. He shook his head sadly. It was another illusion.

But it wasn't. Both men saw a Bedouin on a camel. They began shouting and waving as loudly and as wildly as their exhausted bodies would let them. But the Bedouins did not see or hear them and disappeared behind a sand dune. Then another Bedouin appeared and approached them. To the delirious men he looked like a god as he walked toward them.

Fortunately for Saint-Ex and Prévot, the Bedouin knew exactly what to do with two parched, exhausted men. Placing his hands on their shoulders he made them lie in the sand. Then he unstuck their parched lips with a feather and gently rubbed mashed lentils into their gums, to moisten their mouths. Only then did the Bedouin allow them to drink from a basin of water, but he had to keep pulling back their heads, as if they were two over-eager dogs, to stop them from drinking too fast. Later, Saint-Ex would reflect that he and Prévot were lucky not to have stumbled on some source of water on their own. In their delirious state they would have drunk frenziedly, and split their parched mouths open.

The two exhausted airmen were placed on a camel and taken to a nearby settlement. From here they were able to make their way back to France. Their final desperate gamble had paid off. Against all expectations, they had survived for over three days in the fierce heat of the desert.

After the ordeal

Following his desert rescue, Saint-Ex spent the rest of his life continuing to enhance his reputation as both a writer and pioneer aviator. His experiences in the Sahara are recounted in his book *Terre des hommes* (*Wind, Sand and Stars*) published in 1939, on which this survival story is based. His most famous book, *Le Petit Prince* (*The Little Prince*) was published in 1943. It tells the story of a pilot who crashes in the Sahara, and who meets a magical prince.

During World War Two, Saint-Ex served in the French Air Force, and fled to New York when France was defeated. Returning to serve in the Free French

Forces in North Africa, he was shot down and killed during a reconnaissance flight over Corsica. He was 44. After his death, the French government awarded him the medal of *Commandeur de la Légion d'Honneur*.

Shark's breakfast

One summer morning in 1991, a 32-year-old surfer named Eric Larsen sat astride his surfboard just off the coast of Davenport Landing, in Northern California. Alone in the water, he was enjoying a moment of solitary tranquillity, and waiting for the next big wave to ride to shore. A cool breeze blew across the surface toward the beach, and he felt glad he was wearing a rubber wetsuit and gloves to keep him warm.

But as his thoughts ebbed and flowed, he noticed a huge shape drift effortlessly beneath his board. Larsen immediately snapped out of the pleasant haze he had allowed himself to drift into, and instinctively knew he was in serious trouble. But before he could begin to swim to the safety of the shore, he felt a sharp, agonizing pain. His left leg had been seized by a Great White shark.

Capable of growing to a terrifying 5.34m (17.5ft) long and weighing an unstoppable 2,043kg (4,500lb), Great Whites are one of the most feared creatures on Earth, and in their watery world they are unrivalled. So perfect are these ocean killers they have ruled their domain since the days of the dinosaur.

Ordinarily, a Great White hunts fish, dolphins and seals, and will even chew a lump from a much larger whale. Maybe the one that was now gnawing Larsen's leg mistook him for a seal, because Great Whites usually leave humans alone.

Why he was being attacked was the last thing on Eric Larsen's mind. Without thinking, he thrust his hands down to wrench away the shark's massive jaw. The Great White's jaws slowly eased apart and Larsen was able to free his damaged leg. But, in an instant, the shark took another lunge at him, and snapped both his arms into its jagged mouth.

The Great White's triangular, serrated-edge teeth, are the biggest of all fish, and no other animal on Earth has a more powerful bite. Right now Larsen was getting a horrific close-up of this mighty mouth in action. He could see the ugly gums of the shark, whose upper jaw protruded from its uplifted snout as it bit into him. The eye sockets were eerily sightless. When it attacks, the Great White protects its eyes with a thin membrane, which closes over the eye like an eyelid at the moment it strikes.

Larsen was an exceptional athlete, and he would now need to summon every ounce of his great physical strength to save his life. First, he managed to pull his shredded right arm out of the shark's mouth, and then smashed his fist into the animal's belly. The startled shark released its grip and launched itself at Larsen's surfboard. The unfortunate surfer was tethered to his board by a short cord, and for a few frantic seconds he was dragged through the water.

Then, as quickly as the shark had arrived, it was gone. Calm once again settled on the bay, and Larsen was faced with the task of returning to the shore with extremely serious injuries. His left leg and both arms were shredded to the bone, and he was bleeding badly from the main artery on his left arm. For many people, such injuries received out at sea would be a virtual death sentence, and Eric Larsen had mere minutes left to live. But Larsen had one great advantage – he was a trained paramedic, and he knew exactly what he needed to do.

First of all, he had to stay calm, although the temptation to panic and get out of the water before the shark returned was overwhelming. But instead, he swam slowly to his surfboard and struggled up onto it. Then he began to paddle slowly towards the beach. Larsen knew if he swam as quickly as possible, his heart would beat faster, and he would lose even more blood.

He also knew that the more he bled, the more likelihood there was that the shark would return. In fact, a large amount of blood in the water might even lure other cruising sharks to his board, and the luckless surfer would be devoured in a horrific feeding frenzy. Fortunately, his measured pace paid off, and he eventually reached the safety of the beach.

Being on dry land was a start, but now Larsen had to find some other people to help him, and quickly. Leaving a sickly red trail of blood in the sand, he began to drag himself painfully up the beach towards a row of nearby houses, calling out for help as he made his way.

Clamping his right hand firmly over the spurting gash of his bleeding artery, Larsen also held both arms above his head, because he knew that wounds bleed less when blood has to flow against gravity. But the effort of reaching the beach and dragging himself up it had exhausted him.

Larsen had also lost so much blood that he was beginning to lose consciousness. Just as he reached the edge of the row of beach houses, his head began to spin and he collapsed. But fortunately two local residents who had heard his cries had come running out toward him.

Larsen saw his last chance for survival and summoned his final reserves of strength. He explained exactly what his two helpers needed to do. His shredded leg needed to be raised above his body, to slow down the flow of blood. He also showed one of the helpers where to press down on his arm to restrict the flow of blood still pouring from his artery.

One of the locals rushed off to call for an ambulance, which arrived within minutes. He was in a hospital accident and emergency department within an hour. Here, he was given a blood transfusion and five hours of surgery to repair the shredded muscle and bone of his arms and leg. Then he was patched up with 200 stitches. Eric Larsen, shark's breakfast, had survived to tell the tale.

After the ordeal

Despite his brush with death, Eric Larsen returned to surfing as soon as he recovered from his injuries. He credited his escape from one of nature's most ferocious predators to the unpleasant taste of his rubber wetsuit.

Although shark attacks are rare (less than 260 people in the world have been attacked by Great Whites since records began), the local surfer's website for Davenport Landing reports that shark sightings are common there. One sailboarder named Mike Sullivan fell from his board in 1995, and watched it being ripped to pieces by a shark. Fortunately he was not attacked himself.

Lucky 13

On April 11, 1970, *Apollo 13* blasted off from Earth on the 13th minute of the 13th hour of the day. More superstitious men would not have volunteered for the flight, which was the third manned mission to the Moon. But if commander Jim Lovell and his fellow astronauts Fred Haise and Jack Swigert had any lingering doubts about tempting fate with unlucky thirteen, these would have probably vanished by the evening of the second day of the trip. Things were going so smoothly that mission headquarters on Earth radioed up: "The spacecraft is in real good shape as far as we are concerned. We're bored to tears down here."

But on the morning of the third day, completely out of the blue, there was a violent explosion. In the ship's tiny command module the crew heard a loud bang and felt their craft shudder. An alarm instantly filled the capsule and control panel lights began to flash, indicating that vital power and oxygen supplies were quickly ebbing away.

The astronauts had been trained to keep a cool head, but their first radio message to NASA*

* America's space agency, the National Aeronautics and Space Administration.

headquarters in Houston, sounded distinctly edgy.

"OK, Houston, we've had a problem."

They'd had an extremely serious problem. An oxygen fuel tank in the service module had blown up when a heating switch malfunctioned. The trouble this caused immediately doubled when another oxygen tank linked to it also emptied out into space.

It was April 13, after all.

Apollo 13's crew, and the staff at Mission Control, Houston, were baffled. At Houston, where every aspect of the flight was being closely monitored by hundreds of technicians, instrument readings suggested that either the explosion should never have happened, or it should have destroyed *Apollo 13*.

There was no emergency procedure for an accident like this. When NASA had designed the Apollo craft, many safety features and back-ups had been built in. But engineers had assumed that anything which knocked out two oxygen tanks would also destroy the spaceship. One senior engineer summed up their thinking should this happen: "You can kiss those guys goodbye." But now it had happened, and the astronauts were still very much alive.

Apollo 13

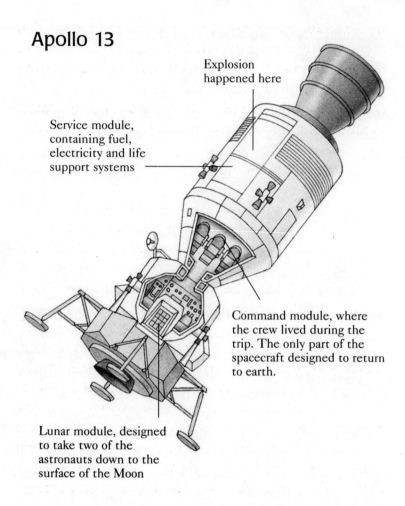

Explosion happened here

Service module, containing fuel, electricity and life support systems

Command module, where the crew lived during the trip. The only part of the spacecraft designed to return to earth.

Lunar module, designed to take two of the astronauts down to the surface of the Moon

At first Lovell, Swigert and Haise did not understand just how seriously their ship had been damaged. But 14 minutes after the explosion, Lovell noticed a cloud of white gas drifting past a command module window. This was the oxygen leaking away from the ruptured tanks. So much had been lost that it now enveloped the ship like a ghostly mist. This was the moment when Lovell realized how serious their situation actually was. They were alive, for now, but *Apollo 13* could become their tomb, locked in a perpetual orbit between Earth and the Moon.

But not everything was stacked against them. Lovell, who was 42, was on his second trip to the Moon, and was America's most experienced astronaut. He had a reputation for good fortune.

"If Jim fell into a creek," said a colleague, "he'd come up with a trout in his pocket."

Even now, he was living up to his reputation. Lovell's crewmates were both new to space, but he could not have hoped for a more appropriate crew to cope with the disaster that had overtaken them. Swigert, the command module pilot, was an expert in Apollo emergency procedures. Haise, the lunar module pilot, had spent 14 months in the factory that built his spacecraft. He knew this complex machine inside out.

As *Apollo 13* continued on its Moon-bound trajectory (flight path), instruments indicating power and oxygen supplies were now all heading stubbornly to zero. The command module, which was to have been their home for the journey between Earth and the Moon and back, was close to breaking down. Lovell estimated it would only keep his crew alive for another two hours.

To survive they needed to move to the lunar module, the part of the spacecraft designed to take two men down to the Moon's surface. This part of *Apollo 13* had so far remained unused on this flight. Now hundreds of switches had to be operated to bring it to life.

Aboard the dying command module, Lovell, Swigert and Haise began these painstaking procedures. Complex coordinates were logged into the lunar module's navigation computers, life support systems whirred into operation, and instrument panels flickered into life. The men worked as quickly as they dared. A mistake made here could prove fatal.

Finally, the lunar module was ready. When they had shut down the fading power supplies of the command module, the three moved through a small connecting tunnel and into its cramped interior. But there was still much work to do. All three men now realized there was no chance of landing on the Moon. Their only priority was to get home alive. Swigert insisted their first task aboard the lunar module should be to make a course correction. This would shorten their journey by a day or so, taking them around the Moon and back to Earth as quickly as possible. So, five hours after the explosion, Lovell ignited the lunar module's engines in a 30 second burst. Everything went as intended. Now their supplies would not have to last so long.

With one essential task out of the way, the crew took a long hard look at their circumstances. The lunar module had been designed to keep two men alive on the Moon for two days. Now it would have to keep three men alive for the four-day return journey to Earth.

Lovell and the crew discussed each aspect of their supplies. The situation looked like this:

Their power supplies (electricity and fuel) were looking bad. This was where the explosion had done most damage.

Their food supply was also looking grim. Most of their food was freeze-dried and needed hot water to make it edible. With their power supplies so low, hot water was no longer an option.

Their water supplies were also bad. All the craft's electronic systems generated heat, and without water to cool them they would overheat and fail.

The only thing they had in good supply was air. There should be enough of that at least, until *Apollo 13* returned to Earth.

The simple truth was that the most durable items on board *Apollo 13* were the crew. They would be able to keep going on little or no heat or fuel for longer than any of the ship's equipment. The next four days were going to be very uncomfortable. Unfortunately, there was barely enough power to supply their essential equipment, so heating their spacecraft became an expendable and unaffordable luxury.

As the temperature dropped, the astronauts began to suffer. They were ill-equipped for such chilly conditions. All their clothes and sleeping bags were designed for the usually warm environment of their spaceship, and were made of thin, light materials. (The two spacesuits they carried for the Moon walk were too bulky to be worn inside the craft.) The three men improvised as best they could, wearing two sets of underwear under their jumpsuits, and Moon boots on their freezing feet.

The gnawing cold chilled the moisture in their breath, and a clammy dampness settled on the spacecraft's interior. They began to feel, said Lovell, "as cold as frogs in a frozen pool." Balanced on a knife edge between survival and death, they could not even sleep for more than two or three hours at a time, as cold and anxiety kept them awake.

Although they were constantly hungry, thirst was less of a problem. This is because astronauts do not feel the need to drink when they are in space. To conserve as much water as possible, the men drank virtually no water at all for the rest of the flight, but as a result they all became dangerously dehydrated.

On the night of April 14, *Apollo 13* swung around the Moon. Inside, the crew made preparations for a second course correction, which would again involve firing the powerful lunar module engine. These engines were designed to land the module on the Moon, not propel the whole spacecraft, so once again very careful calculations had to be made. As Lovell ran through the complex procedures needed to ignite the engines, he noticed Swigert and Haise busy photographing the Moon's surface from an observation window. Suddenly, he felt very angry.

"If we don't make this next move correctly," he snapped, "you won't be getting your pictures developed."

Swigert and Haise were unrepentant.

"You've been here before," they said. "We haven't."

Despite Lovell's concerns the engine ignited successfully, and *Apollo 13* was placed on a trajectory that would take her right back to Earth. But now there was more to do than just sit and wait for their spacecraft to return. Although there was definitely enough air to get them all home, another huge problem was brewing with their breathing. Every time they breathed out, the astronauts exhaled carbon dioxide. This is a poisonous gas and, in an enclosed area such as a small spacecraft, it can soon build up to fatal levels.

All spacecraft are equipped with filters to remove this deadly carbon dioxide, but those in the lunar module were only designed to cope with the poisonous gases of two men. With all three astronauts currently occupying the lunar module, the filters were failing, and levels of the deadly gas were building up.

Back on Earth, NASA technicians had anticipated this problem, and had come up with an ingenious solution. There were several carbon dioxide filters in the now empty command module. These could be removed, placed in an airtight box, and used to filter the air aboard the lunar module.

There were no airtight boxes on board *Apollo 13*, so the crew would have to improvise. They gathered together storage bags, adhesive tape, air hoses and the covers of *Apollo 13* flight manuals. As instructions were radioed up, the three men managed to cobble together a working filter, and the danger of carbon dioxide poisoning was averted.

Flight to disaster

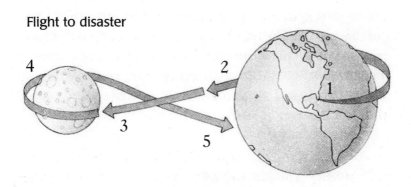

1. Lift off, April 11
2. Leave Earth's orbit, April 11
3. Oxygen tank explodes, April 13
4. Fly around Moon and return to Earth, April 14
5. Prepare for re-entry, April 17

Four days after the explosion, *Apollo 13* was now well on the way home. Looking at the Earth looming ever larger in the spacecraft window, Swigert felt they were "whistling in like a high-speed train".

But the closer they got to the end of their journey, the nearer they got to its most dangerous and challenging moments. Floating in a cold spaceship, on a free-fall flight between the Moon and the Earth, was a walk in the park compared to the flight corrections they would have to make in order to land safely back on Earth.

For any spaceship, crippled or not, re-entry into Earth's atmosphere is one of the most dangerous parts of any space mission. If *Apollo 13* approached the atmosphere at too steep a flight path, then it would burn up like a meteor. But if the flight path was too shallow, it would bounce off into space, like a pebble skimming across the surface of a lake.

Not only that, but *Apollo 13* was designed to land in the Pacific Ocean. (Until the space shuttle's first flight in 1981, all American spacecraft landed at sea.) Rescue vessels had to be close at hand. To land in the right place, Lovell and his crew would have to direct their stricken craft to a minute area above the Earth's atmosphere, known as the "entry corridor". At the end of this 800,000km (500,000 mile) journey, they would have to hit a spot only 16km (10 miles) wide.

All these moves had to be made using the lunar module's engine – a task it was never designed to perform. Then the crew would have to go back into the damaged command module for the final stage of re-entry. This was the most worrying aspect of the whole procedure.

As they got closer to Earth, Lovell went back into the command module. It had been unused for four days, and was now as cold as a refrigerator. Water droplets had formed on every surface – from seat harnesses to instrument panels. Lovell wondered if the electronics behind the panels were just as waterlogged. The command module was so low on power their equipment would have to work the first time – assuming it worked at all.

As Earth loomed even larger, Swigert prepared for re-entry. As pilot of the command module, it was his job to drop them into the atmosphere at the correct angle. Because they were using the lunar module engines rather than the command module to do most of the flight changes here, a whole new set of re-entry calculations and position shifts had to be prepared.

Mission Control technicians worked these out in teams and radioed the instructions up to the spacecraft. Normally, NASA would take three months to prepare such a schedule. This one they put together in two days.

In 1970 fax machines were still too primitive to be worth installing in spacecraft, and emails were unheard of. Swigert took two hours to write down all the hundreds of operations in full. He was not confident he would understand abbreviations in the tense moments to come. But Swigert performed brilliantly. Running though the life-or-death procedure for the first and only time, he placed *Apollo 13* exactly where it needed to be.

As re-entry drew closer, the damaged service module was finally uncoupled from the rest of *Apollo 13*. The astronauts were able to have a close look at it as it slowly drifted away from them. Here they saw for the first time the damage the explosion had done. One whole side of the module was missing, and the site of the explosion was a tangle of wires dangling from a ruptured metal cavity.

Now only the lunar module remained to be cast away. As they watched it drift off from *Apollo 13*, all three astronauts felt a strong surge of affection for the craft which had returned them safely from the Moon. Then they prepared for the most dangerous 20 minutes of their lives.

Aboard the command module, the astronauts were buffeted and rocked in their cold, damp seats, as the tiny craft began to enter the upper layers of the Earth's atmosphere. Bizarrely, it seemed to start

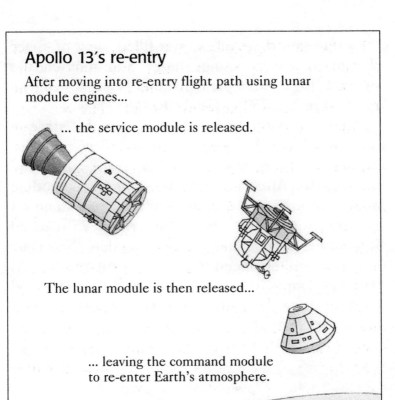

Apollo 13's re-entry

After moving into re-entry flight path using lunar module engines...

... the service module is released.

The lunar module is then released...

... leaving the command module to re-enter Earth's atmosphere.

raining inside the capsule, as the upheaval of re-entry loosened the water droplets behind the instrument panels.

As they plummeted down, the heat shield behind their backs began to glow red hot as it made contact with the gradually thickening air of Earth's atmosphere. Through small observation windows, the crew saw their black, star-filled view of space change to a fiery orange haze. The temperature surrounding their craft quickly reached an extraordinary 2,750°C (5,000°F).

If all went well, they should survive this stage of the journey, which would last around three minutes. But one final uncertainty lay between survival and catastrophe. After re-entry, the command module would drop through the atmosphere like a stone for a further few miles. Then, when *Apollo 13* reached 7,000m (23,00ft), parachutes would slow their craft to a safe landing speed, before they hit the sea. As they lay strapped to their seats, each man worried whether there was enough power left to operate these parachutes.

Re-entry is always a time when communications between ground control and spacecraft are broken. The turbulence of the air around a blazing hot spacecraft makes it impossible to transmit radio signals. While *Apollo 13* dropped to Earth, the technicians of Mission Control waited anxiously by their consuls. Three minutes passed, then four.

Then Swigert's voice crackled over the radio, muttering a terse "OK". They had survived re-entry. Four minutes later, a rescue helicopter in the landing zone relayed live TV pictures to Houston, confirming that the parachutes on board the command module had opened. *Apollo 13* astonished the world by landing only 5.5km (3.5 miles) away from its rescue ship – the closest to date of any Apollo flight.

After the ordeal

One American newspaper remarked of *Apollo 13*'s close escape, "Never in recorded history has a journey of such peril been watched and waited out by almost the entire human race." The three astronauts arrived back at their home town of Houston, Texas, to find US president Richard Nixon waiting to greet them. None returned to space again.

James Lovell retired from NASA in 1973 to work for the Centel Corporation in Chicago. He is still regularly interviewed for TV documentaries on space flight.

Fred Haise faced another disaster in 1973, when a plane crash left him with burns over two-thirds of his body. He recovered and was at the controls of the first space shuttle when it made its maiden Earth flight in 1977, from the back of a specially modified Boeing 747 Jumbo jet. He has recently retired as President of Northrop Grumman Technical Services.

Jack Swigert took up a career in politics. He was elected to public office in Colorado in 1982, but died of bone cancer a month later.

Over the decades, the excitement and drama of the *Apollo 13* space mission was gradually forgotten, until a 1995 Hollywood film, starring Tom Hanks, brilliantly and faithfully told the story. The film was a great success, and made the surviving astronauts famous all over again.

Swallowed by a volcano

During the filming of the Hollywood thriller *Sliver* in 1992, director Phillip Noyce was searching for images to add an air of menace to his picture. He decided shots of the inside of a fiery volcano would do this effectively. After all, there are few things in nature more forbidding than a smoking volcano, all set to unleash massive destruction with a terrifying roar and rumble.

So film cameramen Michael Benson and Chris Duddy were dispatched to Hawaii's Volcanoes National Park, with instructions to capture a steaming volcano in action. Benson was a seasoned professional, and veteran of such Hollywood films as *Patriot Games* and *Terminator II*.

The volcano they chose to film was Pu'u O'o (pronounced POO-oo OH-oh). This had erupted recently and had a jagged, disfigured peak. Beneath this lurked a crater holding a steaming, bubbling cauldron of glowing lava. Corrosive, choking gases venting off the lava curled up through the massive crater, casting thick, smoky clouds which hung ominously over the volcano's summit.

Pu'u O'o was perfect. It was also so menacing that Benson and Duddy took a superstitious precaution as they embarked on their mission. Local folklore told of a fearsome goddess named Madame Pele, who was supposed to lurk within the volcano's fiery cone. Legend had it that she was very fond of gin so, as a gesture of goodwill, the two men brought a bottle with them to throw into the crater. Maybe it would ensure their safety, and good weather, while they were working?

Benson and Duddy decided that Saturday November 21 would be the best day to do their filming. That morning they hired local pilot Craig Hosking, and a Bell Jet Ranger helicopter. Hosking flew them from Hawaii's Hilo Bay airfield to Pu'u O'o. The weather wasn't as good as they had hoped – it was damp and foggy, and showed little sign of clearing as they approached the ash-strewn summit. Thick, sulphurous clouds covered the volcano, making it almost impossible to see.

As the helicopter made its first pass over the volcano summit, the men looked down inside the crater. Even in the relative comfort and safety of the helicopter, they could feel the heat from the lava, and the volcano's fumes caught in their throats. When they crossed the middle of the crater, Benson lobbed in the bottle of gin. They watched it plummet down through the smoke and cloud, and imagined the green glass swallowed by the lumpy red-hot lava, and the gin vanishing in a hissing puff of steam.

Gaps in the cloud came and went, and Benson and Duddy were able to do some filming. But as the helicopter wheeled around to make a final pass over the crater before returning home, the engine started to splutter. Losing power, it began to drop into the steaming volcano.

Benson and Duddy glanced over to Hosking, who was obviously alarmed. They were now losing height rapidly, and the pilot was wrestling with his controls, desperate to avoid a landing inside the crater.

But Hosking was fighting a losing battle. Benson and Duddy sat rigid with fear as the helicopter lurched into the rim, and headed straight for a deep pool of glowing lava in the middle of the crater. Fortunately, the engine had not entirely cut out, and Hosking still had some control over his stricken craft.

As they neared the ground, the pilot directed his helicopter to a flat rock ledge above the lava pool.

Coming into land they pitched and rolled, and the men were flung to and fro in their flimsy seats. Then, the still spinning rotor blades hit the ground and immediately shattered. The helicopter dropped with a sickening thud and broke in half. Benson, Duddy and Hosking, lucky not to have been hit by splintered rotor blades, staggered out from the wreckage, battered but uninjured.

Inside Pu'u O'o

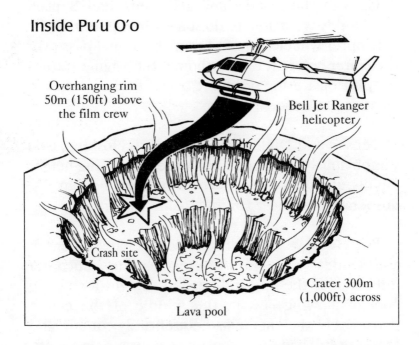

Overhanging rim 50m (150ft) above the film crew

Bell Jet Ranger helicopter

Crash site

Crater 300m (1,000ft) across

Lava pool

The ledge they had landed on was solid rock, but the heat from the molten lava below it still penetrated through their boots. Steam hissed and sputtered from cracks in the ground, threatening to scald anyone unlucky enough to be standing directly above. Clouds of dense, acrid gas drifted around them. The gas was so thick that most of the time the men could barely see their hands in front of their faces.

Then there was the terrible noise. An intense and constant roar filled the air, like the screaming engines of a jet plane, as pools of lava bubbled and boiled around them.

Each man wondered how long they could survive in this smoky inferno. Their immediate chances of rescue were not good. Inside the shattered helicopter cockpit, the radio refused to work. They were not expected back at the airfield for at least another hour, so no one would be wondering where they were for a while yet. They would have to try to make their own way out.

Above them, occasionally visible through the drifting mist, was the summit rim. It was around 50m (150ft) away.

"Let's go for the top," said Benson. "It seems to be the only way out."
But the climb was more difficult than it looked. The rocky surroundings they scrambled up regularly gave way to deep ash and crumbling stone, and the

men found themselves sinking up to their knees in hot, black soot.

After 15 exhausting minutes, they had managed a whole 25m (75ft) – around halfway up the slope. Here the air was slightly clearer, and they could see the slope getting steeper, and then jutting into an overhanging rim at the top. It looked impossible to get over without proper climbing equipment.

Hosking was sure they would never make it.

"Look, I've got an idea," he told the cameramen. "We need to get help, and the only way we're going to do that is to go back to the helicopter and repair that radio."

Benson wasn't convinced.

"I think it's too dangerous. Look down – the 'copter is just covered with poisonous clouds of smoke. If you go back, you'll pass out – or worse."

But Hosking was determined.

"We've got no choice. We stay up here and choke to death. We go down there and choke to death. At least down there there's some chance I can fix the radio and call for help."

He had made up his mind. Wrapping his shirt around his face to keep off the worst of the acrid fumes, he set off back down the slope to return to the helicopter.

Benson and Duddy watched him vanish into the mist, certain they were safer where they were. But they were wrong. Hosking reached the helicopter and began to repair the radio. He could only work on it for short periods, and had to keep coming out of the wreckage to climb to a clearer spot above, to breathe in fresher air. But, piece by piece, he put the radio back together. He also took a battery from one of Duddy and Benson's cameras, and hooked it up to the radio. After a difficult hour, the radio began to crackle. Then a steady roar of static could be heard above the volcano's din, and Hosking knew he'd fixed it.

He tuned into the airfield frequency and was soon speaking to colleagues back at Hilo Bay. An hour later, helicopter pilot Don Shearer, who had often worked on rescue missions in Hawaii, was flying over the volcano.

Shearer radioed down to Hosking.

"Can't see a thing down there, Craig. Smoke's too thick. You're gonna have to guide me in."

"Good to hear you!" said a relieved Hosking, who was now beginning to believe he would get out of this disaster alive. "OK, message understood. I can hear you, so I'll guide you down."

Peering blindly through the swirling smoke, Hosking could faintly hear the dull throb of rotor blades. Gradually he was able to get Shearer to fly close enough to be able to spot the wreckage. As the craft hovered a couple of feet above the ground, Hosking ran up to it and leaped inside. Clouds of smoke swirled away beneath him as the helicopter lifted him to safety. He, at least, had escaped the clutches of Madame Pele.

Crouching on a ledge halfway up the crater, Benson and Duddy had heard the helicopter arrive, although they could not see it through the smoke. They were disappointed to hear its engines recede into the distance, but were pleased to know that at least something was being done to find them.

Hope was closer at hand than they realized. Hosking's radio signals had been picked up by the local National Park rangers. Two rangers had climbed to the tip of the rim and were trying to spot the helicopter crew. The atmosphere around the summit was so deadly they had to wear gas masks, and acidic fumes were corroding their climbing ropes. Every so often, they shouted down into the crater, to try to make contact with the stranded men.

Benson and Duddy heard these faint shouts from their would-be rescuers, above the roar of the lava pits. They sprang to their feet, waving frantically and shouting themselves hoarse. But the cloudy fumes inside the crater were too thick, and their muffled voices just echoed all around the huge rim, making it impossible for either the rescuers or the trapped men to locate each other.

The rangers gave up trying to find the men by shouting. Instead they threw down ropes, in the vague hope that one would land near Benson and Duddy. But the rim of the crater was 300m (1,000ft) across. It was like trying to find a needle in a haystack.

Eventually, darkness fell, and further searching was useless. The rangers gave up, intending to return the next morning.

During the night it rained torrentially, and Benson and Duddy shivered in their soaking clothes. But the rain at least brought some relief from the scorching heat in the crater. When morning came, the weather was even worse. This made a helicopter rescue increasingly difficult. Besides, Don Shearer found that his helicopter had been damaged by the volcano's corrosive fumes when he rescued Hosking, and was now unsafe to fly. Back at the rim of the crater, the rangers could hardly see 3m (10ft) in front of them.

The day wore on, and Benson and Duddy realized they were facing the prospect of another night in the crater, alternately baked by glowing lava and frozen by lashing rain. Choked by fumes, their eyes streaming, the two had only their shirts to wrap around their faces to protect themselves from the poisonous surroundings.

By mid-afternoon of that second day inside the crater, Duddy's patience snapped.

"Maybe there's another way out?" he said to Benson. "Instead of sitting here waiting to be rescued, we ought to be trying to get out ourselves. Whatever, trying to escape is better than sitting here suffocating."

Benson was not convinced. Older and not as fit as Duddy, he doubted his ability to climb further up the slope of the crater to the overhanging rim.

"You go then, Chris," he said, "I'm going to have to stay here."

Benson watched Duddy set off up the slope, and slowly disappear into the cloudy smoke. Inside the crater the light was slowly fading, and now Benson faced a second night in the crater, this time on his own. Duddy did not return. Benson began to think his friend had succeeded, but then he saw a shape fall through the mist. Convinced it was Duddy plunging to his death, Benson was consumed with a terrible mixture of misery, exhaustion and guilt. "Why did I ever bring us to this awful spot?" he said to himself. Weak from lack of food and sleep, he wondered how much longer he could survive.

But, in fact, Duddy had struck lucky. After an exhausting climb through crumbling rock and sooty gravel, he eventually reached a section of the rim where he could scramble out. He soon met up with the rangers who were trying to find them both. They all shouted down to Benson, but their voices were lost in the huge, hollow cauldron.

With night falling, and for want of anything better to do, the rangers tossed food and water packets into the crater, hoping that Benson might stumble upon one. Benson did indeed see one of these packets from a distance. It was this he thought was Duddy plunging to his death.

Luck was not with Michael Benson that night, and he did not find any of these food and water packets. Getting weaker by the hour, breathing was now a painful effort. His mouth was also so dry he could no longer call for help, and the fumes were causing him to hallucinate. He battled with a raging thirst, catching rain in the face of his camera light-meter, and drinking it a mouthful at a time.

Another day dawned. Benson, curled up in a shivering ball, wondered if he would live to see the end of it. But away from the volcano, further action was being taken to rescue him. Overnight, Hosking and Duddy had managed to contact another helicopter pilot named Tom Hauptman, who was famed for his daring rescues. Soon after first light, Hauptman flew over the crater rim. For the first time, through a gap in the clouds, Hauptman managed to spot Benson. The ailing cameraman had heard the helicopter. He was standing up and waving frantically.

Hauptman's helicopter was equipped with a large net, which could be lowered below the craft. Benson was now obscured by cloud again, and Hauptman felt as if he was fishing in a muddy pool. The net went down once, then twice, each time coming back empty. But, on the third attempt, the net landed right in front of the ailing cameraman. Benson grabbed his chance, and threw himself into the net. The helicopter pulled up, and he was lifted away from the crater. Lying in the net, Benson felt deliriously happy. He had escaped from Madame Pele after all.

After the ordeal

Hauptman dropped Benson off with the park rangers, who bundled him into an ambulance and took him to Hawaii's Hilo Hospital. Having been exposed to the volcano's poisonous fumes for over 48 hours, he had seriously damaged his lungs. Fortunately, he was able to make a full recovery. Duddy and Hosking, by comparison, escaped with fairly minor injuries.

The rangers who rescued Benson are convinced he has set a world record for the length of time anyone has managed to survive inside an active volcano.

The film *Sliver* was completed without any shots of smoking volcanoes. One leading character in the film does confess, however, to a great fascination with volcanoes, and admits he has fantasies about flying into one.

Don Shearer and Tom Hauptman, the pilots who flew rescue helicopters into Pu'u O'o, are both thanked in the film's credits.

Terror in the sky

On a crisp December morning in 1942, a Boston bomber took off from Wayzata airfield, Minnesota, USA. Aboard were 29-year-old American test pilot Sid Gerow, and Canadian test observer Harry Griffiths, who was 20.

The aircraft had come to them straight from the factory. It was their job to give it a thorough check-over before it made the long journey across the Atlantic to England, where it would be used to fight in World War Two.

The craft climbed into a cloudless sky, and when it reached 2,100m (7,000ft) the two men began a series of checks and tests. Gerow tried out the controls, pulling the Boston into a slight dive and turning to the left and right, while Griffiths stood beside him, monitoring the instrument panel. Then they tried the two engines, running them at maximum speed, and then pulling back until the Boston was going so slowly, it nearly dropped from the sky.

"No problems here. Everything looks pretty good," shouted Griffiths over the roar of the engines.

He had gone through this drill hundreds of times, and was completely in tune with the workings of the Boston. He knew every rattle and hum of the engines, and every strut and panel of the fuselage, like the back of his hand.

Gerow made a thumbs up gesture in response.

"When you've checked the bombsight I'll take her down," he said.

Griffiths moved swiftly down from the cockpit to the forward section of the plane. The nose of the Boston bomber was made almost entirely of transparent acrylic, giving the bomb aimer an excellent view both of the ground beneath and the skies around the aircraft. Griffiths crouched down and lay flat on his stomach, peering into the telescopic viewer on the bombsight, which was set at the very tip of the bomber's nose.

But, as he checked the mechanism, Griffiths felt the floor beneath him give way. In the Boston, the bomb aimer had to lie across the forward entry hatch to work the bombsight, but the lock on the hatch was obviously faulty.

As he fell through the floor Griffiths instinctively grabbed at the bombsight with both hands, but an immense gust of freezing air sucked the rest of his body out of the aircraft. With the wind and the throb of the Boston's two engines roaring loudly in his ears, he found himself hanging halfway out of the plane, his legs and lower body pressed hard against the fuselage. He yelled at the top of his voice: "Geeeerrrooooowwww!!!!", but knew immediately that there was almost no chance his crewmate could hear him.

Clutching at the bombsight had saved him from plummeting directly out of the aircraft, but the wind was pulling hard at his body, and his fingers soon lost their grip on the polished metal instrument. As his head slipped out of the plane, he clutched desperately at the wooden fitting beneath the sight. Outside the plane the temperature was -25°C (-13°F) and fierce cold gnawed at his battered body.

Harry Griffiths was small, but he was immensely strong. He wrapped his fingers around the wooden fitting and held on with a vice-like grip. Buffeted mercilessly by the plane's turbulent slipstream, few other men could have clung to such a precarious position.

But cling he did, for Harry Griffiths had no other choice. His strength was slowly leaving him and he called feebly for help, but his cries were snatched away by the fierce wind. Very soon his grip would weaken, and he would slip out of the plane and fall to his death.

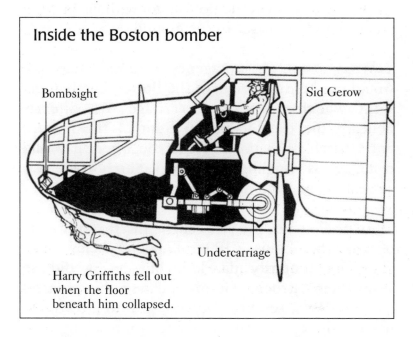

Inside the Boston bomber

Bombsight

Sid Gerow

Undercarriage

Harry Griffiths fell out
when the floor
beneath him collapsed.

In the cockpit above the open hatch, Sid Gerow knew exactly what had happened the moment cold air billowed into the plane, and a severe wind howled around his boots.

"Hey Griffiths, are you all right there?" he shouted down.

There was no reply to his urgent inquiries, but Gerow imagined he could hear his comrade's faint shouts for help. What could he do?

Gerow thought fast. He was in a very difficult situation. If Griffiths had not fallen clean out of the plane, and was clinging on as he suspected, there was little the pilot could do to help. He could not leave the controls of the Boston, for without him the plane would plummet to the ground.

What about an emergency landing? This too would not help Griffiths. In the Boston bomber, the front wheel of the undercarriage was directly beneath the cockpit and in front of the forward entry hatch. If Gerow lowered the wheel it would dislodge his dangling companion. Surely there was something he could do to save Griffiths's life?

As he flew on, the sun caught the frozen waters of Lake St. Louis 2,100m (7,000ft) below. The glare momentarily dazzled, but as it did so inspiration struck. Gerow pushed his control column down, sending the Boston into a dive. He headed directly toward the lake, approaching it as low and as slow as he dared. Anyone falling from a speeding plane onto earth or water would be killed for sure, but ice. . . maybe that would be different?

Beneath the plane, Griffiths was fighting for his life, and struggling just to keep breathing. He was numb with cold, and his grip was going. But as he saw the lake loom before him, he knew at once what he needed to do. The Boston was now skimming over the smooth ice, which was racing below him at 160kmph (100mph). Griffiths knew Gerow could not go any slower, as the plane would stall and both men would be killed.

Griffiths hesitated, plucking up his courage for this last desperate gamble to save his life. Then he let his frozen fingers loosen from the plane. He half expected to drop like a stone, but for a brief moment he glided above the surface, hurled along by his own velocity.

Then he hit the ice with a sickening thud, which completely knocked the breath from his body. Instinctively, he curled into a ball and careered across the frozen surface, hoping that he would not hit a half-submerged log or any other kind of obstacle that would kill him in an instant. Gerow had been right about ice. Its slipperiness prevented the sudden impact that would have killed Griffiths. Gradually, his speed across the ice began to lessen, and eventually he slowed to a halt.

Circling above, Gerow reckoned his crewmate had slid a whole 1km (half a mile). He saw the tiny figure come to a stop and lie quite still. But then, miraculously, he hauled himself to his feet and began to walk cautiously toward the shore.

After the ordeal

Sid Gerow's quick thinking and Harry Griffiths's tough flying overalls had saved his life. He was rushed to the nearest hospital, where he went into a dazed stupor. The next eight days of his life were a complete blank. But, apart from severe bruising and mild frostbite, he survived his extraordinary ordeal without serious injury.

Lost in a polar wilderness

It would be difficult to imagine a more hopeless situation. In November 1915, 29 men stood on the frozen Weddell Sea in the Antarctic, 1,900km (1,200 miles) away from the nearest human settlement. Before them lay the mangled remains of their ship *Endurance*. Especially built to withstand the harsh seas and drifting pack ice of the Antarctic, *Endurance* had been built of greenheart – a wood heavier than iron. But the ship had become caught in the ice a mere day's sailing away from the Antarctic coast. Now, after months of relentless pressure, the hull was being crushed by the ice.

As the crew stood a safe distance away, *Endurance* screeched and groaned in such an eerie fashion, many of the men watching thought she sounded like a dying animal. As the hull gave way, the boat collapsed. Over the last few days, all of the useful equipment and supplies on board had been taken off and placed on the ice. Now all that remained of their boat was a tangled mess of wood, wire, rigging and metal, slowly sinking into the icy water.

Marooned in one of the worst environments on Earth, with no radio and no chance at all of human help, many people would have given up in despair. But the crew of the *Endurance* had one priceless asset – the man who had led them there in the first place. His name was Sir Ernest Shackleton, but everyone just called him "the Boss".

Shackleton was a professional adventurer. He had been to the Antarctic before with the ill-fated British explorer Robert Falcon Scott, who died there in 1912. When Shackleton was not exploring, he made a living writing books and giving lectures about his expeditions. In the late 19th and early 20th centuries, explorers such as Shackleton excited great public interest, making highly dangerous expeditions to the world's wildest places. By 1914, though, there were few challenges left. Although the South Pole had been reached in 1912, no one had ever crossed the Antarctic. Shackleton, now aged 40, was determined to make this 2,415km (1,500 mile) journey, and announced plans to lead the grandly named "Imperial Trans-Antarctic Expedition" to do this.

Five thousand letters of application immediately flooded into Shackleton's central London headquarters in Burlington Street. He had already decided on some of the key members of his expedition, picking men who had worked with him before. But the rest of his crew he picked on instinct, often taking just seconds to hire complete strangers.

Expedition scientist Reginald James, for example, was asked if his teeth were good, if he had a good temper, and if he could sing. When James looked bewildered by this question, Shackleton explained that he wanted someone who could "shout a bit with the boys". On a trip like this, getting along with other people was just as important as scientific expertise.

Endurance's captain Frank Worsley joined the team after a strange dream. "One night I dreamed that Burlington Street was full of ice blocks and that I was navigating a ship along it," he later wrote. Next morning he went at once to Burlington Street where a sign saying "Imperial Trans-Antarctic Expedition" caught his eye. Worsley remembered: "Shackleton was there, and the moment I set eyes on him I knew he was a man with whom I would be proud to work." "The Boss" hired him on the spot, and Worsley became one of the expedition's most valuable members.

The hand-picked crew of seamen, scientists and craftsmen left London in the late summer of 1914, just as the First World War was beginning. Also aboard were 70 dogs to pull their sleighs, and a cat called Mrs. Chippy. On the trip down to the Antarctic they were joined by a stowaway – an 18-year-old Canadian named Percy Blackboro. When Blackboro was discovered, he was brought before Shackleton, who told him, "If anyone has to be eaten, you'll be the first."

When the *Endurance* reached Antarctic waters, icebergs soon surrounded the ship. As they sailed gingerly through, Shackleton described their surroundings as "a gigantic and interminable jigsaw". But shortly after crossing the Antarctic circle, the ice closed in and packed itself tightly around them. They were stuck "like an almond in a piece of toffee", remembered one crew member. Soon they could move neither forward nor backward, and there they stayed for nine months, waiting for the ice to clear.

Although conditions on board the *Endurance* were cramped but comfortable, this was a terrible place to be stranded. Not only was it immensely cold, but at that time of year in the Antarctic, there were only a few minutes of light a day.

In previous voyages, sailors whose ships became trapped in pack ice had fallen prey to deep depression or madness, brought on by this relentless darkness. On one stranded ship in the 1890s, this madness turned men deaf and dumb, or made them hide, thinking the others were trying to kill them. Most spent the time walking in a wide oval on the deck, in what became known as the "madhouse promenade".

Shackleton was determined this would never happen to his crew. *Endurance*, for example, had been equipped with a well-stocked library precisely in anticipation of such a wait. "The Boss" also kept his crew busy organizing dog training, soccer and hockey matches, party games and lectures. The men even carved elaborate, beautiful dog kennels from blocks of ice.

But, despite their patience, the ship never did break out of its icy prison. Now it had sunk, and the members of the crew were forced to camp out on the frozen sea. Surrounded by an untidy mixture of three lifeboats, salvaged equipment and supplies, they christened their new home "Camp Dump". Every one knew they were too far from civilization to be rescued.

A couple of days after the ship sank, Shackleton gathered his companions around him. If they were to survive, he told them, drastic measures were called for. But he had a plan which had every chance of success.

Their only option, he explained, was to haul their lifeboats through the ice to the open sea, and then sail 1,300km (800 miles) back to a whaling station at South Georgia, the nearest inhabited island. To have any chance of success, they would have to leave almost everything behind. Each man, in fact, could only bring 1kg (2lbs) of his own possessions, plus a sleeping bag, a metal cup, knife and spoon, and the heavy clothes he stood in.

To emphasize this point, Shackleton threw to the ground his watch and chain, and a pocketful of gold coins. Then, to everyone's amazement, he also threw down a Bible the Queen had given him at the start of the expedition. He could not have made his point more clearly.

On top of this single kilogram, men were allowed to keep their diaries. Shackleton felt it would be good for morale for each man to record their forthcoming struggle in detail. Leonard Hussey, the expedition meteorologist, was told he should keep his banjo, as a sing-song was always good for morale.

One of the most difficult decisions about what to take and what to leave faced the expedition photographer Frank Hurley. In the days before celluloid film, photographs were made on glass plate negatives, which were twice the size of this page, and very heavy. Shackleton and Hurley chose the best shots between them and smashed the rest, to remove the temptation of taking them all back.

But another, even harder decision also had to be made. Food supplies were so limited that there would not be enough both for the members of the expedition, and most of the animals they had brought along. Some of the dogs, and the ship's cat, had to be shot. It was kinder than abandoning them and leaving them to starve to death, but some of the men had become so attached to the ship's animals, they broke down in tears.

By the time the expedition was ready to set off on their trek, it was almost Christmas, and well into the Antarctic summer. Shackleton, impatient to begin, decided they would celebrate Christmas on December 22, then leave the next day. Despite the shortages, a huge feast of ham, sausage, jugged (stewed) hare, pickles and peaches was prepared. It was a wonderful send-off. The men, fortified by their food, and in good spirits, loaded the boats and sleighs and began towing them toward the sea.

Hauling it all was hot, exhausting work, even in the Antarctic, so most of the travel was done at night when the temperature dropped below zero. But in the first five days they managed only 14km (nine miles). Shackleton's men became grumpy and dispirited, especially when sickness swept through the party. A few of the dogs they had spared were unable to pull the boats and sleighs through the rough, icy landscape, so they too had to be shot. Things were going very badly, right from the start. Fierce arguments broke out between the crew and "the Boss", and Shackleton even had to remind mutinous men that their pay, which they would all receive in a lump sum at the end of the expedition, could be stopped.

Somehow Shackleton managed to drive them on, and for three months the Trans-Antarctic Expedition slogged through the pack ice, stubbornly determined to emerge from the polar wilderness alive. But, slowly and surely, their food and fuel supplies dwindled until they were almost gone, and still the men had not reached the sea.

Then, one morning, their luck changed. A huge leopard seal poked its head out of a crack in the ice and stared at Seaman Thomas McLeod. Both eyed the other as a potential meal, but McLeod was sharper. He began flapping his arms like a penguin – the seal's juiciest prey. It lumbered out of the ice and began chasing him, and was quickly shot. This was a godsend for the expedition. Along with their scant supplies, they had been living off tiny Adele penguins, which were too small to provide much nourishment. Seal meat made a welcome change, and there was also now plenty of blubber – which they could burn in their stoves as fuel. The leopard seal that had chased Thomas McLeod had 50 undigested fish in its stomach, which was an unexpected bonus.

Finally, in early April 1916, Shackleton's men came to the end of the ice and reached the open ocean. After months of pushing and trudging, they were finally able to board their three lifeboats and put to sea. But, although the hauling was over, life was no better. The boats were small, crammed with men and provisions, and open to the worst weather imaginable. At night, if the men slept in the boats, schools of killer whales would surround them. If they set up camp on an ice floe, the ice would sometimes crack. Sleeping men would plunge into the freezing sea, and had to scramble out before the ice closed above them.

They spent 12 days freezing and soaked to the skin, constantly bailing water from their boats, in a desperate effort to keep them from sinking. Eventually, land was sighted. But this was not South Georgia, as they had hoped, but Elephant Island, which was much further west. They were still 1,100km (700 miles) from South Georgia, and other human beings.

Despite it all, the men were deliriously happy. They had survived an appalling journey and, for the first time in nearly one and a half years, they could rest their feet on solid ground.

Elephant Island was a narrow 37km (23 miles) long crop of bare rock. There were no trees, but there were plenty of birds and elephant seals to eat. As the expedition lacked any other shelter, the two smaller boats the men had sailed to the island were turned upside down and made into huts. These huts were primitive but comfortable. The boats were placed on stones, and gaps were filled with moss and fabric to make them windproof. Stoves were placed inside to provide a little heat, and even small windows were carefully built into the sides of the huts, from glass salvaged from other equipment.

Although the *Endurance* expedition never did run out of food, everyone became terribly bored with their monotonous diet. During the day they would huddle around a blubber stove and fantasize aloud about trifles and sticky puddings. At night they dreamed of salads and scrambled eggs.

No one would find them on Elephant Island, as it was too remote, so Shackleton decided to take the biggest boat, the James Caird, and a small crew, to try to reach South Georgia. The rest of his men would have to wait on the island for rescue.

One of Shackleton's greatest talents as a leader was his ability to pick the right people for a job, and for this trip he chose a mixture of the most able and most troublesome men. These he took with him to prevent them from annoying the men that would be left behind on Elephant Island.

Patched up with canvas and paint from the supplies of expedition painter George Marsten, the James Caird and a crew of six set out to travel 1,100km (700 miles) to the whaling station at Grytviken in South Georgia. Once again they had to battle through blizzards and gales. And again they were constantly soaked and freezing, but this time they all suffered from raging thirst, as salt water had contaminated their water supply.

After 17 days at sea, the James Caird finally reached South Georgia. But, just off the coast, a terrible gale ripped away their rudder. Unable to steer the boat, they were washed up on the side of the island furthest away from the whaling station.

South Georgia was long and narrow, like Elephant Island, but it was also very mountainous. As the boat was no longer fit to sail, and the walk around the coast was over 240km (150 miles), Shackleton decided they would have to go over these uncharted mountains.

So, on May 19, 1916, taking only 15m (50ft) of rope and a carpenter's blade, Shackleton, *Endurance*'s captain Frank Worsley, and officer Thomas Crean began their climb into the unknown. Two other men, who were too weak to go on, were left behind with a third to look after them.

Shackleton, Worsley and Crean pressed on through the mountains, up and down for two days, one time tobogganing down a steep ice slope on their coiled-up rope, another time climbing down a waterfall. Once, when they stopped to rest, Shackleton let them sleep for five minutes, and then woke them, telling them half an hour had passed.

On May 21, at 7:00 in the morning, the men heard a factory whistle at Grytviken whaling station. For the first time since December 1914, here was evidence that other human beings were close by. This was the moment they realized they had escaped from the Antarctic with their lives. Their spirits lifted and they arrived at Grytviken by 1:00 that afternoon.

As they walked toward the factory, two small boys, terrified by the sight of these ragged men, ran away screaming. Shackleton asked to be taken to the home of factory manager Thoralf Sorlle, whom he knew well. Sorlle gawped at them in astonishment and said, "Who on Earth are you?" Like everyone at Grytviken, he had assumed that the *Endurance* had been lost with all aboard nearly two years before. When Shackleton told him their tale, Sorlle burst into tears.

Despite the extreme hardship of their voyage to South Georgia, and their dangerous trek through the mountains, a hot bath and a hearty meal was all Shackleton's party needed before they set off to rescue their stranded companions on the other side of South Georgia. These men were picked up the next day, but the rest of the expedition, stranded on Elephant Island, would be more difficult to reach.

Shackleton sailed out on a relief ship on May 23, but ice blocked his route. He made a second attempt to reach the island shortly afterward, but was driven back by fog. On the third attempt rough weather forced them to turn back.

Finally, after 14 frustrating weeks, Shackleton and his relief ship reached Elephant Island on August 30, 1916. A small boat was launched toward the shore, and Shackleton, standing on its bow, anxiously counted the 22 men he had left behind. They were all there. At least no one had died.

The four month wait on Elephant Island had been a tedious ordeal – best summed up in a diary entry by one of *Endurance*'s officers, Lionel Greenstreet: So passes another miserable rotten day.

Although the men had suffered from infections and boils, the only real casualty of the entire two-year adventure had been the ship's stowaway, Percy Blackboro. He had lost the toes of his left foot to frostbite. Shackleton had managed, through good judgment, and great leadership, to bring his entire expedition back alive.

After the ordeal

Shackleton was justifiably proud of his achievement. He wrote in his account of the adventure that they had been through terrible times and yet not a single life had been lost. The survivors of Shackleton's Imperial Trans-Antarctic Expedition returned home to a Europe ensnared in the horrors of World War One. Their story, which then must have seemed like a foolhardy venture, excited little interest when millions of men were dying in the trenches.

Almost all the *Endurance* crew volunteered for the armed services and two, a junior officer and a seaman, were killed in action. Shackleton, his deputy Frank

Wild, and *Endurance's* captain Frank Worsley were sent to the North Russian front, where their knowledge of polar conditions would be useful to Britain's ally Russia. Many of *Endurance's* crew served on minesweepers.

In 1921, Shackleton returned to the Antarctic, with many of his *Endurance* shipmates, on yet another expedition. He died of a heart attack at Grytviken, South Georgia, in January, 1922, and is buried on the island.

South Georgia was not crossed again for nearly 40 years. A British expedition of experienced, well-equipped climbers finally crossed the mountains again in 1955.

Today, Shackleton and his extraordinary story still continues to fascinate. Bookshop shelves are still full of Shackleton biographies and accounts of the voyage of the *Endurance*, many of them lavishly illustrated with Frank Hurley's beautiful, haunting photographs. Exhibitions, TV documentaries, and even a recent Hollywood movie keep his story alive. His brilliant leadership skills are even studied in business training courses. Shackleton "defines what you'd like people to do in a crisis", says one New York business guru. "Don't be afraid to change your plans. Don't be afraid to do nothing when that's the best thing to do. Prepare, prepare, prepare. Plan, plan plan."

"The Mighty Hood"

In the chilly waters of the North Atlantic, just below the perpetual ice field of the Arctic Ocean, a grey May dawn broke before 2:00am. Pitching through a rolling grey sea, scything wind and flurries of snow, a great grey battleship headed relentlessly toward its prey. The year was 1941.

The ship was *HMS Hood* – the most famous vessel in the British Navy. For 20 years the *Hood* had been the world's largest battleship. She had toured the oceans as a symbol of Britain's naval power, and was known all over the world as "The Mighty Hood".

The 1,421 men on board the *Hood* had been ready for battle throughout the night. Most had found it impossible to sleep, for they were about to engage in a life or death struggle with two of Germany's most powerful warships – *Bismarck* and *Prinz Eugen* – which had been sent out to the Atlantic to hunt for British cargo ships.

High above the deck, in the dimly lit compass platform, sat Vice-Admiral Lancelot Holland. Surrounded by his chief lieutenants – the ship's

captain, and navigation, signal and gunnery officers –
Holland scoured the horizon, his fingers tapping
anxiously on his binoculars.

Waiting on the *Hood*'s masters in this lofty perch
was 18-year-old signalman Ted Briggs. His job was to
carry messages to other parts of the ship. Briggs had
first set eyes on the *Hood* on a trip to the Yorkshire
coast in 1935, when he was 12. It was love at first
sight, and he had decided then and there to join the
Navy to sail on her. Now, six years later, here he was,
watching the calm deliberations of her senior officers
with a mixture of fear and fascination.

The *Hood* had never before had to fight another
ship. Briggs knew it would be a bloody, dangerous
business, but he was confident that his beloved *Hood*,
and the battleship *Prince of Wales*, which was sailing
alongside her, would soon destroy any ship that
crossed their path.

But Briggs's faith in the *Hood* was misplaced.
Bismarck was the most powerful ship in the German
fleet. Heavily armed and well protected, the
aggressive angles and sweep of the ship made a
striking contrast with the stately elegance of the
Hood. Like the *Hood*, she was over 3km (5 miles)
long, but she was also 20 years younger, and the very
model of modern naval technology. Compared to the
Bismarck, the *Hood* looked quaintly old-fashioned.

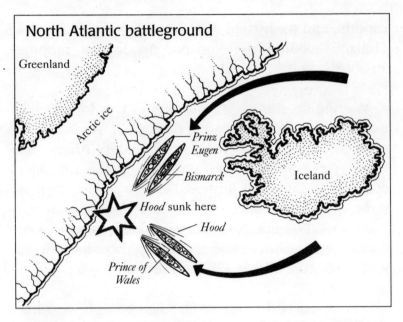

North Atlantic battleground

The two German ships were sighted at 5:35am. Ominous black dots 27km (17 miles) away, they would soon be within range of the *Hood*'s huge guns. The British and German ships continued to speed toward each other, and 23 minutes later, at 5:58am, and at 20km (13 miles) apart, the battle began. *Hood* opened fire, her shells hurtling toward *Bismarck* and *Prinz Eugen* at over twice the speed of sound. Nearly half a minute passed before huge plumes of water, as high as tower blocks, rose around the two approaching ships. The *Hood* had missed.

Up on the compass platform, Briggs watched the *Bismarck*'s guns return fire. Gold flashes with red cores winked from the distant ship. A low whine built to a howling crescendo, as the shells made a 20 second journey between the two ships.

Briggs's terrified anticipation ended when four huge columns of foam erupted to the right of the ship. Then an explosion knocked him off his feet.

The *Hood* had been hit at the base of her mainmast and fire spread rapidly. On deck, anti-aircraft shells set alight by the heat exploded like firecrackers. On the compass platform, the screams of wounded men trickled from the voice-pipes that kept the ship's commanders in touch with their vessel.

As the *Hood* turned to give all four of its main gun turrets a better view of the approaching enemy, another huge explosion rocked the ship, and Briggs was again thrown off his feet. A shell from *Bismarck* had penetrated deep within the hull and detonated the *Hood*'s main ammunition supplies.

Aboard the *Prince of Wales*, the men saw an eerily silent explosion – like a huge red tongue – shoot four times the height of the ship. Pieces of the mainmast, a huge crane and part of a gun turret tumbled through the air.

When Briggs got up he felt in fear for his life and knew instinctively that his ship had been fatally damaged. The *Hood* listed slowly to the right and the helmsman shouted through the voice-pipe that the ship's steering had failed.

To Briggs's relief, the *Hood* rolled slowly back to level. But this relief was short-lived. The ship lurched to the left and began to roll over. What Briggs, and no one else on the compass platform could know, was that the *Hood* had been broken in two by the explosion. The rear of the ship had sunk almost immediately, and now the rest was being claimed by the sea.

There was no order to abandon ship. As the floor became steeper and steeper, the crew on the compass platform headed unprompted to the exit ladder. An officer stood aside to let Briggs go first. Slumped in his chair, Vice-Admiral Lancelot Holland sat stunned and defeated.

Briggs climbed down a ladder to a lower deck on the tilting ship, but the sea was already gushing around his legs. With desperate haste he began to shed any clothing that would weigh him down, managing to discard his steel helmet and gas mask before being sucked into the icy water. Dragged deep beneath the ship, he felt an intense pressure in his ears and realized he was going to die.

Unable to reach the surface and desperate to breathe, he gulped down mouthfuls of water. As he drowned, his panic subsided. A childlike, blissful security swept over him. Briggs pictured himself as a little boy, and thought of his mother tucking him into bed. But his state of peaceful resignation was interrupted. A great surge of water suddenly shot him to the surface.

Choking and spluttering, Briggs gasped down great lungfuls of air, and took in a scene of unimaginable horror. All around were blazing pools of oil. What remained of the *Hood* was 45m (150ft) away. Her bows were vertical in the sea, the guns in her forward turrets were disappearing fast into the water. Bizarrely, these guns had just fired a final salvo toward the *Bismarck*, perhaps triggered by an electric short-circuit, as the bow lurched wildly into the air.

As she sank, the *Hood* made a horrific hissing sound, as white-hot metal and bubbling, blistering paint and wood made contact with the icy water. The *Prince of Wales* sailed close by, nearly colliding with the wreckage. The bow of the *Hood* towered over her like a nightmarish spire.

Realizing he was close enough to be sucked down again by the whirlpool currents the huge sinking ship was making, Briggs swam away through the oily sea as hard as he could. All around were dozens of small wooden rafts which had floated away when the *Hood* capsized, and he hauled himself onto one.

Perched precariously on the raft, he turned to look at the *Hood*, but she had vanished. Now nothing remained except a small patch of blazing oil where the bow had been. Beneath the waters, the huge 42,672 tonne (42,000 ton) ship was beginning a last terrible journey to the ocean floor, 2,500m (8,000ft) below. Once the *Bismarck*'s guns had found their target, his ship had sunk in a mere three minutes.

Briggs was still in terrible danger. Shells from *Bismarck* and *Prinz Eugen* were falling around the *Prince of Wales*, only yards away, and the oil that surrounded him could catch fire at any moment. As he paddled away from the oil, he looked for other survivors. Two were close by. All three paddled toward one another and held their rafts together by linking arms. On one raft was Midshipman Bill Dundas, who had been on the compass platform with Briggs. When the *Hood* capsized, he kicked his way out of a window and swam away from the ship.

The other man was Able Seaman Bob Tilburn, who had been manning a gun position at the side of the ship. His had been the luckiest escape. On deck, he had survived exploding ammunition lockers, and had been showered with falling debris and the bodies of men from the decks above. When the *Hood* capsized, he jumped into the water only to have the ship come down on top of him. Radio wiring had wrapped itself around his sea boots and he had cut himself free with a knife.

Alone in the ocean, the three men were now in danger of freezing to death. To stop them from falling asleep and dying of exposure, Dundas made them sing "Roll out the barrel" – a wartime pop song. Fortunately they did not have to wait too long for help to arrive. The British destroyer *Electra* had spotted the three men and was now heading toward them.

Ted Briggs was too cold to haul himself up to the ship and had to be lifted aboard. In *Electra*'s sick bay, frozen clothes were cut from his body and he was given rum to warm him up.

The *Electra* and three other ships had been sent to look for survivors. There was so little sign of life when they arrived at the scene of the sinking that they thought they must have gone off course.

Briggs, Dundas and Tilburn, and a few wooden rafts, were all that was left. The *Hood* had taken the rest of her 1,421 crew – from Vice-Admiral to engine room stoker – to the bottom of the North Atlantic.

After the ordeal

The destruction of the *Hood* stunned the British public. She was believed to be unsinkable, and many people in Britain remember the moment they heard the news as the single greatest shock of the war. Prime Minister Winston Churchill recalled: "*HMS Hood. . .* was one of our most cherished naval possessions. Her loss was a bitter grief."

A Royal Navy inquiry concluded the *Hood* had been sunk because her protective steel plating was too weak to defend her from plunging shells fired by the German battleships. Tragically, the *Hood* was due to have had all this strengthened in a major renovation, but this had been postponed when war broke out in 1939.

The *Bismarck* did not survive the exchange with *Hood* and *Prince of Wales* unscathed. Minor damage, including leaking fuel tanks, prompted her commander Admiral Lutjens to return to base, in the German-occupied French port of Brest. But on the journey back, *Bismarck* was attacked and crippled by British torpedo planes. Finally, on May 27, 1941, she was sunk by British battleships, a mere four days after her victory over the *Hood*.

Prinz Eugen survived the war, and was surrendered to the British in May 1945. She was handed over to the Americans, who used her for atomic bomb trials at Bikini Atoll in the Pacific. She eventually capsized and sank in December 1946.

The *Prince of Wales* was sunk in the Pacific Ocean by the Japanese Navy, later in 1941.

Following their rescue by the *Electra*, Ted Briggs and his crewmates were taken to Reykjavik, Iceland, and then flown back to England to be reunited with their families for one week's "survival leave". Briggs's mother received a telegram telling her he was safe, only an hour after radio reports announced that the *Hood* had sunk with little chance of survivors.

Briggs, Dundas and Tilburn all survived the war. Serving for 35 years in the British Royal Navy, Briggs rose to the rank of lieutenant. He now lives in Hampshire, and is a prominent member of the Hood Association – an organization set up to preserve the memory of his former ship. He still gives interviews to researchers and documentary producers, and in 2000 he appeared in a Discovery Channel documentary about the sinking of the *Hood*.

TRUE STORIES OF HEROES

Paul Dowswell

CONTENTS

Catastrophe at Chernobyl

The long, thin, red and white chimney of Chernobyl nuclear power station towered over the flat, swampy landscape of the Pripyat Marshes. Just over an hour's drive north of the Ukrainian capital of Kiev, the station was constructed in the 1970s, when it was hailed as one of the Soviet Union's greatest scientific achievements. Its four reactors, with two more being built, made it the largest nuclear power station in the world.

The chief engineer at the plant, Nikolai Fomin, assured visitors that the chances of an explosion in this marvel of modern technology were about the same as being hit by a comet. But he was mistaken. Poor design, bad planning and inadequate staff training meant that Chernobyl was a disaster waiting to happen. And happen it did, on April 26, 1986, when the number four reactor exploded.

A nuclear power station makes electricity in a process known as nuclear fission. Energy is created in a reactor, a specially strengthened chamber inside the power station, by splitting the atoms of a substance called uranium. This process gives off invisible rays called radiation, which can be harmful to living things. In humans, for example, radiation can cause burns and cancer, so power stations have to shield their workers and surroundings from these dangerous rays. The explosion at Chernobyl released huge amounts of radiation into the atmosphere. This caused terrible radioactive pollution, especially to the area immediately surrounding it.

Chernobyl's Number Four Reactor

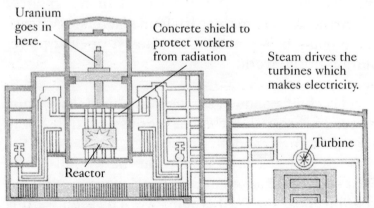

Uranium goes in here.

Concrete shield to protect workers from radiation

Steam drives the turbines which makes electricity.

Turbine

Reactor

Water is heated into steam in the reactor.

Today a huge, ugly, concrete block covers part of the number four reactor. For about 20 miles in all directions, stark branches on dead trees point at the sky, and farmland lies in ruins. In this area of the greatest radioactive pollution, deserted villages and towns slowly crumble and decay, and their empty roads and squares are choked with weeds.

The disaster began on the night of April 25, 1986, when a team of technicians were carrying out routine tests on equipment in the number four reactor. In order to do this, they had to slow the reactor down. Unfortunately, they reduced the reactor's power so much that, like a smoking fire about to go out, it began to shut down.

Chernobyl was supplying power to two and a half million people in nearby Kiev. If the reactor stopped working, the city could be hit by a massive power cut. So the manager on duty that night, Anatoli Dyatlov, ordered workers to restart the reactor, even though doing this when it was so close to shutting down was known to be dangerous.

Control room staff argued that the reactor should be allowed to shut down, which would have been a totally safe procedure. But Dyatlov became enraged at their questioning his decision, and insisted they restart it. He was concerned that he would be held responsible for any loss of power to Kiev, and this might lead to his demotion or even dismissal. Besides, as far as he was concerned, he was just enacting the procedures he had been trained to follow.

Dyatlov's orders were obeyed, but an air of hysteria took hold of the control room as technicians began to grapple with tremendous forces they sensed were running out of control. They were right to feel afraid. As part of the tests, the emergency water cooling system had also been deliberately cut off. In their rising panic, technicians forgot that they had done this, and the reactor began to overheat like a kettle boiling dry.

In the control room, technicians heard a series of ominous thumps, which made the ground tremble beneath their feet. A worker rushed in with the terrifying news that heavy steel covers on the reactor access points were jumping up and down in their sockets.

Then there was a huge thunderclap, the walls shook, and all the lights went out. Dust and smoke billowed in from the corridor, and the ceiling cracked open. A sharp, distinctive smell filled the room, like air after a thunderstorm, only much, much stronger. It was now 1:23am on April 26.

The reactor had disintegrated. It had exploded with such force that it shattered a vast concrete shield, weighing more than a jumbo jet, which lay above the reactor to protect power station workers from radiation. Other equipment, such as a massive fuel machine, had collapsed on top of it.

The reactor just before the explosion

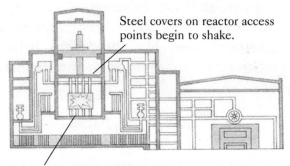

Steel covers on reactor access points begin to shake.

Water cooling system is cut off, causing the reactor to overheat.

The reactor after the explosion

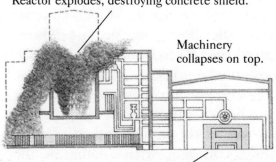

Reactor explodes, destroying concrete shield.

Machinery collapses on top.

Turbine Hall escapes destruction.

Back in the control room, foreman Valeri Perevozchenko's first thoughts were for his colleague Valera Khodemchuk, who he had last seen in the reactor hall. He dashed into the dark corridor, picking his way through clouds of dust and piles of blazing rubble, and made his way to the site of the explosion. The air seemed very thick, and he was also aware of another more sinister sensation. Deadly radiation released by the explosion was passing through him. He could feel it burning his throat, lungs and eyes. His mouth tasted of sour apples.

His blood ran cold and Perevozchenko was seized by panic. He knew that his body was absorbing lethal doses of radiation, but instead of fleeing he stayed to search for his colleague. Peering into the dark through a broken window that overlooked the reactor hall, he could see only a mass of tangled wreckage.

By now he had absorbed so much radiation he felt as if his whole body was on fire. But then he remembered that there were several other men near the explosion who might also be trapped.

Perevozchenko pressed on, running over floors that cracked with the sound of broken glass. He passed a colleague with a radiation monitoring tool, who told him one of his measuring instruments had already burned out, and the one he was using was showing a reading that was completely off the scale.

Still Perevozchenko hurried on into the huge reactor hall. Looking far up to the ceiling, he could dimly see that the roof had been blown off. Firemen summoned to tackle the blaze had already arrived, and their shouts rang across the huge hall. Small fires cast eerie shadows around the mangled mass of pipes and machinery. Streams of water gurgled and splattered from burst pipes. Oddest of all was the strange moaning sound of burning graphite, which was scattered around the floor. This material had come from the very heart of the reactor and was intensely radioactive.

Perevozchenko ran a flashlight over the scene and wondered what on earth he was doing in such a dreadful place. Although he could not see it in the dark, the escaping radiation was rapidly turning his skin brown.

Still, he stopped to listen, in case Khodemchuk was crying for help, then shouted desperately: "Valera! Valera! I've come to rescue you." The echo of his voice died away, and all he could hear was the crackle of the flames and the trickle of running water.

Ahead lay a pile of rubble, and Perevozchenko tore his hands pulling aside concrete and graphite chunks trying to make his way forward. But neither Khodemchuk nor any other colleague was anywhere to be found. Exhausted, he wandered back to the control room, passing the reactor itself on the way. He could see it had been completely destroyed in the explosion and was spewing out deadly radiation.

Perevozchenko knew that his comrades in the control room still believed the reactor was intact, and were struggling to open water vents to try to cool it down. He also realized that the best action to take was to get as many people as possible away from the radiation.

Back in the control room, he struggled to remain conscious. He confronted shift foreman Alexander Akimov and begged him to get everyone to leave the building. But Akimov would not believe the reactor had been destroyed. Perevozchenko's bravery had been in vain. He had not been able to rescue his colleagues, nor warn others to escape before they too became fatally affected by radiation. He was taken to Pripyat Medical Unit and died soon afterwards.

The failure to recognize what had actually happened to the reactor was to cost several more lives, including that of Akimov himself. As he and others struggled to operate valves which would send water to cool a reactor that was no longer there, they too exposed themselves to fatal doses of radiation. Their bodies soon became dark, blistered and swollen, they lapsed into fever and coma and died cruel, painful deaths.

But other workers who endangered their lives had greater success. In the aftermath of the explosion, power station workers in the turbine room were able to drain highly inflammable fuels and gases from storage tanks near to the blazing wreckage. Four received lethal doses of radiation, and another four were hospitalized with painful injuries. But if they had not succeeded, an even greater disaster would have struck Chernobyl. There were another three working reactors at the station. If the fire had spread, these too could have been destroyed, releasing a much greater amount of deadly radiation into the surrounding area.

Unlike poor Valeri Perevozchenko, others who took great risks were able to rescue injured colleagues. Laboratory chief Piotr Palamarchuk and Nikolai Gorbachenko, who were both in the control room at the time of the explosion, began searching for their colleague Vladimir Shashenok. He had been working in a room next to the reactor.

They found him quickly enough, but Shashenok was trapped by a fallen girder and had been badly burned by radiation and scalding steam. They heaved the heavy girder from his body, and carried their injured comrade to the power station infirmary. Palamarchuk and Gorbachenko had exposed themselves to heavy doses of radiation, and they too remained at the infirmary for treatment.

Some of the older staff at the station deliberately chose to carry out the most dangerous tasks to spare their younger colleagues. Alexander Lelechenko, the head of the electrical workshop at Chernobyl, went three times into areas of lethal radiation to disconnect dangerous electrical equipment. Standing next to piles of radioactive rubble, or knee deep in contaminated water, he absorbed enough radiation to kill five people. He stopped briefly to be given first aid for radiation burns, but went immediately back to work for several more hours, only stopping when he was too ill to continue.

Perhaps most of all it was the courage of the Chernobyl firemen that prevented the explosion from causing even worse damage. Lieutenant Vladimir Pravik and his crew dashed to the fire moments after the explosion. Within minutes they were on the roof of the reactor hall, pouring water down on the inferno.

Almost immediately they began to feel sick with radiation poisoning and felt unbearably hot both inside and outside their bodies. But every one of them continued fighting the fire. The roof could collapse at any moment. The tar that lined it was melting, releasing dense toxic smoke and sticking to the firefighters' boots. Radioactive dust fell on their uniforms. One by one they began to falter.

Fire station commander Major Leonid Telyatnikov arrived on the scene soon afterwards. He immediately recognized the scale of the disaster and called out every available fire crew within the area. Telyatnikov issued orders to his men to stand by their posts until the fire had been defeated, and they did not let him down.

For many firemen, fainting and vomiting spells made it impossible to continue but, due to their heroic efforts, the fires caused by the explosion did not spread to Chernobyl's other reactors, and had been extinguished by dawn. The firemen paid a heavy price. Later that day, 17 were taken to a Moscow hospital for specialist treatment.

Treating the injured was Dr. Valentin Belokon. He had been working on the night shift at Pripyat hospital and was called over to Chernobyl shortly after the explosion. As soon as he arrived a guard asked: "Why don't you have special protective clothes?" Belokon realized at once there had been a radiation leak and he was in danger, but as he was the first doctor on the scene he immediately set to work.

He spent all night and all of the next day treating radiation victims, many of whom were very disturbed and near hysteria. By late afternoon of the next day, he too began to suffer from headaches and nausea caused by radiation sickness. He was very much aware of the dangers he faced, but he reasoned: "When people see a man in a white coat, it makes them quieter." He stayed on the site until the next day, when he was too weak to continue working.

By now, the greatest danger was over, but the tragedy still continued to run its course. The nearby town of Pripyat, where most of the Chernobyl workers lived, was completely evacuated. 21,000 people were taken away in convoys of buses, leaving their homes and possessions, never to return. 30,000 had already fled as soon as the disaster happened.

Family pets had to be left behind as large doses of radiation had collected on their fur. Dogs ran behind the convoy until they could keep up no longer and slunk dejectedly back to the empty town. Away from human contact the animals quickly returned to their natural, savage state. Within a day the dogs had formed into packs and hunted down the cats. Within a week they had begun to attack visitors to the town, and teams of soldiers had to be called in to shoot them.

Over a hundred people were taken to hospital after the first night of the disaster. Thirty one of them died over the next few weeks. Some lost their lives because they had tried to rescue injured colleagues. Others died because they had successfully prevented the fire from spreading to the power station's other three reactors. Without their heroism, Chernobyl and the world would have faced a much greater catastrophe.

Afterwards

The Chernobyl accident alerted the world to the fact that a nuclear disaster would never just be a local problem. The immediate area around the explosion became completely uninhabitable, and radiation from Chernobyl even went on to contaminate many other parts of Europe. Traces, for example, were found in Scandinavian salmon and Welsh sheep.

Map showing how Europe was affected

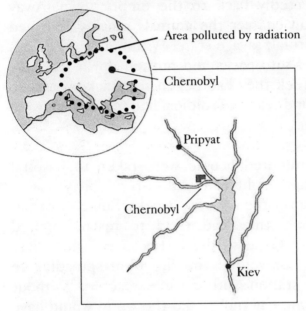

Area polluted by radiation

Chernobyl

Pripyat

Chernobyl

Kiev

Firefighters and construction crews continued to work at Chernobyl for years after the accident. In the immediate aftermath of the explosion, their main task was to prevent radiation from pouring out of the ruptured reactor. Helicopters flew over, dropping sand and other materials onto it. Eventually a huge concrete casing was built around the site.

At least 116,000 people in the surrounding area had to be rehoused in other parts of the Soviet Union. Although accurate statistics have been difficult to verify, it is thought that around 70,000 people have suffered health problems due to exposure to Chernobyl's radiation leaks.

Today, local scientists are concerned that an earthquake could cause the protective concrete casing around the reactor to collapse, releasing more radiation into the surrounding area. The casing itself is also causing alarm, as it is becoming badly cracked and worn.

The accident has had a positive effect on Russian's nuclear power station industry though. Safety measures and procedures have improved immensely, and there is now a much greater willingness to share ideas with European and American scientists.

12 seconds from death

An icy blast roared through the Skyvan transport plane as the rear door opened to the bright blue sky. On an April morning in 1991, above the flat fields of Cambridgeshire, England, three skydivers were about to make a parachute jump they would never forget.

Richard Maynard was making his first jump. He had paid a substantial fee to plummet from 3,600m (12,000ft), strapped to Mike Smith, a skilled parachute instructor. Expecting this experience (known as a "tandem jump") to be the thrill of a lifetime, Maynard had also commissioned instructor Ronnie O'Brien, to videotape him.

O'Brien leaped backwards from the plane to film Maynard and Smith's exit. The pair plunged down after him, speeding up to 290kmph (180mph) in the first 15 seconds. They soon overtook O'Brien, and Smith released a small drogue parachute to slow them down to a speed where it would be safe to open his main parachute, without it giving them a back-breaking jolt. But here disaster struck. As the chute flew from its container, the cord holding it became entangled around Smith's neck. It pulled tight, strangling him, and he quickly lost consciousness.

Watching from 90m (300ft) above, O'Brien saw the two men spinning out of control, and when the drogue parachute failed to open he knew something had gone terribly wrong. Both men were just 45 seconds from the ground. If O'Brien could not help them, they both faced certain death.

O'Brien changed from the usual spread-eagled posture of a skydiver, and swooped down through the air toward the plummeting pair, with his legs pressed tightly together and arms by his side. He had to judge his descent very carefully. If he overshot, he would have little chance of saving the two men, but this veteran of 2,000 jumps knew what he was doing.

Positioning himself right in front of them, he quickly realized what had happened, and tried to grab hold of Smith so he could release his main parachute. But diving at the same speed was extremely difficult. O'Brien would be within arms length of the falling men and then lurch out of reach. Then suddenly, he fell way below them.

How it all happened

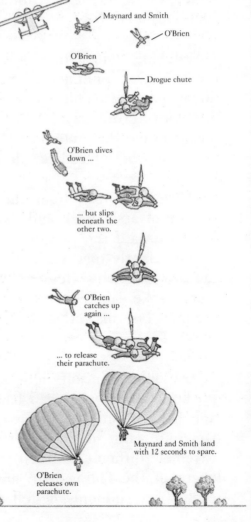

3,600m (12,000ft)
O'Brien jumps from
aircraft, followed
immediately by
Maynard and Smith.

3,000m (10,000ft)
Smith deploys drogue
chute which becomes
tangled around his neck.

2,300m (7,500ft)
Smith loses
consciousness. O'Brien
dives down to help.

2,500-1,500m (7,000-5,000ft)
O'Brien catches up with
tandem divers but slips
underneath them
(25 seconds to impact).

900m (3,000ft)
O'Brien catches up again.

700m (2,500ft)
Parachute released
(12 seconds to impact).
Smith recovers
consciousness.

650m (2,250ft)
O'Brien deploys
own parachute.

Maynard and Smith

O'Brien

O'Brien

Drogue chute

O'Brien dives
down ...

... but slips
beneath the
other two.

O'Brien
catches up
again ...

... to release
their parachute.

Maynard and Smith land
with 12 seconds to spare.

O'Brien
releases own
parachute.

Time was fast running out. The ground was a mere 20 seconds away and O'Brien knew he had only one more chance to save their lives. He spread his arms and legs out to slow his descent, and this time managed to connect with the pair. Whirling around and around, O'Brien searched frantically for the handle that would release Smith's parachute.

With barely 12 seconds before they hit the ground, O'Brien found the handle, and the large main chute billowed out above them. Slowed by the chute, Smith and Maynard shot away as O'Brien continued to plunge down. He released his own parachute when he was safely out of the way, a few seconds before he himself would have hit the ground.

By the time the tandem pair had landed, Smith had recovered consciousness, but collapsed almost immediately. Only then did Maynard realize something had gone wrong. Caught up in the excitement of the jump, with adrenaline coursing through his body and the wind roaring in his ears, he had had no idea that anything out of the ordinary had happened.

Odette's ordeal

On a May day in 1943, several German officers sat beneath a cut-glass chandelier in an elegantly decorated room filled with sunlight. The room served as a court at 84 Avenue Foch, Parisian headquarters of the German Gestapo, the Nazi secret police, whose brutal methods were feared throughout Europe.

The court's attention was focused on a bedraggled French woman who sat before them. She had just spent a month in prison, where she had been forbidden to bathe, exercise or change her clothes. Her feet were bandaged where she had been tortured, but she looked far from broken – in fact she seemed to project a curious, detached kind of dignity, as if she were indifferent to her surroundings. Her name was Odette Sansom, housewife turned British spy, and she was on trial for her life.

Odette, who spoke no German, soon became bored, and her eyes wandered around the room. But when the bemedalled colonel who was obviously in charge of the proceedings stood up and read a statement to her, she knew the trial had ended.

She shrugged wearily and told the court she did not speak German. The colonel frowned and explained in halting French that she had been sentenced to death on two counts. One as a British spy, the other as a member of the French Resistance.

Odette looked on the stiff, pompous men before her with scorn, and a giggle rose inside her. "Gentlemen," she said, "you must take your pick of the counts. I can die only once."

Odette had led a life that hardened her to the tribulations she now faced. She was born Odette Brailly, in Amiens, France, in 1912. When she was four, her father had been killed in the First World War. At seven, she caught polio and was blinded for a year, and then spent another year unable to move her limbs. These disabilities turned her into a fiercely independent character. The teenage Odette was remembered as a loyal friend and merciless enemy.

During the First World War, her mother had provided lodgings for English officers. Odette had liked them all immensely, and grew up determined to marry an Englishman. At 19 she did. His name was Roy Sansom. They moved to England in 1932. Odette's years before the Second World War were spent raising three daughters and living the life of an English housewife in Somerset.

War broke out in 1939 and, in less than two years, Nazi Germany had conquered almost all of Europe. When France fell in 1940, it caused Odette much grief. Cut off from her family, she worried constantly about their safety.

In the spring of 1942, Odette heard a government radio broadcast appealing for snapshots of French beaches. An invasion of France from Britain was being planned, and such photos would help decide which beaches were best for landing troops. Odette had spent her childhood by the sea, so wrote to offer her help.

Shortly afterwards an official letter arrived asking her to come up to London. Here she met a man in a shabby back room office, in a building off Oxford Street. They talked for a while and she placed an envelope of her photos on his desk. To Odette's surprise, he pushed them to one side and looked at her closely.

"Actually," he said with a brisk smile, "we're not really interested in your photos. What we'd really like you to do is go to France as a spy."

Odette was flabbergasted.

"Look, I'm a housewife," she said with some exasperation. "I'm not particularly bright and I don't know a thing about spying. I'm sorry. I'll have to say no to you."

"Very well," said the man, who seemed quite unperturbed. "That's quite understandable. But, here, take my number. If you change your mind, just telephone."

Over the next week Odette could not decide what to do. She was torn between her own patriotic feelings for France, and the responsibility she felt for her three children in England. Eventually she decided she would train as a spy, and found a convent boarding school for her daughters. Odette's work was so secret she could not even tell her family and friends what she was doing. She told them instead that she had joined the Army to work as a nurse.

She joined a branch of the British secret service called the Special Operations Executive (SOE), which sent agents overseas. As soon as her training began, the dangers that would face her were made alarmingly clear. "In many ways it's a beastly job," said her commanding officer, Major Buckmaster. "You will be living a gigantic lie for months on end. And if you slip up and get caught, we can do little to save you." In wartime, the fate of a captured spy was almost always execution.

Physical fitness and combat training toughened Odette. She also learned specialized skills, such as which fields were best for aircraft to make secret landings, and how to tell the difference between various kinds of German military uniforms.

Buckmaster had mixed feelings about Odette. He felt she had a temperamental and impulsive nature which could endanger her and any other agents she would work with. "Her main asset is her patriotism and keenness to do something for France," he wrote in a report. "Her main weakness is a complete unwillingness to admit that she could ever be wrong."

In Odette's final days in England, before she went to France, the British secret service made sure her appearance looked as French as possible. She was given a new wardrobe of authentic French clothes, as anything with an English label on it would betray her. But tiny details were taken care of too. The English fillings in her teeth, for example, were taken out and replaced with French ones, and even her wedding ring was replaced with one that had been made in France.

On Odette's last meeting with Major Buckmaster, he supplied her with several different drugs to help with her work. There were sickness pills, energy pills, sleeping pills and, most sinister of all, a brown, pea-sized suicide pill. Buckmaster told her it would kill her in six seconds. "It's rather a horrible going away present," he said, "so I've also brought you this," and gave her a beautiful silver compact.

Odette was flown over to France in November 1942. She began working in Cannes with a group of secret service agents led by a British officer named Peter Churchill. She acted as a courier, delivering money to pay for the work of the Resistance – French men and women who continued to fight the Germans in France even though their country had surrendered. The British secret service worked closely with the Resistance, organizing bands of guerrilla fighters, assisting in sabotage operations and sending back information to England.

Odette picked up stolen maps and documents from the Resistance to pass back to Britain. She found "safe houses" for other spies and suitable locations for aircraft to land with agents or drop weapons by parachute. Peter Churchill was impressed with her. His new agent was quick-thinking, and capable. He thought she was very funny and seemed to possess an unstoppable determination.

Her job was very difficult and danger lurked at every turn. The Germans were constantly arresting Resistance members, and anyone Odette met in her work could be a double-agent. Eventually the group was betrayed by a traitor named Roger Bardet, who worked for German Military Intelligence – the Abwehr. Churchill and Odette were arrested on April 16, 1943. Even as they were being bundled off at gunpoint, Odette had the presence of mind to hide Churchill's wallet, which contained radio codes and names of other agents, by stuffing it down the side of a car seat on their way to prison.

There was no point denying they were British agents, but Odette spun a complex tale for her captors, hoping at least to save Peter Churchill's life. She said that that they were married to each other, and Churchill was related to the British Prime Minister, Winston Churchill. This was a complete lie. Her "husband", she went on, was an amateur dabbler who had come to France on her insistence. It was she who had led the local resistance ring, and she who should be shot. She told the story so convincingly the Germans swallowed it completely.

A month after their arrest, both of them were taken to Fresnes – a huge jail on the outskirts of

Paris. Odette was placed in cell No. 108, and a campaign to break her spirit began. Outside her door a notice read: "No books. No showers. No packages. No exercise. No privileges."

This was where Odette's interrogation by the Abwehr began in earnest. But she also began her own campaign to survive. With a hairpin she carved a calendar on the wall and marked every day. A grate set high in the wall covered an air vent which led to the cell below, and she was able to talk to a fellow prisoner named Michelle. This was a great comfort, as part of her punishment was that she was allowed no contact with other prisoners. Apart from frequent visits to her interrogators, she had no human contact other than an occasional visit by a German priest named Paul Heinerz.

The window in Odette's cell was made of opaque glass. Michelle whispered up to her: "Break that glass pane at once! If you can see even a little blue sky,   or the crescent of the Moon, it will be a wonderful sight in your dreary cell. The guards, they'll punish you to be sure. They'll probably stop your food for a few days. It's tasteless slop anyway! Believe me, when you can see outside, you'll feel it's been worth it." Odette didn't think twice.

After two weeks of interrogation, the Abwehr realized their prisoner was not going to tell them anything useful and Odette was taken instead to Gestapo headquarters at 84 Avenue Foch. On her very first visit she was given a large meal. But despite her ravenous hunger, she only ate a little. She knew the meal was intended to make her sleepy and dull-witted.

Her interviewer this time was a sophisticated young man, with Nordic good looks, who smelled of cold baths and eau de Cologne. He was polite, but Odette knew she was dealing with someone who was prepared to be far more brutal than the Abwehr. She was right – this urbane young man was actually a trained torturer. But his questions about Odette's Resistance activity were met with her stock response: "I have nothing to say". The interview came to an end and Odette was returned to Fresnes for the night.

She knew her visit to the Gestapo the next day would be more difficult. The suave young man told her he had run out of patience. Her stomach turned over as a shadowy assistant slipped into the room and stood menacingly behind her. First this man applied a red-hot poker to the small of her back. Still Odette would not talk. Then he removed her toenails one by one.

Throughout this torture Odette gave no cry, although she expected to faint several times. As she was asked the same set of questions, she replied with the same answer: "I have nothing to say."

The young man offered her a cigarette and a cup of tea – a standard tactic by torturers, who hope to catch their victims off guard by showing them unexpected kindness. Although she was in great pain, Odette felt elated. She had kept silent and won her own victory over these inhuman thugs.

Her questioner told her they were now going to remove her fingernails, and Odette's courage wavered. But help came from an unexpected quarter. Just as they were about to start on her hands, another Gestapo man came into the cell. "Ach, stop wasting your time," he said. "You'll get nothing more from this one."

Odette was taken back to her cell at Fresnes, where she bound her injured feet in strips of wet cloth. Then she lay on her cell bed, sick with fear at what the Gestapo would do next. Michelle called throughout the night but she was too weak to answer. Father Heinerz visited. He was so disgusted he could not speak. He kissed her head and left. A few days later, she was summoned to the Gestapo court in the chandeliered ceiling room at Avenue Foch, and sentenced to death.

❖

Returning to her cell after the trial, Odette felt unexpectedly calm. Throughout her torture, she had not betrayed her fellow agents. Most of those she knew were still free to continue their work fighting against the Nazis. Alone on her bunk, she bid a silent good night to each of her three daughters and fell sound asleep. But in the early hours she woke with a start. There was no date for her execution. From now on, every footstep outside her door could turn out to be a guard detachment, arriving to escort her to a firing squad.

Despite this constant threat, Odette was determined not to give up hope. Her story about being related to Prime Minister Churchill had been widely repeated among the prison authorities. Many of the staff who guarded Odette were unusually courteous with her. Like many people in 1943, they had realized the war was going badly for Germany and thought that it would pay to keep on the right side of one of Winston Churchill's "relations".

As summer turned to autumn, Odette fell gravely ill and was moved to a warmer cell. She was also given a job in the prison sewing room and ordered to make German army uniforms. This she refused to do, saying she would make dolls instead. Amazingly, the prison staff let her do this.

Over the winter her health improved but, in May 1944, news came that she was to be transferred to a prison in Germany. As she left, Odette caught sight of one of her interrogators and waved at him gaily, shouting "Goodbye, goodbye." She was determined to let him know he had not broken her spirit.

In the van that took her away were seven other women. They all immediately recognized each other as fellow SOE agents. All instinctively felt they were being taken to Germany to be executed, but they were still delighted to see each other. Their instincts were right. Within a year, all but Odette would be dead.

On the way through Paris, they stopped at Avenue Foch where a Gestapo officer asked if there was anything they wanted. Odette ordered a pot of tea, "... not as it is made in France or Germany, but in the English manner. One spoonful for each person and one for the pot. With milk and sugar please." The tea duly arrived, with china cups and saucers.

Odette was placed on an east-bound train with an armed guard, and spent the next few weeks in several prisons. Once she was presented to a Nazi newspaper reporter who crowed that there were now three Churchills in German prisons, and he was to write a feature on her. Odette dismissed him with a barbed remark, but this was good news. If the Nazis were publicizing her imprisonment, they were hardly likely to execute her immediately.

In July 1944, she was taken to Ravensbrück – a Nazi concentration camp for women on the shore of swampy Lake Fürstenburg. Even the name of the camp, the "Bridge of Ravens", sounded sinister.

Inside its barbed-wire perimeter were row upon row of shabby prisoners' huts, patrolled by guards with whips and savage dogs. All of Ravensbrück's inmates had shaven heads, to cut down on the lice that constantly plagued them. Prisoners who had been there for months or years had been so badly fed they looked like walking skeletons.

Smoke from the camp crematorium constantly filled the sky, scattering a ghastly pall of dust and ashes over the stark, grey interior. The Nazis sent their enemies here to be worked to death and, every morning, those who had died in the night were carried away in crude wooden handcarts. As a young girl walking the cliffs of Normandy, Odette had sometimes wondered where she would die. As she entered Ravensbrück, she felt she knew the answer.

❖

The commandant of the camp, a German officer named Fritz Sühren, was eager to meet Odette. When she was taken before him, she noticed how clean and well fed he looked. Like most of her captors, Sühren was interested in her connection with Winston Churchill. He ordered her to be placed in "the bunker" – the camp's own solitary confinement cells.

Odette's bunker cell was pitch black and for three months she was kept there in total darkness. But she had been blind for a year of her childhood. She was used to the dark. She passed the time thinking about her three daughters, and how they had grown from babies into young girls. She decided to clothe them in her imagination, stitch by stitch, garment by garment. So completely did she fill her days deciding on the fabric, shades and style of these clothes, that whenever she was visited by camp guards, it seemed like an interruption, rather than the chance to make contact with another human being.

In August, southern France was invaded by French, British and American forces. This was where Odette had done most of her Resistance work. As a spiteful punishment, the guards turned the central heating in her cell to maximum. Odette wrapped herself in a blanket soaked in cold water, but this did not stop her from becoming terribly ill. Near death, she was taken to the camp hospital. It was a strange way to treat someone who had been sentenced to execution. Perhaps the Nazis were still hoping they could break her and she would tell them about her Resistance work.

Away from the bunker, Odette recovered her strength and was returned to her cell. On the way back she found a single leaf that had blown into the treeless camp, and scooped it into her clothing. In her dark world she would trace its spine and shape with her hands, and think about how the wind had blown a seed into the earth which had grown to a tree with leaves and branches that rustled in the wind and basked in the sunlight.

Over the next few months she overheard the execution of several of her fellow agents, all of whom were shot during the winter.

On April 27, 1945, Sühren visited her. He stood at the cell door then drew his finger across his throat. "You'll leave tomorrow morning at six o'clock," he said. Odette wondered if the end had come at last. On April 28 she would be 33. It would be a pity to be shot on her birthday.

When morning came she could hear the chaos that had overtaken the camp. Sühren arrived and bundled her into a large black van with a handful of other inmates. Through the window she could see the guards fleeing from the camp.

The van, together with an escort of SS troops (elite Nazi soldiers), drove west. It soon became clear to Odette that the war was almost over. For the next three days Sühren, his SS escort, and his small band of prisoners, drove from one camp to another as Germany collapsed into anarchy. Many of the prisoners in these camps, so near to freedom but so close to death, were almost hysterical. Some whooped and screamed, making huge bonfires of anything they could find to burn. Others collapsed from hunger, or rushed at their guards only to be gunned down. It all seemed like a delirious nightmare.

On the fourth day away from Ravensbrück, a guard grabbed Odette and dragged her before Sühren. She was told not to bring her few belongings, and was certain she was to be executed. Thrown into Sühren's large staff car, and with an escort of SS guards in two other cars, she sped away from the camp.

After two hours, the three cars stopped by a deserted field and Sühren barked, "Get out." But this was not to be Odette's place of execution. Instead Sühren offered her a sandwich and a glass of wine, and told her he was handing her over to the Americans. At first she thought this was a cruel joke, but he seemed serious enough. Clearly he thought safely delivering Winston Churchill's relative would get him off to a good start with his captors.

The SS guards spent the next few hours burning incriminating Ravensbrück documents. Then, at 10:00 that night, they drove into a village which had been occupied by American soldiers. Sühren marched up to an officer and said, "This is Frau Churchill. She

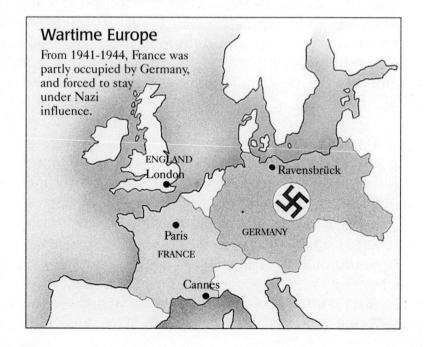

Wartime Europe

From 1941-1944, France was partly occupied by Germany, and forced to stay under Nazi influence.

ENGLAND
London
Ravensbrück
Paris
GERMANY
FRANCE
Cannes

has been a prisoner. She is a relative of Winston Churchill." He handed Odette his revolver and surrendered.

The Americans offered her a place to sleep, but Odette wanted to spend her first night of freedom out in the open. She walked over to Sühren's abandoned open-topped car and sat in the front seat, feeling neither triumph nor elation, just utter exhaustion. Nearby was a party of SS soldiers who had been part of Sühren's escort. One came over and gave her his sheepskin coat to ward off the chill of the night.

To Odette, this act of kindness by a former enemy seemed part of a strange dream, and she expected to wake at any moment and find herself back in the bunker at Ravensbrück. But the dream continued. She nestled into the coat and stared up at the stars. The village clock chimed its quarter hours throughout the night, and it was so quiet she could hear her heart beating.

Afterwards

Following her release, Odette returned to England, after ensuring that Fritz Sühren's American captors were aware that he had been commandant of Ravensbrück. (He was later tried as a war criminal and executed.)

She had several operations on her injured feet before she was able to walk properly again. In 1946, she became the first woman to be given the George Cross, Britain's highest civilian award for bravery, "for courage, endurance and self sacrifice of the highest possible order". She always insisted that the medal had not been given to her personally, but in recognition of the bravery of all French resistance workers.

The medal was stolen a few years later. But following a series of outraged newspaper articles in Britain's national press, it was returned with a letter of apology from the anonymous burglar.

In 1948, after her first husband had died, she married Peter Churchill, the man she had suffered so much to protect. But after eight years they parted, and Odette later married Geoffrey Hallowes, another secret service veteran. In later life she co-founded the British "Woman of the Year" award, worked for charities and spent many hours writing to thousands of people with problems, who had contacted her for advice or inspiration.

Odette Sansom's life as a secret agent was portrayed in the 1950 British film *Odette*, starring Anna Neagle. It was partially shot at Fresnes Prison, Paris, where Odette herself had been held prisoner. She worked as an advisor on the film, but seeing

Anna Neagle relive her worst moments was a very painful experience.

She returned to Ravensbrück in 1994, for a ceremony to unveil a plaque commemorating the courage of the British SOE women who had died there. Looking back on the war, Odette wrote: "I am a very ordinary woman, to whom the chance has been given to see human beings at their best and at their worst."

She died in 1995, aged 82.

Helicopter heroes

The situation outlined in an emergency phone call to Royal Naval Air Station Culdrose, Cornwall, UK, was deeply alarming. On October 28, 1989, a huge Pakistani container ship, named *Murree*, was caught in a severe storm some distance from Start Bay, Dartmouth. Her cargo, piled high on the deck, had shifted in the rough weather. One stack of containers had broken free and fallen into the sea. But one of the heavy steel containers swung back against the hull and split it open. Now vast amounts of water were flooding into the hold. A lifeboat had already been launched from nearby Brixham, but the turbulent sea had made docking all but impossible.

So Sea King helicopters were dispatched from Culdrose to help in the rescue operation. They arrived above the *Murree* within minutes, and two Royal Navy divers, Petty Officers Steve Wright and Dave Wallace, were lowered down onto her heaving deck.

Wright and Wallace were disturbed to discover that there were 40 people on board the sinking vessel, including many of the wives and children of the crew. As gale force winds lashed the sloping deck, they gathered together the terrified crew and passengers. With the bow already underwater, they strapped them two at a time into harnesses so they could be lifted into waiting helicopters. But time was running out.

Just as the last two crew members were being winched off the deck, the *Murree* lurched alarmingly and the bow sank deeper beneath the waves. Wright grabbed hold of a nearby deck railing to stop himself from falling. Wallace was not so lucky and slithered down the tilting deck towards the boiling sea below. Fortunately, his leg caught in a coil of rope. This broke his fall, but he had to struggle frantically to break free.

The *Murree* was going down fast. On the stern of the ship the two divers grabbed desperately at the harness from the helicopter overhead, but it slipped from their grip. There was only one thing left to do. Taking a huge leap from the stern into the heaving waves, they plunged deep underwater and surfaced to see the ship's stern towering over them.

Fearing they would be sucked under as the ship went down, the two swam for their lives. Battered by huge waves and debris from the wreckage, they floundered in the sea until a Sea King helicopter was able to pluck them from the water.

Back on dry land, the *Murree*'s Captain Abdul Ajeeq, who had been the last crew member to leave the doomed vessel, told waiting newspaper reporters: "These helicopter men are fantastic. They gave us our lives."

Afterwards

In 1990, Wright and Wallace's courage was officially recognized when they were presented with the George Medal. The *Murree* still lies deep under the water, halfway between Star Point and Alderney in the Channel Islands. It is now almost totally covered in brittlestars and sea anemones, and is occasionally visited by divers interested in exploring its rusting interior.

Punching a hole in the sky

In the summer of 1947, a huge silver B-29 bomber soared off the windswept runway at Muroc airbase, California. As it climbed into a cloudless August sky, the sun gleamed brightly on a strange bullet-shaped craft slung under its belly. This was the Bell X-1 rocket, a machine designed to fly beyond the very frontiers of aviation science.

The X-1's pilot, a 24-year-old US Airforce captain named Chuck Yeager, knew he was dicing with death every time he took to the sky. But before the year was out, Yeager was determined to fly this rocket beyond the speed of sound – faster than any man had ever flown before.

In 1947, supersonic flight – as any aircraft speed faster than sound is known – was dark, forbidding territory. Yeager joked that it might make his ears fall off. But it was true that some aircraft that had attempted to break the sound barrier had literally disintegrated, shaken apart by invisible forces no one yet understood.

Most aviation engineers thought no aircraft could fly faster than sound. They believed there was a "sound barrier" – an invisible wall of turbulence that would tear apart any plane that tried to break through it.

Military pilots rarely flew on such dangerous experimental missions. A highly paid civilian test pilot, named "Slick" Goodlin, had begun the project. As the X-1 tests had approached the speed of sound, he had demanded a $150,000 bonus for an actual attempt on the sound barrier. The US military could no longer afford him, and recruited a pilot from their own ranks.

Despite the obvious dangers, Yeager volunteered. Flying filled him with an indescribable joy. The chance to pilot a beautiful aircraft like the X-1 was heaven sent. Besides, in the competitive world of the test pilot, the opportunity to become the first man to travel faster than sound was too good to miss. He took the job on his standard captain's pay of $283 a month.

With his slow, West Virginian country drawl, Yeager was something of an oddball in the high-powered world of experimental flying. But his exceptional skill, and quick thinking coolness under pressure, made him by far the best test pilot at Muroc.

Lacking a college education, he had joined the US airforce at 18 years old as a mechanic. Yeager had extraordinary hand-eye coordination and excellent eyesight. This was soon noticed and he was transferred to flight-training school. In World War Two, he piloted fighter planes over Europe, was shot down over France and escaped back to his base in England. He flew nearly 100 combat missions, and once shot down five German aircraft in a single day.

Now, as the B-29 climbed into the sky on this breezy August day, Yeager was about to pilot the X-1 on its first powered flight. He had flown the plane before, but only on glide flights. This time it was brimming with liquid oxygen and alcohol fuel.

At the flick of a rocket ignition switch, his craft could shoot straight to the top of the sky, or it could explode into a thousand flaming pieces. He was nervous, but told himself fear was a pilot's friend. It sharpened his senses and kept his mind focused on the job in hand.

Trying to break through the sound barrier was so dangerous it could only be attempted in small stages. The X-1 would be dropped from the bomb bay of the B.29 at 8,000m (25,000ft), and then

Yeager would ignite the rockets and fly off into the horizon. Being unleashed from the B-29, rather than taking off in the usual way, saved weight on fuel. The less weight the X-1 carried, the faster it was going to fly.

The Bell X-1

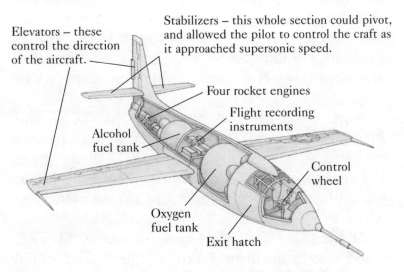

Elevators – these control the direction of the aircraft.

Stabilizers – this whole section could pivot, and allowed the pilot to control the craft as it approached supersonic speed.

Four rocket engines

Flight recording instruments

Alcohol fuel tank

Control wheel

Oxygen fuel tank

Exit hatch

Yeager didn't sit in the X-1 at take-off, in case it accidentally dropped out of the B-29 before they reached a safe height for the rocket to fly. Near the drop zone, he left the B-29's cockpit and squeezed through a narrow corridor to the bomb bay. Here he could see right down to the surface of the Earth.

Yeager had to climb down a ladder to a small metal platform and squeeze feet first through the hatch into his craft. At such a height, it was viciously cold and the wind threatened to tear his frozen fingers from the ladder's metal rungs.

Once he was inside, the door to the hatch was lowered down. His flight engineer and good friend, Jack Ridley, stood on the ladder and held it in place as it was locked from the inside. Yeager trusted his flight engineer with his life. Only 29, Ridley had already established a reputation as a brilliant scientist.

Some people said the X-1 was the most beautiful aircraft ever built. Yeager knew it was certainly the coldest. It was so chilly in the darkened bomb bay that he had to bang his gloved hands together to keep them from becoming numb. The X-1 cockpit had no heating, and directly behind the seat sat several hundred gallons of freezing-cold liquid oxygen fuel; the belly of the craft was now coated in a thin film of ice.

But now was no time to worry about the cold. "All set," radioed in Ridley, back inside the B-29. "You bet," said Yeager. "Let's go to work."

The X-1 dropped like a stone. Yeager was blinded by bright sunlight and wrestled to get his craft under control. When the X-1 was flying level, he flicked the rocket ignition switch on his instrument panel. A luminous jet of flame roared from the rocket exhaust and a huge surge of power slammed him

The sound barrier

Mach 0.5
As a plane flies through the air it creates small disturbances, or shock waves, in the air around it.

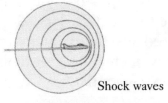

Shock waves

Mach 0.9
Near the sound barrier, shock waves travel at the same speed as the plane, causing buffeting.

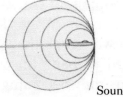

Sound barrier

Mach 1
Above the speed of sound a plane travels faster than the shock waves.

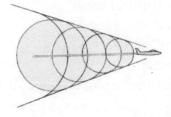

back into his seat. It seemed as if he was heading for the very roof of the sky and was going to punch his way into space itself.

Yeager controlled the X-1's speed by igniting between one and four of his rocket engines. By the time all four engines were lit, he had reached 14,000m (45,000ft). The sky turned from bright blue to dark indigo. Yeager was on the edge of space and flying close to the speed of sound at Mach 0.8.

Down at Muroc, the research engineers and airbase technicians not working on the X-1 showed little interest in the project. In fact, they all thought it was doomed to failure and tragedy. Experienced test pilots had been warned off volunteering for the flights. Most people thought Goodlin had got out just in time.

But up on the roof of the sky, the X-1 was flying beautifully. Yeager had reached maximum speed for this flight and still had half his fuel left. He thought it was time to show the Muroc personnel what his plane could do, so he cut the engines and dived toward the airbase. Lining up the rocket with the main runway he took it down to 90m (300ft) and headed for the control tower. Then Yeager hit the rocket ignition switches.

The four engines burst into life with an enormous streak of flame, making a roar that rattled every roof, window and coffee cup in the base. The X-1 shot back into the sky so fast it reached 11,000m (35,000ft) in under a minute. The fuel cut out, and Yeager glided down to the main runway, so excited he could not speak.

Yeager might have been pleased with himself, but everyone else was furious. His commanding officer Colonel Boyd told him angrily that the X-1 project was one of the most dangerous test-flights ever attempted. There was no space for fooling around.

The next few trips were extremely dangerous. On its sixth powered flight on October 5, the X-1 started to buffet violently as Yeager reached Mach 0.86. Through the window he could see the rocket's wings shaking wildly as shock waves assaulted his craft.

The next flight was even worse. As Yeager pushed the X-1 to Mach 0.94 he found the control wheel jammed. This was serious. At the speed of sound it was assumed that the aircraft nose would either point up or down – something that the pilot would have to correct. If he was unable to do this, the craft could spin out of control and crash.

Yeager returned to base, sure that the X-1 project would be cancelled. Everyone agreed, apart from Jack Ridley, who quickly scribbled some calculations on a piece of scrap paper. The flight engineer explained that the reason the control wheel jammed was that, at such high speed, the force of the air flowing over the rocket prevented the wing and tail elevators from moving. Instead, suggested Ridley, the aircraft could be controlled by moving the stabilizers on the tail, where the force of the air was not so strong. Yeager had not done this before, because he was afraid the tail might rip off, plunging the plane into an uncontrollable spin which would end with his death in a fiery explosion.

There was only one way to test Ridley's theory. Yeager flew back up to Mach 0.94, a whisker away from the speed of sound. Sure enough, Ridley was right. Moving the stabilizer controls was enough to keep the X-1 flying steady, and gave Yeager the confidence to know that he would be able to keep control of his aircraft.

Yeager now felt sure that he could break the sound barrier in the X-1 and survive. The next flight was planned for the following Tuesday – October 14, 1947.

On Sunday evening, Yeager took his wife Glennis out riding, but disaster struck when he was thrown from his horse and fractured two ribs. The pain was intense but Yeager refused to go to the hospital at Muroc. He knew they would stop him from flying and he was determined to finish the job he had started.

So, on the Monday morning before the flight, Glennis drove him to a local doctor who patched him up and told him to rest. But rest was the last thing on his mind. Despite the fact that he could do very little with his right hand, Yeager drove over to Muroc and confided in Jack Ridley. He was convinced he could still make Tuesday's flight. He knew the aircraft really well now, and most of the controls would be no problem to operate.

However, lifting the handle to lock the door of the X-1 required more strength than his painful right arm could muster. In the cramped cockpit he could not reach it with his left hand. But he managed to think of a solution. Ridley found a broom and sawed off 25cm (10in). Yeager could use his good left arm to push the handle up with it. Getting down the ladder would be difficult too, and Yeager jokingly suggested that Ridley could carry him piggyback.

The B-29 took off at 8:00 in the morning that Tuesday. Officially, Yeager was only meant to go to Mach 0.97. But he reasoned that the more flights there were, the more chance there was of an accident. He could be killed or the project could be cancelled. He was going to go for bust.

Getting down the ladder with two broken ribs hurt terribly, but the broomstick worked well on the door handle. As the X-1 dropped from the bomb bay, Yeager felt perfectly in control. He ignited the rocket engines in quick succession and streaked towards the top of the sky. At Mach 0.88, the buffeting started, and Yeager cut two of his engines and tilted the tail stabilizers. They worked perfectly too, and the X-1 stopped shaking. He kicked in rocket engine three and continued to climb. The faster he went, the smoother the ride. The needle in his Mach instrument began to flutter, and then wavered off the scale.

Aircraft flying faster than sound create air turbulence which causes an explosive noise called a "sonic boom." Down at Muroc, a sound like distant thunder rolled over the airfield.

Yeager was elated. He radioed Jack Ridley in the B-29.

"Hey Ridley," he giggled, "that Machmeter is acting screwy. It just went off the scale on me."

"Son, I think you must be imagining things," Ridley responded.

"Must be," said Yeager in his particularly slow drawl. "I'm still wearing my ears and nothing else fell off, neither."

Only his instruments told Yeager he had broken the sound barrier. The X-1 was streaking smoothly along and, as he was flying faster than sound, he did not even hear the sonic boom.

When its fuel ran out, the rocket coasted down to Earth. Yeager landed seven minutes later, to a hero's welcome. His ribs ached terribly, but the desert sun felt wonderful on his face. Not since Orville and Wilbur Wright made the first powered flight in 1903 had an aircraft made such an extraordinary journey.

Afterwards

Yeager's pioneering flight paved the way for all subsequent supersonic jet plane development. Following his record-breaking journey, he spent another decade working as a test pilot.

In the 1960s, Yeager returned to active service, flying bombing missions over Vietnam. He rose to the rank of Brigadier General. Over his life he has logged more than 10,000 hours of flying time, in over 180 different military aircraft. "The best pilots fly more than others," he once said. "That's why they're the best."

His assault on the sound barrier was captured spectacularly in the 1983 American film *The Right Stuff*, starring Sam Shepard. Based on Tom Wolfe's best-selling book of the same title, the film also depicts America's first attempts to launch an astronaut into space. Yeager worked as a technical advisor on the film, and also made a brief cameo appearance as a bartender at an inn near Muroc airbase.

In retirement, Yeager spends his life hunting, flying (anything from hang-gliders to high speed jets) and making regular appearances as an after-dinner speaker. "I'm not the rocking-chair type," he remarked in his 1986 autobiography *Yeager*.

Animal heroes

The following four short stories show how some people owe their lives or freedom to acts of animal heroism.

Jan's best friend

There are many stories about dogs who have saved their owner's lives by pulling them from swollen rivers, or alerting them to house fires or gas leaks. But few people can have had such a loyal companion, nor owed so much to their dog, as Jan Bozdech of Czechoslovakia.

A few years before the Second World War, Bozdech came across a starving German Shepherd puppy who had been abandoned. He adopted the dog, named it Antis, and the two became inseparable.

When the German army occupied his country in 1938, Bozdech fled to France, taking Antis with him. When war broke out he volunteered to become a pilot in the French Air Force and flew several missions, taking his faithful companion with him in his fighter plane. The two were shot down but survived. When France was also conquered by the Germans, pilot and dog left for England, where Bozdech joined the British Air Force.

When the war ended in 1945, they returned home. But Bozdech's troubles were far from over. Czechoslovakia was now controlled by the Soviet Union rather than Nazi Germany. Shortly after he returned, a strict communist system was set up in his country, and citizens were forbidden to leave.

Bozdech had spent most of the last decade fighting such tyranny and was determined to escape. With Antis and two friends he set off for Austria, the nearest non-communist country. His friends were not happy to travel with the dog, but Antis soon proved his worth, alerting them whenever they were close to police or border guard patrols by growling or looking wary.

Along the way, the escapers had to cross a fast-flowing river under cover of darkness. During the crossing Bozdech slipped, bashed his head on a boulder, and was carried away unconscious by the current. Antis bounded after him, grabbed Bozdech's jacket in his teeth, and dragged him to the riverside. As he lay recovering, the German Shepherd trotted off to find his two friends who had vanished into the night.

Near the border, the party stopped to rest in a quiet spot, leaving the dog to keep watch. After a while, a border guard appeared and began to walk directly toward the sleeping men. Antis immediately started to bark and leaped around the guard, distracting him from his route and saving the three escapers from almost certain arrest.

Once they had safely reached Austria, Bozdech and Antis were able to make their way back to England, where Bozdech had many friends. Antis died in 1953 and Bozdech had him buried at Ilford Animal Cemetery in London. His grave is still there today, and you can see these words written on his gravestone:

> *There is an old belief*
> *That on some solemn shore*
> *Beyond the sphere of grief*
> *Dear friends shall meet once more.*

Goose saves guardsman's bacon

Coldstream guardsman Jack Kemp stood to attention on guard duty at a farm outside Quebec. The year was 1837 and Kemp's regiment had been sent to Canada by the British government to defend the territory from French settlers, who were rebelling against British rule.

As Kemp surveyed the countryside before him, he noticed a handsome white goose searching for food. Close by, and watching intently, was a hungry fox. Sensing danger, the goose looked up. Both animals stood frozen, as if in a trance. Then the goose panicked, and ran shrieking between the guardsman's legs. Kemp reacted instinctively, and when the fox came hurtling after, he killed it with his bayonet.

Much to Kemp's surprise, the goose started to rub his head affectionately against his legs, as if to say thank you. From that moment on, the guardsman adopted him as a pet and gave him the name of Jacob. It was an alliance that was to save his life.

Shortly afterwards, Kemp was standing guard again outside the farm when he was attacked by a group of French rebels. As he fought for his life Jacob came squawking to the rescue, flapping his wings wildly and pecking with his sharp beak. While the distracted rebels defended themselves from the angry goose, Kemp grabbed a rifle that had been knocked from his hand and fired. The shot alerted soldiers nearby who came to his rescue and the attackers ran off. Jacob had saved both Kemp and his comrades. The guardsmen gave Jacob a gold collar as a reward for his bravery. They became so attached to their unusual pet that they took him with them when the regiment returned to London.

The snow dog

New Jersey winters can be harsh. When a blizzard strikes, children are sometimes unable to travel to school, as roads become blocked and driving is impossible. On a day like this in February, 1983, Andrea Andersen and her sisters were stuck at their seaside home. Andrea soon became bored and suggested to her sisters that they go outside to play. Putting on their warmest clothes, they walked through a howling gale to the sea front, but the sisters soon returned home, complaining that it was too cold to be out. Andrea, though, was determined to stay.

Alone now, Andrea snuggled deep into her coat and watched the snow tumble down over the choppy waters of the North Atlantic. Suddenly, a howling gale picked her up and blew her into a snowdrift, right on the edge of the icy sea. Andrea was so numb with cold she could hardly move, and became increasingly terrified to discover she did not have the strength to pull herself out. She shouted frantically for help at the top of her voice, but her cries were swallowed by the wind.

But help was at hand. Next door to the Andersen's lived a couple named Dick and Lynda Veit, who kept a Newfoundland dog named Villa. Dogs have much more sensitive hearing than humans, and Villa was able to recognize Andrea's desperate cries above the noise of the raging storm. Immediately, the dog left the house, leaped over a 1.5m (5ft) wall, and set off to look for the girl.

After a brief search among the snow, Villa found Andrea and lowered its big head into the drift. Andrea, who was feeling colder and weaker by the minute, could not believe her luck. She reached up and fastened her freezing fingers around Villa's collar. The Newfoundland pulled her out, and then led the helpless schoolgirl back to the warmth and safety of her home.

When news of the incident broke, Villa was awarded a "Ken-L Ration" medal, for "outstanding loyalty and intelligence", by the Quaker Oats Company, that produces Ken-L dog food. The medal came with a year's supply of dog food.

Heroic homing pigeons

Pigeons have the ability to fly over great distances and return to one particular spot which they think of as home. Soldiers have long made use of this phenomenon by employing these birds to ferry messages, which are carried in a metal tube on the pigeon's leg. Birds used to do this are called homing pigeons, or carrier pigeons.

Some pigeons give up easily in difficult circumstances, but others are determined to return. Pigeons have completed their missions with bullet wounds, or after being mauled by a hawk. One even walked back home with a broken wing.

During the First and Second World Wars, carrier pigeons were used in great numbers and many men owed their lives to the birds. In Italy in 1943, one American carrier pigeon named G.I. Joe flew 32km (20 miles) in only 20 minutes, with a message warning a bomber squadron not to attack a village that had just been captured by American troops.

Another pigeon named Winkie was aboard a British bomber when it crashed in the North Sea. The crew survived but, as no one at their base knew their position, they were in danger of freezing to death. Winkie was covered in oil but this did not prevent him from flying the long journey home, with a message reporting that the plane had crashed in the sea, and a detailed map reference showing where the crew could be found. Thanks to Winkie's perserverance, a search was immediately launched and the crew's lives were saved.

Stauffenberg's Secret Germany

On a spring morning in 1943, American fighter planes screamed low over a Tunisian coastal road, pouring machine-gun fire onto a column of German army vehicles. Fierce flames bellowed from blazing trucks and smeared the blue desert sky with oily, black smoke. Amid the wreckage on the ground lay Colonel Claus von Stauffenberg, one of Germany's most brilliant soldiers. He was badly wounded, and fighting for his life.

Stauffenberg was quickly transported to a Munich hospital and given the best possible treatment. His left eye, right hand and two fingers from his left hand had been lost in the attack. His legs were so badly damaged that doctors feared he would never walk again.

Willing himself back from the brink of death, Stauffenberg was determined not to be defeated by his injuries. He refused all pain-killing drugs, and learned to dress, bathe and write with his three remaining fingers. His recovery was astounding.

Before the summer was over he was demanding to be returned to his regiment.

Hospital staff were amazed by their patient's stubborn persistence, and admired what they thought was his patriotic determination to return to active service. But it was not to fight for Nazi leader Adolf Hitler that the colonel struggled so hard to recover. What Stauffenberg wanted to do was kill him.

Stauffenberg had supported the Nazis once, but his experience in the war had turned him against them. In Poland, in 1939, he had witnessed SS soldiers killing Jewish women and children by the roadside. While fighting in France in 1940, he had seen a Nazi field commander order the execution of unarmed British prisoners. Worst of all had been Hitler's war against the Soviet Union (now Russia). Not only had this invasion been fought with great brutality to Russian soldiers and civilians alike, but Stauffenberg had been sickened by Hitler's incompetent interference in the campaign, and his stubborn refusal to allow exhausted troops in impossible situations to surrender.

After one disastrous battle, Stauffenberg asked a close friend: "Is there no officer in Hitler's headquarters capable of taking a pistol to the beast?" Lying in his hospital bed, Stauffenberg realized he was just the man for the job.

Like most people, Stauffenberg had his flaws. Although he was untidy in his personal appearance, he was incredibly strict about orderliness and punctuality. He had a ferocious temper, and could become enraged if an aide laid out his uniform less than perfectly. But Stauffenberg was blessed with a magnetic personality and he was a brilliant commander. He also had a sensitive nature, which encouraged fellow officers to confide in him. All these aspects of his character made him an ideal leader of any opposition to Hitler.

As soon as Stauffenberg was well enough to come out of hospital, he was appointed Chief of Staff in the Home Army. The Home Army was a unit of the German Army made up of all soldiers stationed in Germany. It was also responsible for recruitment and training. Stauffenberg quickly established that the deputy commander of the Home Army, General Olbricht, was not a supporter of the Nazis either. He too was willing to help Stauffenberg overthrow Hitler. Between them, they began to persuade other officers to join them.

Stauffenberg and his fellow plotters soon devised an ingenious plan to get rid of Hitler. In the previous year, the Nazis had set up a strategy called *Operation*

Valkyrie, as a precaution against an uprising in Germany against them. If such a revolt broke out, the Home Army had detailed instructions to seize control of all areas of government, and important radio and railway stations, so the rebellion could be quickly put down.

But, rather than protect the Nazis, Stauffenberg and Olbricht intended to use *Operation Valkyrie* to overthrow them. They planned to kill Hitler and, in the confusion that followed his death, they would set *Operation Valkyrie* in motion, ordering their soldiers to arrest all Nazi leaders and their chief supporters – especially the SS (elite regiments of Nazi soldiers) and the Gestapo (secret police).

The plot had two great flaws. Firstly, killing Hitler would be difficult, as he was surrounded by bodyguards. Secondly, when the head of the Home Army, General Friedrich Fromm, was approached by the conspirators, he refused to take part. Like everyone in the armed forces, he had sworn an oath of loyalty to Hitler, and he used this as an excuse for not betraying him. Fromm also feared Hitler's revenge if the plot should fail. Without Fromm's help, using Valkyrie to overthrow the Nazis would be considerably more difficult.

But the plotters were not deterred and Stauffenberg still threw himself into the task of recruiting allies. He referred to his conspiracy as "Secret Germany" after a poem by his hero, German writer Stefan George. Many officers joined Stauffenberg, but many more wavered. Most were disgusted by the way Hitler was leading the German army but, like Fromm, they felt restrained by their oath of loyalty or feared for their lives if the plot should fail.

The plotters took care to avoid being discovered by the Gestapo. Documents were typed wearing gloves, to avoid leaving fingerprints, on a typewriter that would then be hidden in a cupboard or attic. Stauffenberg memorized and then destroyed written messages, and left not a scrap of solid evidence against himself. And such was his good judgment in recruiting plotters that not a single German officer he approached to join the conspiracy betrayed him.

But by the summer of 1944, time was running out. The Gestapo had begun to suspect a major revolt against Hitler was being planned. They were searching hard for conspirators and the evidence to condemn them. The longer the plotters delayed, the greater their chance of being discovered.

By this time, the plotters had decided the best way to kill Hitler would be with a bomb hidden in a briefcase. As part of his Home Army duties, Stauffenberg attended conferences with the German leader, who thought the colonel was a very glamorous figure and had a high regard for his abilities. Because Stauffenberg had such close contact with Hitler, he volunteered to plant the bomb himself.

In order to give him time to escape, the bomb would be primed with a ten-minute fuse. This device was quite complicated. To activate the bomb, a small glass tube containing acid needed to be broken with a pair of pliers. The acid would eat through a thin steel wire. When this broke, it released a detonator which set off the bomb.

On July 11, Stauffenberg went to Hitler's headquarters at Rastenburg in East Prussia for a meeting with Hitler, and two other leading Nazis, Heinrich Himmler and Herman Goering. He hoped to wipe out all three, but when Himmler and Goering did not arrive he decided to wait for a better opportunity.

On July 15, Stauffenberg was again summoned to Rastenburg. On this occasion, *Operation Valkyrie* was set in motion before the meeting. But unfortunately, at the last moment, Hitler decided not to attend the conference where Stauffenberg was due to plant his bomb. A frantic phone call to Berlin called off *Valkyrie* and the conspirators covered their tracks by pretending it had been an army exercise.

Their chance finally came on July 20, 1944, when Stauffenberg was again summoned to Hitler's headquarters at Rastenburg. Together with his personal assistant, Lieutenant Werner von Haeften, he collected two bombs and drove to Rangsdorf airfield south of Berlin, and from there took the three hour flight to Rastenburg.

Arriving in East Prussia at 10:15am, they drove through gloomy forest to Hitler's headquarters. Surrounded by barbed wire, minefields and checkpoints, the base – fancifully known as "The Wolf's Lair"– was a collection of concrete bunkers and wooden huts. It was here, cut off from the real world, that Hitler had retreated to wage his final battles of the war.

The conference with Hitler was scheduled for 12:30pm. At 12:15pm, as conference staff began to assemble, Stauffenberg requested permission to wash and change his shirt. It was such a hot day this seemed perfectly reasonable.

An aide ushered him into a nearby washroom, where he was quickly joined by Haeften, and they set about activating the two bombs. Stauffenberg broke the acid tube fuse on one but, as he reached for the second bomb, they were interrupted by a sergeant sent to hurry Stauffenberg, who was now late for the conference.

One bomb would have to do. But there was further bad news. Stauffenberg had hoped the meeting would be held in an underground bunker – a windowless, concrete room where the blast of his bomb would be much more destructive. But instead, he was led to a wooden hut with three large windows. The force of any explosion here would be a lot less effective.

Inside the hut, the conference had already begun. High-ranking officers and their assistants crowded around a large, oak, map table, discussing the progress of the war in Russia. Stauffenberg, whose hearing had been damaged when he was wounded, asked if he could stand near to Hitler so he could hear him properly.

Placing himself to Hitler's right, Stauffenberg shoved his bulging briefcase under the table, to the left of a large, wooden support. Just then, Field Marshal Keitel, who was one of Hitler's most loyal generals, suggested that Stauffenberg should deliver his report next. But with less than seven minutes before the bomb would explode, he had no intention of remaining inside the hut. Fortunately, the discussion on the Russian front continued and Stauffenberg made an excuse to leave the room, saying he had to make an urgent phone call to Berlin.

Keitel, already irritated by Stauffenberg's late arrival, became incensed that he should have the impertinence to leave the conference, and called after him, insisting that he should stay. But Stauffenberg ignored him and hurried off. Like all the conspirators, he hated Keitel, whom he called Lakeitel – a pun on the German word *Lakei* meaning "toady" or "lackey."

There were less than five minutes to go. Stauffenberg hurried over to another hut and waited with his friend General Erich Fellgiebel, the chief of signals at the base, who was one of several Rastenburg officers who had joined Stauffenberg's conspiracy. The seconds dragged by.

Inside the conference room, an officer named Colonel Brandt leaned over the table to get a better look at a map. His foot caught on Stauffenberg's heavy briefcase, so he picked it up

The Wolf's Lair Conference Room

Map table

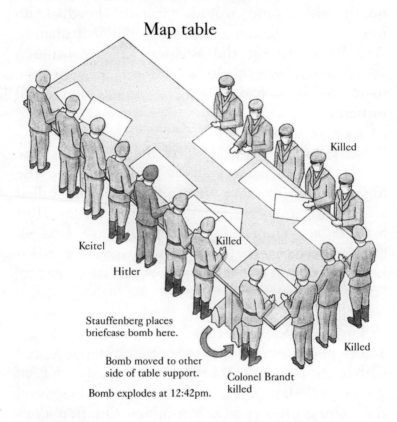

Killed

Killed

Keitel

Hitler

Stauffenberg places
briefcase bomb here.

Bomb moved to other
side of table support.

Bomb explodes at 12:42pm.

Colonel Brandt
killed

Killed

and moved it to the opposite side of the heavy, wooden support. An instant later, at 12:42 precisely, the bomb went off.

At the sound of the explosion, Haeften drove up in a staff car and Stauffenberg leapt in. The two of them had to escape to the airfield quickly, before "The Wolf's Lair" was sealed off by Hitler's guards. The hut looked completely devastated and, as they drove away, both felt confident no one inside could have survived.

They were wrong. Brandt and three others had been killed but, in moving the briefcase to the other side of the wooden support, Brandt had shielded Hitler from the full force of the blast. The German leader staggered out of the hut, his hair smoldering and trousers in tatters. He was very much alive.

Fellgiebel watched in horror. Hitler's death was an essential part of the plot. But, nonetheless, shortly before 1:00pm he sent a message to the War Office in Berlin, confirming the bomb had exploded and ordering Olbricht to set *Valkyrie* into operation. He made no mention of whether Hitler was alive or dead.

But back in Berlin, Olbricht hesitated because he was uncertain whether Hitler was dead. Until he knew more, he was not prepared to act. Meanwhile Stauffenberg, flying back to Berlin, was cut off from everything. During the two hours he was in the air, he expected his fellow conspirators to be carrying through *Operation Valkyrie* in a frenzy of activity. In fact, nothing was happening. Unfortunately for the plotters, Stauffenberg could not be in two places at once. He was the best man to carry out the bomb attack in Rastenburg, but he would also have been the best man to direct *Operation Valkyrie* in Berlin.

At Rastenburg, it did not take long to realize who had planted the bomb. Orders were immediately issued to arrest Stauffenberg at Berlin's Rangsdorf airfield. But the signals officer responsible for sending this message was also one of the conspirators, and the order was never transmitted.

Only after an hour and a half, at 3:30pm, did the Berlin conspirators reluctantly begin to act. Home Army officers were summoned by Olbricht and told that Hitler was dead and *Operation Valkyrie* was to be set in motion. But General Fromm was still refusing to cooperate, especially after he phoned Rastenburg and was told by General Keitel that Hitler was alive.

At 4:30pm, the plotters grew bolder and issued orders to the entire German army. Hitler, they declared, was dead. Nazi party leaders were trying to seize power for themselves. The army was to take control of the government immediately, to stop them from doing this.

Stauffenberg arrived back in Berlin soon afterwards. He too was not able to persuade Fromm to join the conspiracy. Instead the commander-in-chief erupted into a foaming tirade against him. Banging his fists on his desk, Fromm demanded that the conspirators be placed under arrest and ordered

Stauffenberg to shoot himself. When Fromm began to lunge at his fellow officers, fists flailing, he had to be subdued with a pistol pressed to his stomach. Then he meekly allowed himself to be locked in an office. Other officers at Home Army headquarters who were still loyal to the Nazis were also locked up.

Stauffenberg's final day

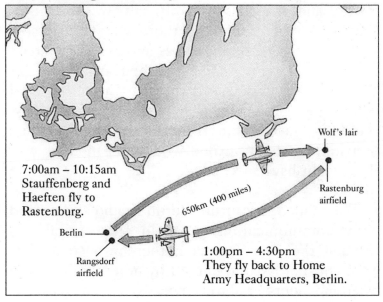

7:00am – 10:15am
Stauffenberg and
Haeften fly to
Rastenburg.

650km (400 miles)

Wolf's lair

Rastenburg
airfield

Berlin

Rangsdorf
airfield

1:00pm – 4:30pm
They fly back to Home
Army Headquarters, Berlin.

Stauffenberg now began to direct the conspirators with his usual energy and verve. For the rest of the afternoon, they worked with desperate haste to carry out their plan. Stauffenberg spent hours on the phone trying to persuade reluctant or wavering army commanders to support him. He was still convinced

Hitler was dead, but many of the people he spoke to would not believe him. At the time, it was widely believed that the Nazi leader employed a double who looked and acted just like him. What if Stauffenberg had killed the double rather than the real Hitler, they thought.

From Paris to Prague, the army attempted to take control and arrest all Nazi officials. In some cities such as Vienna and Paris there were remarkable successes, but in Berlin it was another story. Here, the plotters were foiled by their own decency. They had revolted against the brutality of the Nazi regime and, ironically, only a similar ruthlessness could have saved them. If the conspirators had been prepared to shoot anyone who stood in their way, they might have succeeded.

They failed to capture Berlin's radio station and army communication bases in the capital. All through the late afternoon, their own commands were constantly contradicted by orders transmitted by commanders loyal to the Nazis.

By early evening it became obvious to Stauffenberg that the plot had failed yet, true to his character, he refused to give up. He insisted that success was just a whisker away and he continued to encourage his fellow plotters not to give up hope. But the end was near.

The War Office was now surrounded by hostile troops loyal to Hitler and, inside the building, a small group of Nazi officers had armed themselves and set out to arrest the conspirators. Shots were fired, Stauffenberg was hit in the shoulder and Fromm was released.

Fromm could only do one thing. Although he had refused to cooperate with the plotters, he had known all about the plot. No doubt the conspirators would confirm this – under torture or of their own free will. Fromm had to cover his tracks. He sentenced Stauffenberg, Haeften, Olbricht and his assistant Colonel Mertz von Quirnheim to immediate execution.

Stauffenberg was bleeding badly from his wound, but seemed indifferent to his death sentence. He insisted the plot was all his doing. His fellow officers had simply been carrying out his orders.

Fromm was having none of this. Just after midnight, the four men were hustled down the stairs to the courtyard outside. By all accounts, they went calmly to their deaths. Lit by the dimmed headlights of a staff car, the four were shot in order of rank. Stauffenberg was second, after Olbricht. An instant before the firing squad cut Stauffenberg down, Haeften, in a brave but pointless gesture, threw himself in front of the bullets. Stauffenberg died moments later, shouting: "Long live our Secret Germany."

There would have been more executions that night, had not Gestapo chief Kaltenbrunner arrived and put a stop to them. He was far more interested in seeing what could be learned from the conspirators who were still alive.

Still, the Gestapo torturers had been cheated of their greatest prize. Stauffenberg and his fellow martyrs were buried that night in a nearby churchyard. They had failed, but their bravery in the face of such a slim chance of success had been truly heroic.

Afterwards

If Stauffenberg and his conspirators had succeeded with *Operation Valkyrie*, the war in Europe might have ended much earlier. As it was, it continued for almost another year. In those final months of the Second World War, more people were killed than in the previous five years of fighting.

Hitler described the conspiracy as "a crime unparalleled in German history" and reacted accordingly. Although Stauffenberg, von Haeften, Olbricht and Mertz were dead and buried, Hitler demanded that their bodies be dug up, burned, and the ashes scattered to the wind.

Following brutal interrogation, the main surviving conspirators were hauled before the Nazi courts. They refused to be intimidated, knowing the regime they loathed was teetering on the brink of defeat. General Erich Fellgiebel, who had stood with Stauffenberg as the bomb exploded at Rastenburg, was told by the court president that he was to be hanged. "Hurry with the hanging Mr. President," he replied, "otherwise you will hang earlier than we."

Gestapo and SS officers investigated the plot until the last days of the war. Seven thousand arrests were made, and between two and three thousand people were executed. Among them was General Fromm. Although he had never joined the conspirators, he was shot for cowardice in failing to prevent them from carrying out their revolt.

Stauffenberg's personal magnetism continued to exert an extraordinary influence, even from beyond the grave. SS investigator Georg Kiesel was so in awe of him, he reported to Hitler that his assassin was "a spirit of fire, fascinating and inspiring all who came in touch with him."

Alexei Stakhanov – Soviet superstar

During the First World War, the Russian Empire collapsed into chaos and, in 1917, a revolution swept away the old regime. Russia's new rulers renamed their country the Soviet Union. They set up a communist society where citizens were supposed to have equality, and the state took control of all the country's farms and industry.

A decade later Russia was still very poor. Dictator Joseph Stalin, who ruled his people with an iron grip, was determined to transform his country into a powerful nation ready to defend itself from enemies.

In 1931 he broadcast a speech to the whole Soviet Union, saying: "We are 50 or 100 years behind the advanced countries," meaning the capitalist nations of Europe, the United States, Japan and others. "We must make good this distance in ten years. Either we do it, or they crush us."

He gave orders for huge factories, steel works and coal mines to be built. In Stalin's plan, workers on these projects, fired with enthusiasm for their new communist nation, would go on to produce record levels of materials.

But most workers in these new plants and factories were peasants. In the 1920s and 30s, 17 million of them moved from villages and farm work to towns and industry. Packed into unfamiliar cities, away from their close-knit country communities, many felt disoriented and unsettled. New to the routine of factory jobs, they were ill-disciplined and apathetic.

Execution or imprisonment was Stalin's usual method of persuading people to do what he wanted, but for this situation he had another tactic. If other countries made heroes of film stars or royalty, then the Soviet Union would have heroes of industry. His henchmen were dispatched to find a suitable candidate.

On September 1, 1935, Soviet citizens woke to read in their morning papers that coal miner Alexei Stakhanov had dug out an extraordinary amount of coal in a Donbass mine during the night shift of August 30-31. It was fourteen times the amount a miner was expected to produce in a single shift. The papers talked of his efforts in heroic, military terms.

He was a "shock worker" who had made a "breakthrough" on the "coal production front." The message was clear, the papers said. If an ordinary miner could perform such superhuman work, then "there are no fortresses communism cannot storm."

In a carefully set-up media campaign, Stakhanov was overwhelmed with attention. He spoke on the radio, starred in newsreels, appeared in propaganda posters and was awarded the Order of Lenin, the Soviet Union's most prestigious medal. He moved to Moscow where he became the figurehead for the so-called "Stakhanovite" movement, which encouraged other workers to follow his example.

How could one man do the work of 14? Stakhanov told the Soviet people he had been inspired by a speech of Stalin's, which he had heard on the radio the evening of his heroic shift. The truth was that his feat was a confidence trick set up by the Soviet authorities. Two other miners had actually helped him dig the coal. Then a team of workers had carried it from the coalface, and done a range of other jobs a miner would usually have to do for himself on an ordinary shift.

The truth was that Stakhanov was not even an exceptional worker. He had been selected for hero status because his handsome face would look good in photographs and, equally important, because he was a docile, easy-going fellow, unlikely to question what he was being asked to do.

The "Stakhanovite" movement created other heroes, from steel workers to milkmaids whose cows produced record levels of milk. ("Storm the 3,000 litre level" ran one slogan.) They starred in newsreels and were celebrated in biographies. "Stakhanovites" were rewarded with extra pay or prestigious apartments. But many were unpopular with their fellow workers, who felt their exceptional workmate showed up the rest of them in a bad light. Some "Stakhanovites" were attacked or even murdered.

And what of Stakhanov himself? The Soviet superman who exchanged the Donbass coal fields for a desk in Moscow proved to be a poor organizer. When other workplace heroes sprang up to replace him, he was quietly dropped from his post, and vanished into obscurity.

Afterwards

Stalin's attempt to build a powerful industrial nation succeeded just in time. The Soviet Union was invaded by Nazi Germany in 1941. The Nazis nearly overran the country but the Soviet army, fighting with great heroism and determination, drove them off. However, the army could never have defeated the Nazis without the guns, tanks and aircraft built in Stalin's new factories.

Stakhanov enjoyed his moment of fame, but adjusted badly to life away from the spotlight. He turned to drink, and died a bitter man in 1977. Despite the obscurity of his later years, he still featured prominently in Soviet school history books and it was only in 1988 that the Soviet people were finally told that his legendary record was a sham.

Blackbeard meets his match

The years between 1690 and 1730 were the "Golden Age of Piracy". Cargo ships sailing from Europe to North and South America and Africa were regularly plundered by gangs of pirates, most of which were British.

These pirates were much feared by the sailors they preyed upon, none more so than Edward "Blackbeard" Teach. A whole head taller than most and built like a bear, Teach's nickname came from his huge, black beard. Stretching down to his chest, it was usually braided with bright ribbons, and covered a face that was in constant contact with a bottle of rum.

Originally a slave trader from Bristol, England, Teach did have a certain roguish charm. But the string of women who married him (14 in all) usually came to regret their decision – especially when he insisted on sharing them with the rest of his crew. He was certainly never dull company. Once, during a lull in plundering, he suggested to his crew that they create tortures of their own, to see who could last the longest. He and three shipmates had themselves sealed into the ship's hold with several pots of blazing, foul-smelling gas. Naturally, Teach won, and emerged on the deck to announce they ought to have a hanging contest – to see who could last the longest dangling from a noose.

It was all good training for his crew's likely prospects. "A merry life and a short one shall be my motto" wrote another pirate captain, Bartholomew Roberts. The risks of piracy, after all, were great – death in battle or public execution. Yet the rewards were extraordinary. A successful pirate, who in everyday life might struggle to earn a pittance as a sailor, mill worker or miner, could make as much in a year as a wealthy aristocrat.

Teach was not all fun and games. He usually went into battle with several slow-burning fuses woven into his hair. With his already terrifying features cloaked in a haze of smoke, he looked like a demon from his lair and frightened his opponents witless.

Captured crews who had put up a fight could expect no mercy. Teach even cut off the nose of one Portuguese captive and made him eat it. His own companions sometimes fared no better – he was reputed to have killed one of his crew just to remind them how evil he was.

This was all above and beyond the needs of ordinary piracy, but it served a purpose. As his reputation spread, few of the merchant ships he attacked dared to oppose him. Hoping to make as much profit as possible, greedy traders manned their ships with small, badly paid and badly armed crews. Faced with a horde of ruthless pirates, many were not willing to defend their cargoes with their lives.

Teach's hunting grounds were the coastal waters of North America. Here his plundered wealth brought him friends in high places, who alerted him to the whereabouts of Navy ships or soldiers, and allowed him to trade his stolen goods in coastal settlements. But by 1715, his activities – and those of other pirates in the Caribbean and Atlantic coast of America – were having such a bad effect on trade that he could no longer be ignored. Cargo ships had to travel with naval escorts, and the cost of insuring their goods became so expensive it was hardly worth transporting them. Something had to be done, but who could be found to fight such a formidable foe?

Alexander Spotswood, Governor of Virginia, put up a reward of £100 (then nearly 10 years wages for an ordinary seaman), hoping to attract someone whose lust for wealth or glory outweighed his fear of this most evil of pirates. As well as advertising this reward, he also called in the Royal Navy, and paid for a search party of two ships from his own personal fortune.

So, on November 17, 1718, Lieutenant Robert Maynard, commander of the Royal Navy warship *HMS Pearl*, set sail from Virginia to look for Teach, together with a smaller ship *HMS Lyme*. Altogether he had 60 men under his command. Maynard had been told that Teach had based himself in Ocracoke Inlet, North Carolina, and his small search party arrived there just before dusk four days later.

Maynard soon spotted Teach's ship, the *Adventurer*, and dropped his anchor some distance away. He planned to attack the next morning. That night the pirates had a party, and their drunken curses drifted across the water between the two ships. Maynard's anxious crew wondered what sort of men they would have to fight on the coming day.

Daybreak finally came, and Maynard ordered his attack to begin. It started very badly. Ocracoke Inlet is shallow, and no sooner had Maynard's ships moved against the *Adventurer* than they became stuck in

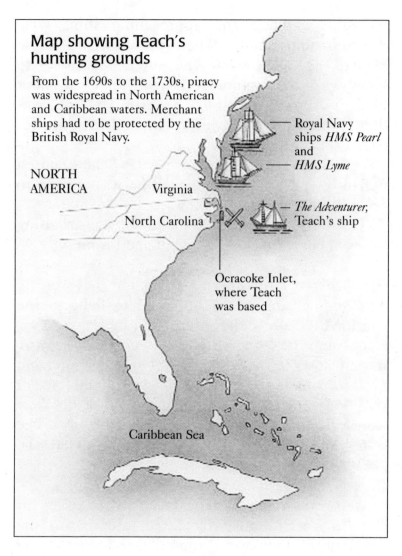

Map showing Teach's hunting grounds

From the 1690s to the 1730s, piracy was widespread in North American and Caribbean waters. Merchant ships had to be protected by the British Royal Navy.

NORTH AMERICA

Virginia

North Carolina

Royal Navy ships *HMS Pearl* and *HMS Lyme*

The Adventurer, Teach's ship

Ocracoke Inlet, where Teach was based

Caribbean Sea

sandbanks. Only when several heavy weights had been thrown out of the vessels were they able to move on.

Teach watched the approaching ships with drunken amusement. When the *Pearl* was close enough, he called across the water, demanding to know what they wanted. Maynard knew all about Teach's reputation, but nevertheless he was determined to inspire his frightened men with a courageous response.

"You may see we are no pirates," he shouted defiantly, and boldly announced he was coming to seize Blackbeard and his crew.

Teach was enraged and bellowed a hair-raising series of curses back at Maynard and his men.

Teach's crew was only 19 strong, but they were all seasoned villains and determined to fight to the death. After all, if they were captured alive, they would only be hung as pirates. As the *Adventurer* moved closer to the Navy ships it swung around and fired its cannons. *HMS Lyme* caught the full force of this broadside. Its captain and several of his crew were killed and the ship floundered helplessly in the water. Maynard and the *Pearl* pressed on to face the *Adventurer* alone.

Worse was to come. Blackbeard's next volley hit the *Pearl* with similar force. So intense was the fire that 21 men were injured and Maynard had to order his crew to take cover below. Teach's ship came alongside the deserted deck of the *Pearl* and his pirate crew tossed aboard blazing bottles stuffed full with a mixture of gunpowder, buckshot and scrap iron.

Smoke shrouded the deck of the shattered *Pearl*, and Teach was confient that he had already won an easy victory. His pirates swarmed aboard to take possession of the ship. But, at that moment, Maynard unleashed a counter-attack, and led those of his crew who could still stand out onto the deck. Bayonets flashed and pistols cracked as the two sides clashed in hand-to-hand fighting.

Battling through the chaos Maynard fought his way toward Teach, and both men fired their pistols at point-blank range. Teach's drinking had blurred his senses, and only Maynard found his target. But the bullet that struck the huge pirate seemed to have no effect on him, and he lunged forward with his cutlass. Maynard raised his own sword to deflect the blow, but to his horror it broke in two. Teach towered over him with a rabid leer and raised his cutlass to cut him dead. But the blow never fell.

One of Pearl's crew, rushing to defend his captain, slashed at the pirate's throat. Yet even this was only a distraction. Spurting fountains of blood, Teach drew another pistol from his belt and aimed again at Maynard. Then a strange, faraway look came into his eyes. He swayed, and toppled over like a fallen oak.

The death of the mighty Blackbeard was the turning point of the struggle, and the rest of the pirates were soon killed or surrendered. Ten of *Pearl's* men lay dead, and all but one of the seamen had been injured.

After the battle, Teach's head was cut off and hung from the Pearl's bow. But such was his fearsome reputation that his body, which was thrown overboard, was said to have swum several times around the ship in brazen defiance before it sank to the bottom of the sea.

Afterwards

Although his victory over the fearsome Teach marked the virtual end of piracy in North America, Maynard was poorly rewarded. Alive, Blackbeard had a price of £100 on his head. Once he was dead, the government authorities refused to pay up.

Four years of legal wrangling followed, as the navy lieutenant tried to secure a fair reward for his crew. He was eventually given a measly £3 for his trouble, and those who fought with him were given half that amount.

The story of Blackbeard and his final battle with Lieutenant Maynard still continues to entertain and intrigue. Several movies have been made about Blackbeard's life. The most well known is the 1952 American film *Blackbeard the Pirate*. Here, Robert Newton plays the infamous villain, and charges around waving pistols and rolling his eyes with immense enthusiasm. The plot takes great liberties with the known facts. Instead of Lieutenant Maynard, reformed pirate Sir Henry Morgan is hired to rid the high seas of the pirate menace. Morgan still has something of a wicked streak in him and Blackbeard comes to a suitably gruesome end. Buried up to his neck on a sandy beach, he is slowly drowned by the incoming tide.

Owens 4,
master race 0

American athlete Jesse Owens was fresh off the ocean liner *Manhattan* on his way to the Berlin Olympics. The year was 1936. As his motor coach rolled south-east towards the German capital, he stared out from the window with increasing amazement. The streets of Germany were like nothing he had ever seen before. The old buildings fascinated him, as they did any American who had grown up in a town or city that had only recently been built. But most striking of all were the swastika flags that seemed to hang from almost every window or shop front. The crooked black cross on a blood-red banner was the symbol of the German Nazi Party. Its ubiquitous presence spoke silently of a country in the total control of its political masters.

The 1936 Olympics were held in troubled times. Italy had just conquered Ethiopia; mass unemployment plagued Europe and America; Brazil was so politically divided it sent two teams to the games (both were disqualified); civil war had broken out in Spain that very summer. Most ominously of all, a regime of alarming brutality had taken control in Germany.

The Nazis believed that the German people were the "master race" – superior human beings who were destined to rule the world. To them, the huge 110,000 capacity Berlin Olympic Stadium was to be a grand stage, where German athletes would assert their claims to racial superiority. The whole occasion was one big advertisement for their regime and its sinister beliefs.

The Nazis had strong views about other races too, especially Jews and Black people. Nazi leaders blamed Jews for every evil that had overtaken their country that century, and Jewish people in Germany were subjected to daily abuse and violence. The Nazi attitude to Black people was less complicated – they simply thought of them as subhuman.

Many people throughout the world were disgusted by the racist attitudes of the Nazis, and felt their country should boycott the Olympics. Aware of this disapproval, the Nazis had softened their extremist policies in the months leading up to the Olympics – for example, racist street graffiti, billboards and political newspaper articles denouncing Jews disappeared. For a while it looked as if the Nazis were softening their policies. Eventually 52 nations agreed to attend the Berlin Olympics.

Owens too had wondered whether he should go to Berlin. But at 22 he was one of America's most promising athletes. He was a phenomenal runner and long jumper – in May 1935, at an athletics meeting in Michigan, USA, he had broken three world records in one amazing hour. The Olympic Games offered him the opportunity to show his skills to the entire world.

His coach had warned him to expect racist abuse from Nazi supporters among the Berlin crowds. But Owens had come to the Olympics determined not to allow this to affect his performance. But their expectations were wrong. The German people were fascinated by Owens, and no sooner had he arrived in the country than he was mobbed by sports fans who had read about his record-breaking performances.

Owens made an ideal hero. Being tall and handsome obviously helped, but the athlete had a boyish charm and modesty that made him particularly likable. As he posed for photographs and signed endless autographs, he talked to the crowd in the few words of German he had taken the trouble to learn. Curiously, his popularity proved to be just as much a problem as the hostility he had expected. At night, Owens was kept awake by fans who came to his bedroom window to take photographs or demand autographs.

The Games began on August 1 with a massive celebration designed to glorify the Nazi regime as much as it did the Olympics. Then the founder of the modern Games, Pierre de Coubertin, made a speech to the Berlin spectators, saying: "The important thing at the Olympic Games is not to win, but to take part ... the most important thing about life is not to conquer, but to struggle well." It was a philosophy the Nazi hosts of the Games would not be taking seriously.

Owens' first race, the 100m, was on the day after the opening. This brief event is one of the most glamorous and exciting in athletics, and is always the cause of tremendous interest.

Owens felt under enormous pressure in the tense moments before the race he had worked so hard to win. As he arrived at the starting line for the final, he realized that the other five athletes there were the world's fastest human beings. All of them wanted to beat him. Dismissing these thoughts from his head, he focused instead on the finishing line ahead, and reminded himself that the next 10 or so seconds of the race would be the climax of eight years of training.

On that cold, wet afternoon the crowd held its breath, the sound of the starting pistol echoed around the stadium, and Owens shot from the line. He was ahead by the first 10m (30ft). Described by one journalist as having "the grace and poise of a deer", he had a natural style that made running look easy. Sweeping to a new Olympic record and an ecstatic reception from the stadium crowd, he won the race in 10.3 seconds. He would look back on the moment he was presented with his first Olympic gold medal as the happiest of his career.

In his private stadium box, Nazi leader Adolf Hitler, a regular spectator at the Games, was not amused. His dream of German athletes dominating the games was fading before his eyes. When an aide suggested he invite Owens up to congratulate him (as he had with successful German athletes), Hitler was outraged. "Do you really think I will allow myself to be photographed shaking hands with a black man?" he hissed.

The next day Owens competed in the long jump, but his three preliminary jumps nearly ended in disaster. Back home in America, athletes were allowed to make a trial run up to the long jump pit, as a warm-up exercise. Here in Germany, the rules were different. When Owens did this and ran into the sand, the judges indicated that he had failed his first jump. Badly riled, he went on to fail his second jump too.

As he prepared for his vital third jump, help came from an unexpected quarter. A fellow long jump competitor named Lutz Long, who was one of Germany's star athletes, whispered a few consoling words. Encouraged, Owens jumped successfully. The competition ended with Owens jumping to victory against Long in the final. The German just could not match his stupendous, record-breaking 8.06m (over 26ft) leap. "I just decided I wasn't going to come down," Owens later told reporters. The record remained unbeaten for 24 years.

Long and Owens left the stadium arena arm-in-arm, and that evening they met again at the Olympic Village and talked through the night. Long's blond, Germanic good looks and perfectly proportioned athlete's body were the epitome of the Nazi German racial ideal. But Long did not share his leader's racist notions. He and Owens found they had much in common. They were the same age and from similar, poor backgrounds, and both saw athletic success as a passport away from their humble origins. Long too was disturbed by the prejudice he saw all around him in Germany.

There were more successes to come. On August 5, Owens took to the field to run in the 200m final. By now Nazi hopes that their athletes would sweep away all competition had evaporated. The Nazi press had started to ridicule Owens, and German officials were heard complaining about "non-humans" being allowed to take part in the Games.

Owens refused to let himself be intimidated by this atmosphere of petty spite, and won the 200m in a record-breaking 20.7 seconds. He had a particular technique for getting off to a good start. He noticed that the starting official would make some small gesture, a flexing of the legs, or tensing of the facial muscles, just before he fired the starting pistol. From the corner of his eye, Owens would watch for these signs. Forewarned, he would shoot from the starting line the instant the gun fired.

For Owens, the 200m was the final event, and he settled back to enjoy the rest of the Games, free from the pressure of further competition. But the U.S. coaches had other plans for him. He was on such top form they insisted he take part in the 4 x

100m relay. (Here four athletes run 100m each, passing a baton between them.) It was an unhappy decision, which caused a lot of hard feelings, as the coaches dropped American Jewish athlete Marty Gluckman. Owens himself protested. He'd won three gold medals already, he told the coach, and someone else should be given a chance. The coach was unmoved. "You'll do as you're told," he growled.

So Owens took to the field. The American team was unbeatable. Starting the race, Owens was ahead by several paces by the time he passed the baton on to the second runner. Once again an Olympic record was set by the team, and Owens added a fourth medal to his collection. It was a wonderful end to a wonderful performance, although Owens, with characteristic modesty, insisted another athlete occupy the top spot of the podium during the medals ceremony.

The Berlin Olympics made Owens world-famous. When the games finished he left Germany for a short tour of Europe, surrounded by press photographers and well-wishers. Hitler was deeply irritated by it all. The 1936 Olympic Games were supposed to have been a great victory for the German Master Race. Now no one was going to forget the soft-spoken Black American who had quietly ridiculed Nazi boasts of German racial supremacy.

Afterwards

Back in the Olympic Village, events were taking a more sinister turn. As they left, athletes could hear machine gun fire from nearby fields. The Village was already being turned into an army training camp. Days later, billboards and newspapers in Germany were again filled with anti-Jewish propaganda. The next Olympics were due to take part in 1940. The host nation would be Germany's ally, Japan, but by then, Europe was at war and the Games did not actually take place again until 1948. Hitler fantasized that, following the Nazi conquest of Europe, the Games would be held in Germany forever, and black athletes would be forbidden to compete.

Owens and his Olympic triumph were captured on film by the eminent German director Leni Reifenstahl in *Olympische Spiele 1936*. This sinister but beautiful film is seen by many as a hymn to Germany's Nazi regime, but Reifenstahl made no attempt to play down the victory of Black American Owens over the pride of Germany's athletes.

The long jump record set by Owens remained unbeaten until 1960, but his fame did not bring him happiness. Deluged with showbusiness and business offers, Owens displayed his athletic ability at sideshows and exhibitions, where he would run against racehorses or play with the celebrity basketball team, the Harlem Globetrotters. Badly advised and cynically exploited, the money he made was invested in businesses that collapsed.

After the Second World War, Owens found a new role for himself, and his life picked up again when he worked for children's charities and went around the world as a goodwill ambassador for the United States. He died in 1980.

His friend and Olympic rival Lutz Long was killed in 1943, fighting with the German army in Sicily.

Rubble and strife in battlefield Beirut

In 1975, a civil war broke out in Lebanon when Christian and Muslim groups fought to decide who would have the most political power. Beirut, a city of many cultures and religions, was the main battleground, and the situation there soon became extremely complex. There were various competing factions, known as "militias", each with their own soldiers. Ten years later, in 1985, a British surgeon named Pauline Cutting took a job with the charity Medical Aid for Palestinians, and was sent to work in Beirut. This is her story.

On a dank December morning, a taxi bounced down a road strewn with debris and pockmarked with potholes. The route, between Beirut airport and its outer suburbs, ran parallel to open drains. The stench was appalling, but the passenger in the taxi, British surgeon Pauline Cutting, told herself she had better get used to it. She was experienced in accident and emergency work, and felt her expertise would be useful in Beirut. It was turning out to be far worse than she ever expected. A decade of civil war had ruined the once beautiful Mediterranean city, and 50,000 people had been killed. There seemed to be no solution to the savage fighting, which flared up or died down unpredictably.

The car passed a block of bomb-damaged apartments. One side had collapsed. Crumbling concrete floors and stairways hung precariously over the road, spilling out tangled wiring and seeping streams of water. The other side of the block was still occupied, and Cutting could see people peering uneasily from cracked or broken windows.

Deeper into the bustling city the buildings closed around the taxi in a maze of dark streets and dirty alleys. Clustered on corners were small groups of young men carrying machine guns and grenade launchers. Occasionally the sinister silhouette of a tank could be glimpsed, skulking behind a burned-out factory or lurking in a side street. Chaos reigned. Here government had no control. There were no traffic signs, no policemen, no laws. Beirut was a battlefield.

Cutting was taken to the Palestinian camp of Bourj al Barajneh. It was not really a camp as such, more a shanty town of tiny alleys. Once 30,000 people had lived here. By the time Cutting arrived, only 9,000 remained. Amid the alleys there were little shops selling food and clothes, hardware stores, and even a hairdresser and a garage.

In the middle of the camp was Haifa Hospital, a five-floor concrete building where Cutting would be in charge of the surgery department. When she arrived at the hospital, she was greeted warmly by a Palestinian doctor and taken on a tour of her new workplace. It was a dispiriting experience. Like all the other buildings in Bourj al Barajneh, it had been seriously damaged in the fighting. The top two floors had been so badly shelled they were beyond repair.

The entrance hall was littered with homeless families and their belongings, and children milled around the muddy floor. The hospital's most vital departments were sheltered in the relative safety of the basement. Here there was the emergency room, operating room, X-ray department and laboratory. Wards and staff living-quarters were scattered around the remaining inhabited floors.

Over the next few days, Cutting was introduced to the rest of the staff. There were six Palestinian doctors, 30 nurses (who worked in three shifts of 10), 10 office workers, and 10 cooks and cleaners.

Cutting spent these first days in a daze, wondering if coming to Beirut had been a terrible mistake. Equipment was primitive and the staff felt demoralized, but she had so much responsibility and so much to learn, there was barely time to worry about it.

Most of her work involved treating day-to-day illnesses, and diseases caused by the camp's damp living conditions and dirty water. On top of this, there were the casualties of the war. Cutting was used to handling harrowing hospital cases such as car crash victims, and now she had to learn to deal with injuries caused by bombs, shells and bullets.

Working in the camp, Cutting also learned more about the plight of the Palestinians. Driven from their homeland following the creation of the state of Israel in 1947, they lived as refugees, unwanted and in great poverty, in nearby Arab states. Cutting had known little about this when she agreed to come to Beirut. After a few months at Haifa, she could see the difference her work made to the lives of the people she treated, and she became determined to stay and help.

But in early 1986, the situation in Beirut grew worse. Violence simmered among rival groups. Most troubling of all for Cutting were the kidnappings and murders of American or European residents. One United Nations worker was hanged, and his kidnappers released a video of his execution. Cutting saw the tape and was haunted by the fuzzy pictures of a hooded body swaying from a tree.

But not everything was grim. Cutting made many friends during her stay, especially a Dutch nurse named Ben Alofs, who also worked in the camp. He was tall and amiable, and he seemed to know a lot about the complex politics of Beirut. Their friendship grew, and one day he gave her Ernest Hemmingway's *Farewell to Arms* – a novel about a passionate romance between an ambulance driver and nurse during World War One. It was something of a hint. Alofs was transferred to another part of the Lebanon soon after, and left a letter for Cutting saying he was falling in love with her.

It was around this time that Bourj al Barajneh began to be attacked again. The camp was surrounded by Amal militia men. Amal was one of several armed Muslim groups, and they wanted to drive the Palestinians from their city. Now, anyone venturing outside the camp could be kidnapped or killed. Inside Bourj al Barajneh, sniper fire and shelling became a daily danger.

On May 26, 1986, Amal soldiers stormed the camp. As the Palestinians fought to defend their territory, a steady stream of injured and dying men was brought into the hospital, and Cutting and her staff struggled to save the wounded. The following two days were just as difficult. As well as soldiers, children were also maimed in the fighting.

This was Cutting's first experience of all-out battlefield surgery. Apart from the daily danger of being killed, she had to make harrowing decisions about who to save and who to leave to die, and work with only the most basic supplies and equipment. There were no experts to consult, and no back-up facilities, and at times she felt very alone.

❖

Worse was to come. On May 31, as Cutting lay asleep, a shell exploded above her room. The blast hit her like a punch in the chest, and thick black soot and rubble filled the hospital. The direct Amal attacks on Bourj al Barajneh had not succeeded, so instead they launched a week-long bombardment by tanks and artillery.

During this terrifying time, Cutting became good friends with two Belgian doctors who had also arrived at the hospital. They noticed how she read Ben Alofs' letter every time she lay down to sleep, and offered to teach her some Dutch, so she could speak to Ben in his own language.

At the end of June, after negotiations between the two sides, the shelling stopped. Government soldiers from Syria and Lebanon surrounded the camp, to prevent more attacks by Amal soldiers. For a while there was peace. There was other good news too. Ben Alofs was back in Beirut, working in another camp. Now Cutting was not so busy, she was able to spend time with him, and also travel to England for a break.

She returned to the camp in late August, to be joined soon afterwards by Scottish nurse Susie Wighton. Another round of fighting was brewing. The next few months were going to be very difficult.

Amal soldiers were still determined to drive the Palestinians from Beirut. At the end of October, they attacked Bourj al Barajneh and other Palestinian camps, in a campaign that became known as "The Camp War." Again, it became impossible for Palestinians to enter or leave Bourj al Barajneh. The fighting grew fiercer, and electricity to the camp was cut off. The hospital had to rely on diesel-powered generators. Hospital staff coped the best they could with ingenious improvisations. Headlight bulbs and batteries, for example, were removed from cars and rigged up to provide light in the darkened building.

During this ruthless campaign, the hospital became a target for the shelling. Sometimes direct hits shook the building to its foundations. When this happened, Cutting found herself trembling with fear. One shell explosion left her partially deaf for three weeks. Another shell shattered a water tank at the top of the building. Water trickled down the walls, collecting in deep pools in corridors and rooms throughout the hospital. On top of all their other troubles, the hospital staff had to cope with having constantly wet feet.

By mid-November, the Lebanese winter had taken hold. Cutting often worked 18 hours a day. In the rare moments she had to relax, she would fantasize about sitting in front of a burning coal fire, eating stew and dumplings. Ben Alofs, braving sniper fire and shells, and loaded with supplies of cakes and custard, crept into the camp whenever he could.

The bombardment increased, so staff moved their living quarters to the basement. They slept in a tiny room next to the operating surgery. It was warmer here, and everybody was friendly, but the strain of having no privacy was difficult to endure.

Despite the hardship, hospital staff still managed to work wonders. In November, a little boy was brought in with a terrible head wound. He was so disturbed that when anyone roused him he would cry like a cat. After a few days he started to speak, but would not open his eyes. Cutting was deeply moved by the courage that injured children showed. This boy had begun to learn English and, every morning when she visited, he would greet her with a formal "Good morning" and say, "I'm fine thank you". He went on to make a full recovery.

On another occasion, a Palestinian fighter was brought in close to death. Cutting and her team struggled all day to save him, removing 500 shell fragments from his body. He too survived. Successes like these strengthened Cutting's resolve to stay in the camp until the siege was over.

But the hospital was collapsing around them. Fuel was running out and the generators could only run for four hours at a time. In the cold, damp building the winter wind howled along corridors from one broken window to another, and black mildew crawled down the walls. To heat water, staff had to pour lighter fuel onto cotton on the stone floor and set it alight.

One of the men in the camp had worked in a filling station near to its perimeter. He began to wonder if a tunnel could be dug out to the fuel storage tanks that were built beneath the station. The idea was worth a try. A 40m (130ft) tunnel was carefully constructed. The burrowers did their job well. The tunnel went straight to the storage tanks and over 18,000 litres (4,000 gallons) were siphoned off. This escapade lifted everyone's spirits, solving at least one of the problems the camp faced.

The shortage of food just got worse. Cutting, along with everyone else, faced the winter months with a constant gnawing hunger, and sometimes she would faint while operating.

By the end of December, the third and fourth floor had collapsed under the shelling. The drainage and sanitation system had been destroyed, everyone had lice, garbage piled up in every corridor and rats scurried underfoot.

But there were still happy moments. January 19 was Cutting's birthday and Ben sneaked into the camp to present her with a siege survival kit – clean socks, soap, toothpaste, two candles and a packet of cigarettes. It was the best present she had ever had.

Cutting found the people of Bourj al Barajneh were exceptionally kind. Most days a little boy would bring her food from his family. When she said he was being too generous, he told her: "When we have a little, I will bring you a little. When we have nothing, then I will bring you nothing."

The camp was being starved and bombarded into submission. Worst of all was the fear that if Amal soldiers did break into Bourj al Barajneh, they might massacre its inhabitants. Palestinians had been slain in their thousands when rival militias had entered other refugee camps. Ben Alofs had nearly been killed himself when he had been caught up in such an attack. Cutting began to have terrible nightmares about these killings.

It seemed that nobody was prepared to help them. Intending to draw attention to the situation in the camp, Cutting, Ben Alofs and Susan Wighton prepared a formal statement to the international newspaper and broadcast journalists who were covering the fighting in Beirut. Their declaration, detailing the dreadful conditions of everyday life for Bourj al Barajneh's thousands of inhabitants, was transmitted over the hospital two-way radio.

Identifying themselves like this took a great deal of courage. They knew the American and

European media would be more interested in the siege if they knew westerners were suffering too. But this also made them a target for Amal gunmen.

The declaration was broadcast on Arab radio stations, but it caused little international interest. The situation grew worse. Starvation in the camp became so bad that people were forced to eat rats, dogs, cats – even grass. Their spirits at rock bottom, Cutting and her staff radioed out another declaration calling for the siege to be lifted. This time, the BBC World Service broadcast their statement.

Friday, February 13, was the worst day of the siege. A shell landed among a group of people who had ventured from their shelters. Many were terribly wounded. With the barest amount of equipment and supplies, the starving doctors operated on two patients at a time throughout the day.

As Cutting lay exhausted on her bed at 11:00 that night, she was roused by a message on the hospital radio. A BBC World Service reporter named Jim Muir, whose voice they all instantly recognized, was trying to contact her. Over a crackling radio link, they talked about conditions in the camp. Then, to Cutting's great surprise, her mother and father spoke to her. The BBC had arranged a radio link-up, so they could talk to their daughter. Muir came back on the radio and asked if they wanted to be rescued. Cutting was determined not to leave her patients. "I'm not coming out until it's finished," she replied.

After Jim Muir's report on the camp was broadcast, more journalists began to take an interest. Cutting also learned that other militia groups in Beirut were beginning to side with the Palestinians against Amal. The increasing news coverage that followed their declarations had generated some support in Beirut for the camp's inhabitants.

On February 17, a cease-fire was negotiated and a few trucks full of food were allowed into the camp. Women were permitted to go out for a brief period each day to buy food. They were still shot at by snipers, and had to put up with brutal treatment by Amal forces. "We know all about Pauline Cutting and we are going to cut her to pieces," they told the women who passed through their checkpoints.

But now, television crews and newspaper journalists were frequent visitors to the camp. The plight of Bourj al Barajneh's inmates had become a focus for the world's media. On April 8, prompted by an international outcry, Syrian government troops came to patrol the perimeter. For the first time in five and a half months, there were no casualties admitted to the hospital. The International Red Cross arrived, along with new medical staff for the hospital. After 163 days the siege was truly over.

It was time to go home. After many sad farewells, Pauline Cutting, Ben Alofs and Susie Wighton made their way out of the camp. Cutting was still uneasy about Amal death threats, so at least 50 people surrounded her, to make sure she was not seized as she left. As she got into a waiting car, she turned to look back at the camp. All the hundreds of people who had come to see her off were smiling and waving. It was a heartbreaking sight. She was walking away. They had nowhere else to go.

The next day they took a ferry to Cyprus, where they were met by TV crews and journalists. All of a sudden the whole world wanted to know about these three medics from Bourj al Barajneh. In their hotel that evening they celebrated their survival with a bottle of wine, and entertained themselves by turning taps and lights on and off. It seemed unreal to be in a place where everything actually worked.

Afterwards

In 1987 Cutting was awarded an OBE (Order of the British Empire) by the British government, in recognition of her work in Bourj al Barajneh. She is a member of the board of Medical Aid for Palestinians, and returned to Beirut in October 1995, while reviewing the charity's projects in Lebanon.

After a spell in a hospital in Amsterdam, she now works in Ysbyty Gwynedd Accident and Emergency unit in North Wales. She is married to Ben Alofs, who has qualified as a doctor. They have two children.

Susie Wighton was awarded an MBE (Member of the British Empire) in 1987, and continued to work as an emergency relief worker in both Lebanon and Bosnia. She recently took a Master's Degree in community health, and now lives in Perthshire, where she works as a staff nurse. In 1999, the "Nursing Times" ran a cover story on her, with a special tribute from Cherie Blair (wife of Britain's Prime Minister).

Cosmonaut number one

In the dead of night, April 12, 1961, on a windswept plain in central Russia, a towering green rocket named *Vostok 1* sat pointing at the sky. Its task: to hurl a man into outer space. Airless and endless, home to lethal radiation, meteorite storms, and perils unknown to science, no deadlier environment ever awaited human exploration.

Technicians swarmed around the concrete launch pad, illuminated by powerful floodlights. Alongside *Vostok 1* rose huge steel gantries carrying fuel pipes and electricity cables which snaked into the rocket's thin metal casing. *Vostok 1* creaked and groaned as liquid oxygen and kerosene boiled away from access vents and into the cold night air.

As the first rays of the sun caught on the rocket's pointed tip, a small bus drew up beside it. Several figures emerged, including one dressed in a hefty orange protective suit and a large spherical helmet. The technicians stopped work for a moment as this man made a brief speech. As they began to applaud, he stiffly raised a hand to thank them.

Then he boarded an elevator, which took him to a small instrument-packed capsule at the top of the rocket. Here he was strapped into a couch, and 30 nuts were screwed in around an exit hatch to seal him in. One by one the technicians retired to the safety of nearby concrete bunkers, leaving him alone with his thoughts. Today would be a day of endless waiting.

The man cocooned in this tiny capsule was former jet fighter pilot Yuri Gagarin, officially known as "Cosmonaut number one." (The Russians called their spacemen "cosmonauts" – a word made up from *cosmos*, meaning "the universe", and *nautes*, a Greek word for "sailor".) Gagarin, an amiable 27 year-old, who was the son of a carpenter and a dairymaid, had been selected from over 3,000 volunteers to be the first man in space. No one on the project doubted he was the best person for the job. He was a cool and clear thinker, with great stamina and personal courage. If anyone was going to survive the hardships of space, Gagarin had the physical and mental ability to succeed.

Like the great European seafarers who had first explored the world's oceans three centuries before, he was venturing into the unknown. They had feared storms, sea monsters or savage tribes. The fears Gagarin faced were far stranger.

Space, as an environment, was extreme enough. But any visitor there also had to cope with the phenomenon of weightlessness. On Earth, gravity holds everything in its place. In space its effect is unnoticeable, and everything floats. In the years before Gagarin's journey, animals had been sent into orbit. They had coped well with weightlessness, but many scientists still wondered how a human would survive without gravity. Would blood still flow around his body? Would he choke on food? Worst of all, would his mind become so disoriented by this alien sensation that it would cease to function? (At the time it was a commonly held fear that space voyagers would return to Earth as burned-out zombies.)

There were other more obvious worries. To escape the pull of Earth's gravity, and place a capsule in orbit, *Vostok 1* needed to reach a speed of 40,000kmph (25,000mph). A cosmonaut would have to travel at speeds no human had experienced before. The physical damage this might cause could only be guessed at.

To reach this speed required a huge amount of fuel, and *Vostok 1*, like all rockets, was basically a huge fuel tank with a capsule on top. In the days before the Space Shuttle, rockets had several sections, known as stages, which would be discarded when the fuel inside them had been used up. *Vostok 1*, for example, had three stages.

Sending *Vostok 1* into Space

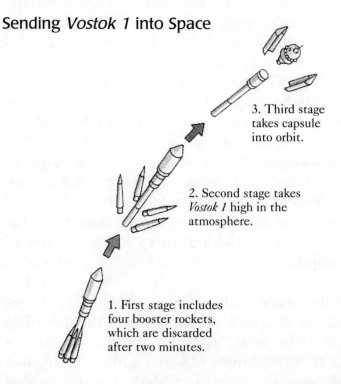

3. Third stage takes capsule into orbit.

2. Second stage takes *Vostok 1* high in the atmosphere.

1. First stage includes four booster rockets, which are discarded after two minutes.

The business of sending a vehicle into orbit by igniting thousands of tons of highly inflammable, explosive fuel was never going to make going into space particularly safe. Even today, over forty years later, space travel is still extremely dangerous. In 1961, rocket science was in its infancy, and the seven months prior to Gagarin's flight had seen some terrible disasters.

One rocket, aimed at the planet Mars, had blown up on the launch pad, killing Russia's space project director Marshall Mitrofan Nedelin and scores of his best technicians. More ominously still, several unmanned flights in the *Vostok*-type craft that Gagarin now sat inside had ended with the capsule locked in an endless orbit around the Earth, or burning up on its return through the atmosphere.

For three hours Gagarin sat waiting, as rocket engineers ran through final checks. Then, at 9:07am, it was time to go. Four metal gantries, which supported the rocket, unfolded, its engines ignited, and *Vostok 1* rose slowly into the air. In his capsule Gagarin heard a shrill whistle and then a mighty roar. As the rocket built up speed, he was pressed hard into his seat. After a minute the acceleration was so great he could barely move. Technicians on the ground, monitoring his physical reactions, noted his heart rate rise from its usual 64 beats a minute to 150.

After two minutes, the protective cover around the capsule was jettisoned and Gagarin could see out of the small portholes. The view of the Siberian landscape below was so stunning it took his mind off the unpleasant feeling of being squashed into his seat.

The crushing sensation began to lessen as *Vostok 1* gradually escaped the clutches of gravity, and entered into orbit. Only minutes after take off, Gagarin was flying around the Earth at an incredible speed: around 8km (5 miles) a second.

The first thing he noticed was how he had begun to rise in his chair as far as his harness would allow. He was the first human being to experience the sensation of weightlessness. Initially he found it unpleasant, but adapted very quickly. It was not nearly as uncomfortable as scientists had predicted. Gagarin unbuckled his belt and hung in the air. It felt as though his arms and legs did not belong to him, and his map case, pencil and notepad floated by. The whole sensation was very dreamlike. Strangest of all, he noticed, was the way in which liquids behaved. Water leaking from a drink container formed into a sphere and floated in mid-air until it reached a solid surface where it settled like dew on a flower.

Now he was safely in space, the Soviet authorities decided to release the news to an unsuspecting world. Radio Moscow interrupted its usual schedule with a burst of patriotic music and a solemn voice which announced: "The world's first spaceship with a man on board has been launched in the Soviet Union on a round-the-world orbit." Throughout the country, factory, farm and office workers listened intently, immensely proud of the fact that their country could perform such a scientific miracle.

Vostok 1

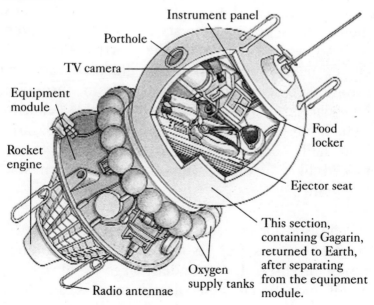

Instrument panel

Porthole

TV camera

Equipment module

Rocket engine

Food locker

Ejector seat

This section, containing Gagarin, returned to Earth, after separating from the equipment module.

Oxygen supply tanks

Radio antennae

There was very little actual flying to be done. Flight corrections were made automatically. The discarding of stages, the flight-path of the capsule, the speed it moved, even the conditions inside the cabin, were all controlled from the ground, or by computer. This left Gagarin free to concentrate on what he saw and felt. He quickly realized that weightlessness was not going to affect the way he worked, so he began to jot down observations and report what he could see.

The orbit of *Vostok 1* took it between 181km (112 miles) and 327km (203 miles) above the surface of the Earth. From here, coastlines, mountain ranges and forests could easily be seen, as well as the curve of the Earth. Along this curve, the pale blue atmosphere gradually darkened into a series of rich shades – from turquoise, blue, violet and finally black. Above this beautiful sight hung the dark eternity of space. For Gagarin, who had been brought up on a farm, space looked like "a huge black field sown with star-like grain".

The Sun looked very different. Without Earth's atmosphere to soften its rays, it seemed a hundred times brighter. It reminded Gagarin of molten metal, and when it shone directly into his capsule he had to shield his portholes with protective filters.

Suddenly, *Vostok 1* plunged into pitch dark as the capsule flew from the rays of the Sun and into the Earth's shadow. Below him, Gagarin could see only blackness, but quickly realized he must be flying over an ocean.

Although the cosmonaut was neither hungry nor thirsty, he ate a small meal – carefully sucking pulped food from a tube-like container, and drinking a little water. He had to be careful transferring both food and liquid from the container to his mouth, in case it floated off and attached itself to his instrument panels.

Soon *Vostok 1* emerged again into the light, the horizon blazing from bright orange through all the shades of the rainbow.

Gagarin's mind began to wander. He thought of the bustling streets of Moscow, where he had visited his wife and two daughters a couple of days before the flight. But in less than 90 minutes *Vostok 1* had orbited the entire Earth, and now it was time to return. This was the most dangerous part of the flight. If something had gone wrong at take-off, Gagarin had at least a small chance of ejecting to safety. If anything went wrong now, the first man in space could be marooned forever or burned to a cinder. Until this time, Gagarin had had every faith in his spacecraft, but now, in the most dangerous part of his trip, he began to wonder if it would work properly.

On-board equipment placed the capsule in the correct flight path, using the Sun as a guide, and *Vostok I* began its giddy descent. As it plunged down into the upper layers of the atmosphere, the outer skin of the craft began to glow red-hot. Fiery crimson flames licked along the heat-shield underneath the capsule, and flashed past his small portholes. Gagarin was once again pinned to his seat. Coming back was much more unpleasant than going out, and when his ship began to tumble around he became immensely worried.

Things had in fact gone seriously wrong. Before re-entry, his small capsule was supposed to separate from a connected equipment module. What Gagarin did not realize was that this had not happened properly, and both craft were still tethered to each other by electrical wiring. Fortunately the heat of re-entry burned away the wire cables. The two craft separated and disaster was averted.

When the equipment module broke free from Gagarin's capsule, the tumbling finally stopped, and descent parachutes opened to slow down the speeding capsule. As soon as this had happened,

Gagarin realized that the most hazardous part of his journey was finally over. He had taken an enormous risk on his life for the glory of his country and now he was going to live to tell this extraordinary tale. Overcome with sheer relief, he began to sing at the top of his voice.

Around the world in 108 minutes

Vostok 1 made a single orbit before returning to Earth.

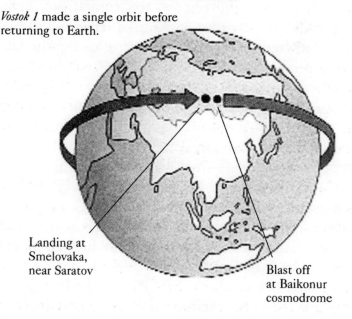

Landing at
Smelovaka,
near Saratov

Blast off
at Baikonur
cosmodrome

There was still one final, dangerous step to take. 6,000m (20,000ft) from the ground, Gagarin braced himself in his seat and was ejected from the capsule. Once outside *Vostok 1* he floated back to Earth by parachute. Soviet rocket engineers thought that landing inside the capsule would be too jarring, and that parachuting down separately would be safer.

At 10:55am, less than two hours after he had taken off, Gagarin landed in a field near the village of Smelovka, watched by two startled farm workers. They walked toward him, anxious to help, but slowed uncertainly as they approached. His unusual, bright orange spacesuit, and large white helmet, clearly frightened them. One, a woman named Anna Takhtarova, asked: "Are you from outer space?"

Gagarin took off his helmet, to show the farm workers he was a man and not an alien. He reassured Takhtarova that he was a fellow Russian, but yes, indeed, he had come from outer space. Then other farm workers arrived. Unlike Takharova, they had been listening to their radio. "It's Yuri Gagarin! It's Yuri Gagarin!" one shouted, completely astonished to be meeting the remarkable man he had heard about minutes before.

Gagarin and the excited farm workers embraced and kissed like long-lost relatives. This was indeed an extraordinary moment. For the first time in history, a man had left the planet and returned safely to Earth.

Afterwards

In 1961 space exploration was a matter of intense rivalry between nations. The communist Soviet Union (now Russia) and capitalist United States vied with each other to demonstrate their technological superiority to the world. There was great competition to see who would be the first to put a man into orbit, as this would be a good advertisement for each nation.

On his return Gagarin was declared a "Hero of the Soviet Union". His 1961 space flight made him an instant global celebrity, and he spent the next five years touring the world, even visiting the Soviet Union's arch-rival, the United States. He was an excellent ambassador for his country, and his amiable modesty made him hugely popular with the thousands who turned out to see him.

In 1968 he began to train for another space flight, but was killed when a jet he was flying swerved to miss another aircraft and hit the ground. A massive funeral ceremony was held in Moscow, but only in 1984 did the Soviet authorities reveal that Gagarin's body had never been found.

Death or glory for the "last gladiator"

There never was a hero quite like Robert "Evel" Knievel – the world's most famous motorcycle stuntman. Knievel (pronounced Kuh-nee-val) was a self-made legend from the top of his cracked skull to the bottom of his broken toes. By 1974, 10 years of jumping across snake pits, lion cages, fountains and rows of trucks had brought Evel a Rolls-Royce, half a million dollars a year, and a reputation as one of America's most swashbuckling celebrities.

The stories they told... how he was a reformed bank robber, how he'd broken every bone in his body, how he washed down painkillers with his own "Montana Mary" cocktail of beer, tomato juice, whiskey and engine oil...

Well, some of it was true. Knievel hadn't broken *every* bone in his body, just 35 of them. One jump had put him in a coma for 29 days. 14 major operations had left him with one leg shorter than the other, and his body was held together with steel plates and screws. Once, when quizzed by a reporter who asked him why he did it, he swaggered, "I'm a competitor. I face the greatest competition any man can face, and that, my friend, is death".

But Knievel was married with three children. He was growing weary of his 'death or glory' lifestyle. Still, there was one final challenge the great competitor had yet to face. For years he had dreamed of hurtling up a ramp at full throttle, and sailing clean across the Arizona Grand Canyon. It was a perfect spot – a national landmark and the greatest chasm on the face of the Earth. But the Navaho Indians, who owned the land, considered it sacred, and would have nothing to do with Knievel. Even $40,000 wouldn't make them change their minds. The Snake River canyon in Idaho was chosen instead. It was 1.6km (1 mile) across, and its dark, jagged walls made it a suitably sinister spot for Knievel's last stand.

A former rocket engineer was hired to design a vehicle to cross it. He presented Knievel with the *Sky Cycle*. It may have been called a cycle, but it was actually one million dollars worth of steam-powered rocket. The plan was simple. Knievel would sit in the rocket, and be fired up a ramp and over the gaping mouth of the canyon. Once across, a parachute would slow the *Sky Cycle* to a safe landing speed. The day was set for September 8, 1974, and Knievel played up the stunt for all it was worth. He told reporters he would survive "...if the heater doesn't blow up and scald me to death, if the *Sky Cycle* goes straight up and doesn't flip over backwards, if I reach 3,000ft, if the parachute opens, and if I don't hit the canyon wall at 300mph".

Within weeks the event had captured the imagination of the world. Fifteen businesses invested in it. There were toys, T-shirts, records, even silver and gold commemorative statues. As the day drew near, 50,000 spectators gathered at the Snake River site, paying a hefty $25 a ticket. Most lucrative of all was the plan to broadcast the action to several million paying customers in movie houses throughout the world. Knievel's fans called him "the last gladiator", and many believed he was actually going to die. According to his publicity men, his jump would most likely "leave behind the richest widow in America".

But to others, the stunt was a con. A bright teenager, they said, could have calculated the rocket's flight path, and see that it would land perfectly safely. One cynic, regarding the mob of desperado bikers who made up the bulk of the Snake River audience, suggested that the crowd was more dangerous than the *Sky Cycle*. Even the man himself was unsure... "I don't know if I'm an athlete, a daredevil, a promoter, a hoax, or just a nut."

So it was, on the afternoon of September 8, 1974, that Evel Knievel mounted his *Sky Cycle* and launched himself into the clean blue sky. The omens were not good. Two test runs had seen unmanned *Sky Cycle*s crash into the canyon's far wall. Showing uncommon courage, Knievel was undeterred. Just before the jump he told reporters he'd "spit the canyon wall in the eye just before I hit".

He was right to expect the worst. As the rocket sped up the launch ramp, a parachute accidentally opened behind the steam-powered thruster. The flight of the *Sky Cycle* was now fatally flawed, and it lurched into the canyon, parachute billowing behind. Knievel, struggling to escape, could not free himself in time to jump to safety. The *Sky Cycle* grazed the craggy wall of the canyon, and then dumped the hapless stunt man in the Snake River.

Quickly rescued, Knievel was shaken but uninjured. His stunt had turned out to be hair-raisingly dangerous after all, and there was worse to come. Disappointed by his poor performance, sections of the crowd rioted. They stormed the press enclosure and had to be beaten off by policemen. But injured pride was a small price to pay. On that day, Knievel's dare-devil heroism had captured the imagination of the world and made him around five million dollars. Even today, Knievel Web sites are full of messages from adoring fans, and his own site still does a lucrative trade in toys and other memorabilia.

TRUE
SPY
STORIES

Paul Dowswell
and Fergus Fleming

CONTENTS

This charming man...

Everyone liked Gordon Lonsdale – the handsome Canadian seemed to have friends all over London. In the late 1950s his face was familiar in the capital's best clubs and restaurants, and his car, an expensive white model imported from America, made a splash in a country still recovering from the hardships of World War Two. He lived in a beautiful apartment block called "The White House", just by Regent's Park. Here, he gave extravagant parties and charmed a succession of girlfriends attracted to his dark good looks.

Behind the playboy image, though, Lonsdale was a hard-working businessman. He ran a company which leased jukeboxes, vending machines and car security equipment. His work took him all over the country. But there was yet another side to the playboy businessman – one that would have astonished every single girlfriend, business associate and restaurant owner who thought they knew him well. His real name was Konon Trofimovich Molody and he was a Soviet spy.

Molody had led an extraordinary life. He was born in Russia in 1922, but he had been sent to live with an aunt in California when he was only seven years old. Nine years later, he spoke English like a native. Returning to Russia in 1938, he joined the Communist Youth Movement and fought heroically during World War Two. When the war ended Molody was recruited by the KGB, the Soviet Union's security service. He had a fanatical faith in his country's communist ideology and a brilliant flair for languages – two major qualifications that would make him an ideal spy.

By the age of thirty two, he had reached the rank of commander and had been sent on numerous foreign missions. In 1954, with Cold War hostility between the Soviets and Western enemies such as the United States and Britain approaching a peak, he was given his most important mission yet.

A new form of warfare had developed after World War Two – submarines carrying nuclear missiles. Such vessels lurked unseen beneath the seas of the world. Impossible to track and destroy, they were capable of inflicting nuclear destruction on their nation's enemies. Molody was to be sent undercover to Britain, to discover all he could about the Royal Navy's nuclear submarines, which were among the most advanced in the world. To do this he would have to establish contacts with other Soviet spies, and find members of the British armed services or government who would be prepared to sell him such secret information.

An assignment like this asked a great deal of an agent. Molody was now thirty three. He would have to leave everything he possessed in the Soviet Union behind him, and go to live in a foreign land as a total stranger. He was given a new identity and nationality – that of Gordon Lonsdale. There had been a Canadian named Gordon Lonsdale, but he had disappeared in Finland – possibly murdered – and his doctored passport, and past life history, was now in Molody's hands. He was sent to Canada in 1954. After a year living his life there as Lonsdale, he arrived in Britain in March 1955. He was to play out his new identity extraordinarily well.

Gordon Lonsdale had two very good friends out in London's western suburb of Ruislip – Peter and Helen Kroger. A quiet American couple in their 50s, they ran a business dealing in antique books. One time, friends on the street asked them to a dinner party. Helen arrived wearing a long black dress, and their hostess exclaimed: "Why Helen, you look like a Russian spy!" If she hadn't been laughing so much at her own little joke, she would have seen the Krogers exchange a terrified glance. Helen

Kroger was indeed a Russian spy, and so was her husband. Their house at 45 Cranley Drive was a major threat to British security.

Under the kitchen floor was a cavity containing a high-frequency transmitter and a high-speed tape recorder for sending coded messages at more than 240 words a minute. An internal 23m (74ft) antenna stretched into and around the attic. In the sitting room was a radio which could receive signals from anywhere in the world. Beside it stood a typewriter, tape recorder and some headphones. The bathroom could be converted into a photographic darkroom, complete with a gadget for making and reading microdots – a technology which could reduce large photographs to a size smaller than a pinhead.

There were surprises everywhere. A copy of the Bible in the sitting room concealed light-sensitive cellophane for making microdots. In the bedroom was a microscope for studying them. Rolls of microfilm were hidden in a hipflask. In the bathroom, a container of powder unscrewed to reveal a microdot reader rather like a small telescope. A large cigarette lighter on the table concealed a secret compartment full of coded messages.

The Krogers had led lives just as extraordinary as Molody's. Peter Kroger had been born Morris Cohen, of Russian-Jewish parents in New York. He met and married Helen at the University of Illinois. Her real name was Leona Petka. During the 1930s both had become communists, and Peter had gone to fight against the fascists in the Spanish Civil War. He had returned to the United States and worked for various Soviet trade organizations there before serving in the American army in World War Two.

After the war the couple began to spy for the Soviet Union, and helped to pass on American atomic bomb secrets to the Russians. They fled from America in 1950, suspecting they were about to be arrested, and surfaced again in Britain in 1954. This time they were known as the Krogers, having taken their identity and backgrounds from a New Zealand couple who had died earlier in the century.

Lonsdale was a frequent visitor to Cranley Drive – he came to dinner at least one Saturday of every month. Of course that was not all he did. The Krogers were Lonsdale's link with the Soviet Union. It was there, in their quiet suburban house, that the fruits of his spying work were transmitted to the KGB in Moscow.

Lonsdale's best contact was a Royal Navy clerk at the top-secret Admiralty Underwater Weapons Establishment in Portland, Dorset. His name was

Harry Houghton. He had access to a variety of "classified" (secret) material, and better still for Lonsdale, he had a shady past. In 1951 he had been posted to the British Embassy in Warsaw, Poland. There he had disgraced himself by keeping a mistress and dealing in black market goods. He was sent home with a severe reprimand. Yet despite his suspect character, he had been posted to Portland.

The British authorities were not the only ones keeping tabs on Harry Houghton in Warsaw. The Polish secret service had been watching him too. They told the KGB he was likely to be easily corruptible. The KGB passed on this titbit to Lonsdale, who wasted no time introducing himself.

Lonsdale told Houghton he was Commander Alex Johnson from the American Embassy. As they chatted away, he realized Houghton was just the man he needed. He was willing to do almost anything for money. It was easy to trick him into becoming a traitor. Lonsdale said the Americans needed certain information from him. He need not worry about the Official Secrets Act – a document guaranteeing confidentiality that all armed forces personnel were required to sign – after all, weren't Britain and the United States on the same side?

When Lonsdale mentioned money, Houghton's eyes lit up. He also came up with a clever scheme for smuggling documents out of Portland. Houghton had a girlfriend at the base, a middle-aged woman named Ethel "Bunty" Gee. She was a filing clerk with high level security clearance – meaning she handled top secret documents. Although there were spot checks on male employees as they came in and out of the building, to make sure they were carrying no secret documents, female staff were never searched. This bizarre lapse in security meant that Bunty would be a perfect accomplice.

Soon all sorts of files, from charts of navy docks to details of shipbuilding projects, were being smuggled out of Portland. Their contents were dictated onto a tape recorder, then transmitted in high speed radio bursts from Cranley Drive, or they were photographed to be smuggled on to Moscow as microfilm. Then Bunty returned them before anyone noticed they were missing. It all worked like a dream. Lonsdale and the Krogers were able to smuggle secrets on from Houghton and Gee, as well as other military and intelligence organization contacts they had made, for six years.

But all good things come to an end. Houghton may have been Lonsdale's best source, but he was probably also the most unreliable person the Soviet spy had to deal with.

Routine checks by MI5 – Britain's counter-intelligence agency – showed that the Portland navy clerk was living way beyond his means. In 1960 his official earnings were only £714 – a modest salary at the best of times. Yet he had just bought a flashy new car, laid out £10,000 on a house, and was spending £20 a month on drink alone. Where was this money coming from? MI5 were determined to find out. Checks on Houghton's bank account gave nothing away though. Lonsdale paid him in cash, so the police would never be able to trace the source of this new-found wealth back to him.

In July 1960 an MI5 operative started to tail Houghton and Gee. He followed them on a trip to London, to the Old Vic theatre in Waterloo. He watched them meet Gordon Lonsdale, who handed over an envelope in exchange for a grocery bag. Then Houghton and Gee left, taking an odd, roundabout route back to their car. It was all highly suspicious.

Then a month later, Houghton went up to London again. Here he met Lonsdale at the Old Vic, and the two of them retired to a café. The MI5 man slid into the table next to theirs and strained to hear the conversation.

"These will be the first Saturday in each month," said Lonsdale, "especially the first Saturday in October and November."

Something was definitely being planned.

They left the café, and the MI5 man followed at a distance. Then, both men crammed into a phone booth. But instead of making a call, Houghton gave Lonsdale a file wrapped in a newspaper. Then they parted. Houghton disappeared into the crowd, but the MI5 man followed Lonsdale, who got into a car and drove off. Another couple of MI5 men followed him in their own car and watched him as he stopped outside a bank. He got out, handed over a brown suitcase to a bank official, and drove off.

After he had gone the MI5 men moved in. They discreetly explained to the bank manager that they were employed by the government on work of a highly sensitive nature, and that they needed to look inside the suitcase. The manager understood, and they found that Lonsdale's case contained a Russian-made camera, a magnifying glass, two films and an assortment of keys. It was all very curious.

Then there was a lull in investigations. Lonsdale went away to Europe for two months on business, but when he returned from his trip, MI5 agents were waiting for him. They tailed him as he picked up the suitcase from the bank, and then got on a train to Ruislip.

Over the next few weeks, as MI5 watched, a pattern emerged. On the first Saturday of each month, Houghton would meet Lonsdale in London.

They would exchange packages, and that evening Lonsdale would go to Ruislip, arriving at the Kroger's house about 7:15pm. After three months MI5 decided to swoop. The man in charge of the operation was Detective Superintendent George Smith of London's Special Branch police force.

On January 7, 1961, Harry Houghton made his journey to London. On this occasion Bunty Gee came with him, carrying a big shopping bag. They arrived at Waterloo Station where no less than 15 agents, including George Smith, loitered on the platform disguised as passengers and newspaper sellers. The train was 45 minutes late. Maybe it was the delay that made Smith's men sloppy, maybe it was the cold. Whatever the reason, they were taken by surprise when the couple reached the station exit and dashed for a bus. Only one man managed to get on the bus with them.

Houghton and Gee had taken a spur-of-the-moment sightseeing trip, and after an hour or two they returned to Waterloo Station and went over to the Old Vic theatre, as they usually did. Here Smith's men were waiting for them again. Lonsdale was waiting there too, to greet them. When they arrived, he took Gee's bag, as if making a gentlemanly gesture of carrying it for her. That was enough for Smith. He ran up to all three and said: "I'm a police officer, and you're all under arrest."

At that instant, three unmarked cars screeched to a halt in front of them all. Lonsdale was bundled into the first, Houghton the second, and Gee the third. The cars sped off, and a pre-arranged radio signal was sent out: "Lock, stock and barrel." All three had been grabbed without so much as a shout in anger.

Gee's bag was certainly full of interesting items. There were four files from Portland and film containing more than 300 photographs of top-secret material on British nuclear submarines.

At the police station all three were charged under Britain's Official Secrets Act. Their responses varied dramatically.

Harry Houghton was crestfallen: "I've been a bloody fool!" he blurted.

Bunty Gee was indignant: "I've done nothing wrong," she protested.

Gordon Lonsdale was as cool as a cucumber: "As I appear to be going to stay here all night, could you find me a good chess player?"

His request was granted.

(While Lonsdale was in custody, Smith would ensure there was always a first-class chess player among his guards. Smith admired Lonsdale's style, and explained his generous attitude to newspaper journalists, saying: "He had a difficult job to do – so do you and so do I. He did it well. How can I condemn a man for that?")

Later that afternoon Peter and Helen Kroger also received unexpected visitors. Smith and his squad hurried up to Ruislip as soon as Houghton, Gee and Lonsdale were safely in custody. When the police arrived to arrest them, the Krogers were quite calm. They acted as if this visit from the police must be a mistake but, as any decent citizens would do, they were prepared to cooperate fully until they were released.

As they left the house, however, Helen Kroger asked for permission to stoke the boiler for the night, so that the house would be warm when they returned. Smith, who was nobody's fool, said: "Certainly, Mrs. Kroger, but first let me see what's in your handbag."

Helen Kroger looked stony faced. This was the moment she must have realized the game was up. In the bag were typed messages, a glass slide containing three microdots and a five page letter, written in Russian by Lonsdale. This was all intended for the boiler, but now it would become prime evidence for the prosecution case against them instead.

With all five members of Lonsdale's spy ring now under arrest, the police unleashed forensic squads on all of their homes. Naturally, it was 45 Cranley Drive that revealed the most incriminating clues to their activities. The radio and microdot equipment were easily located, but over the next week, as the house was virtually dismantled, police investigators found signal codes, transmission dates, thousands of US dollars, two New Zealand passports in the name of the Krogers, and two Canadian passports as well. Lonsdale's apartment revealed a radio set and microdot equipment, and Harry Houghton and Bunty Gee's respective homes contained equally incriminating secrets – including official documents, a camera and a box of matches with a false-bottom, which held a map of meeting places in London.

The trial started on March 13, 1961, and went on for nine days. Newspapers dubbed the spies "The Microdot Five". All were found guilty of spying and sentences were duly handed out. Houghton and Gee got 15 years each, the Krogers got 20 years. Lonsdale was clearly perceived to be the man in charge of the spy ring and the judge reserved the stiffest sentence for him.

"Gordon Arnold Lonsdale," he said, "you are clearly a professional spy. It is a dangerous career and one in which you must be prepared, as no doubt you are, to suffer. You will go to prison for 25 years."

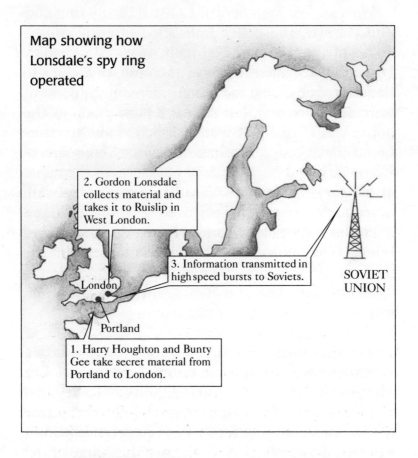

Map showing how Lonsdale's spy ring operated

2. Gordon Lonsdale collects material and takes it to Ruislip in West London.

3. Information transmitted in high speed bursts to Soviets.

SOVIET UNION

London

Portland

1. Harry Houghton and Bunty Gee take secret material from Portland to London.

Standing in the dock, Lonsdale smiled. He knew he would not be behind bars for long; he was too valuable an agent. In the tit-for-tat world of Cold

War espionage he would soon be swapped for a captured English spy. His friends in the KGB would see to that for sure.

Afterwards

Lonsdale was right to be confident. Within three years he had been exchanged for the British spy Greville Wynne (see "The salesman and the superspy", pages 371-386). Back in his home country he was greeted as a hero, and showered with medals. He continued to work for the KGB, although he was now too well known to be sent abroad as a spy. But the stress of his double life in espionage caught up with him and he died young. In October 1970, aged only 48, he had a fatal heart attack while gardening at his Moscow apartment.

The Krogers had to wait longer for their release, but their KGB masters did not desert them. A British lecturer in Moscow was arrested on fake charges in 1969, and exchanged for them. Both of the Krogers lived to a ripe old age, Helen dying aged 79 in 1992, and Peter dying aged 84, in 1995. Later occupants of 45 Cranley Drive dug up yet another of the Krogers' radios in 1981, when they were gardening.

Bunty Gee and Harry Houghton had no one but each other to look after them, and they stayed in prison for nine years. They were released in 1970, six years being taken off their sentences for good conduct. They married in Poole in 1971, and ran a guesthouse in Brankscome, Dorset, under false names. Both of them are believed to have died sometime in the 1980s.

Double agent for the Czar

Desperate times breed desperate men. In the decades before the communist revolution of 1917, Russia had more than its fair share. There were fanatical revolutionaries willing to sacrifice their lives to further their own beliefs. There were supporters of the Russian monarchy, prepared to exercise terror to hold on to their own positions.

In such circumstances there are always people ready to take cold-blooded advantage of the uncertain age in which they live. People like Yevno Azev. Described by a biographer as "one of the most depressing characters in the history of the Russian Revolution", he was happy to betray and destroy anyone who crossed his path. Unlike many spies, who are motivated by strong moral or political convictions, Azev cared for only one thing – money.

His tale begins in Grodnensky province, Russia, in 1869. Born of poor Jewish parents, Azev, like all Russian Jews, faced a life of persecution. Despite the grinding poverty of his childhood, young Azev was bright, and did well at school. But when he left in 1890 he would not settle, and drifted from one job to another. Like many young Russians he dabbled in the fashionable left-wing politics of the day, and in 1892 signed a political manifesto denouncing Russia's ruler, the Czar. This fell into the hands of the Okhrana, the feared state secret police. When the Okhrana began to arrest all those who had signed this document, Azev was forced to flee. He ended up in Karlsruhe, Germany, where he enrolled at the local college to study electrical engineering.

Many of Azev's fellow students were also Russian exiles. He became friends with a group belonging to a political party called the Social Democratic Society, which he joined. Here he met young men and women who were violently opposed to the Czar's regime, and were prepared to give their lives in the struggle to depose him. Unfortunately for them, they met in Azev someone who was all too happy to help them on their way.

So poor he was starving, Azev was desperate to make some money. He wrote to the Okhrana, offering to spy against these revolutionary students. The Okhrana investigated him, and liked what they found. A report stated:

"(He) is intelligent and a clever intriguer. It can be assumed that his greed for money and his present state of need would make him zealous in his duties."

It was a wise assessment. Azev began to receive a wage – 50 roubles a month – which would allow him to live in some comfort. Shrewdly, he hoarded most of his income, and still lived a very frugal life. Whenever he did spend money, he told fellow students that he was receiving help from Jewish charities, to see him through his education.

With a foot in both sides of Russia's political divide, Azev's career blossomed. Within the Social Democratic Society he took up a paid position, organizing and coordinating various revolutionary groups among anti-Czarist exiles throughout Europe. On his travels he came across an even more radical organization called the Union of Social Revolutionaries, and joined it. Meanwhile, making his way from one country to another, he sent back vast sheaves of information to the Okhrana about the Czar's exiled opponents in Europe.

So impressive were Azev's reports that he came to the attention of the Okhrana's chief, a man called S.V. Zubatov. He recognized Azev as a person of considerable cunning and a total lack of morality – someone much like himself, in fact – and he was determined to make more of this prize agent. What he had in mind was using Azev as an *agent provocateur*

– someone who works among revolutionaries, persuading them to commit violent acts, so they can be discredited or punished. Zubatov knew he could pay Azev more than anyone else, so he felt totally secure in his loyalty.

On Zubatov's orders, Azev returned to Russia in 1901, and was given money to move to Moscow to mingle with anti-Czarist revolutionaries. He soon became a popular and trusted member of a group called the Social Revolutionaries, and quickly revealed details to the Okhrana of its leading members, and the location of a secret press which was used for printing revolutionary leaflets and posters. The press was raided and arrests were made, but no suspicion fell on Azev. Instead, the Social Revolutionaries blamed this misfortune on their own poor management and promoted Azev to put matters right. The Okhrana were so delighted that they doubled his salary. Azev rewarded them by betraying the head of his organization. After the head was arrested, Azev's salary went up a dizzy ten times its original level.

The Social Revolutionaries appointed a new leader, a fiery young man named Gershuni. He trusted Azev completely, and together they planned the formation of a terrorist squad which they called the Combat Section. It was here that Azev took his role as an agent provocateur a little too seriously. The first task allocated to the Combat Section was the assassination of Dimitri Sipyagin, Russia's Minister of the Interior.

Despite the fact that he was an employee of Russia's Czarist government, Azev had no qualms at all about planning the assassination of one of its most important ministers. After all, what better way could he prove his loyalty to his fellow revolutionaries? Still, he figured, the Okhrana would not be very happy with one of their own agents killing a government minister. He would have to hoodwink them too.

So, in the week planned for Sipyagin's assassination, Azev took a trip out of Moscow. This way he could tell the Okhrana plans had been changed in his absence, and that he had had no time to warn them of the plot.

On April 5, 1902, a member of the Combat Section duly turned up at the Ministry of the Interior. He was dressed in an officer's uniform, complete with sword and pistol, and carried an envelope which he insisted he must personally deliver to the minister himself. He was ushered into Sipyagin's office and handed over the letter. It was a sentence of death. As the increasingly alarmed minister read the letter, he was shot at his desk. Shortly after the killing, Azev slipped the assassin's name to the police, and this man was arrested.

Azev continued to play this extraordinarily dangerous game. His fellow revolutionaries expected more assassinations, and Azev obliged. His Okhrana employees expected warning of any violent revolutionary activity. Azev gave them enough names to keep them happy, but withheld enough information to be able to continue with his own terrorist activities.

Those Azev betrayed were carefully chosen – anyone who challenged his authority within the Combat Section, or who might learn of his association with the Okhrana. Naturally, Gershuni was selected. He was arrested and sentenced to life imprisonment in a Siberian slave camp. The Combat Section was devastated by this reversal of fortune, and elected Azev to be their leader instead. It was a fine promotion, for now Azev controlled the organization's funds too. Like his Okhrana salary, much of this was squirreled away for the future.

Despite a gradual thinning of the bravest and best of their ranks, the Combat Section chalked up some spectacular successes – some of which were reported all around the world. With Azev pulling the strings and plotting the assassinations in great detail, they managed to dispatch Nicolai Bogolepov, the Minister of Education, N.M. Bogdanovich, Governor of Ufa, and N.I. Bobrikov, Governor of Finland. Azev always apologized to the Okhrana for being unable to notify them of such attacks in advance, but always delivered the names of the assassins after the deed was done. But just to allay Okhrana suspicions, he set up the assassination of Dimitri Trepov, the Moscow Chief of Police, three times. Each time he sent his men to kill Trepov, he tipped off the Okhrana first, and the assassins were arrested before they could carry out the deed.

In 1904, Azev planned the Combat Section's most daring move yet – the assassination of Sipyagin's successor at the Ministry of the Interior, Vyacheslav Plehve. As the minister drove through the streets of St. Petersburg in a horse-drawn carriage, a small, dark man raced across and lobbed a small package into Plehve's lap. What happened next was witnessed by a London journalist, who sent this report to his newspaper:

"Suddenly the ground before me quivered, a tremendous sound of thunder deafened me, the windows on both sides of the broad street rattled and the glass of the panes was hurled onto the stone pavement. A dead horse, a pool of blood, fragments of a carriage and a hole in the ground were my rapid impression."

Plehve was quite a target. A brutal and much hated minister, he had been responsible for the ruthless killing of many of the Czar's opponents, and had banned all political gatherings and meetings in Russia. He was also a fiercely anti-Jewish bigot, and had done much to ban Russian Jews from good jobs and housing.

Azev, of course, cared little for Plehve's political record, even his anti-Jewish racism, just as long as he was getting money from both sides. Once again he apologized to the Okhrana for not being able to prevent the assassination, but passed on the names of those who had carried it out.

More killings followed – another Moscow Chief of Police, a leading Jewish politician, even Grand Duke Sergei, the Governor General of Moscow, and Uncle to the Czar. But Azev also took care to continue to plan assassinations which would be discovered at the last moment, thanks to a tip off from him.

Then things started to go wrong. In 1905 an anonymous letter was sent to a member of the Combat Section, denouncing Azev as a police spy. The Social Revolutionaries held a secret tribunal with Azev in attendance. He bluffed his way out quite coolly. Fellow revolutionaries lined up to defend his character, telling the tribunal that it was absurd to label a man responsible for the deaths of the czarist Minister Plehve and Grand Duke Sergei as a police spy. The charges were dismissed.

It was a lucky escape, but Azev's confidence had been undermined. The source of the anonymous letter was still a mystery. He felt secure enough with the Social Revolutionaries, so he guessed his betrayer must work for the Okhrana. Further disasters followed. The Combat Section's best bomb maker blew himself to pieces. Then the Okhrana seized their entire stock of dynamite. He had certainly not told them about it, which led him to suspect that there was another agent working among them. Perhaps he was being spied on himself? Then, potentially worst of all, an Okhrana agent defected to the Social Revolutionaries, bringing with him the names of two of its members who were spying for the Okhrana.

One of the names was the man he suspected had been sent to spy on him. He was killed immediately. The other name was Azev's. Once again his luck held, and he managed to convince his colleagues that he was on their side.

Shortly after this, Azev was attacked in the street by two thugs. They stabbed him fiercely, and he only escaped serious injury because his fur coat was too thick for the knives to penetrate too deeply. Azev was shrewd enough to realize this was a warning from the Okhrana, to remind him of where his real loyalties lay. His relations with the Okhrana were further soured when another revolutionary group tried to kill the Russian Prime Minister, Peter Stolypin. The strain of his double life became too much, and he closed down the Combat Section and fled to France.

"I have been in fear of my life since the days of Gershuni," he announced. "I have a right to rest."

But life was too interesting to pass Azev by. In early 1907, Gershuni arrived back in St. Petersburg, having escaped from his Siberian prison camp in a barrel of pickled cabbage. Working under a false name, he resumed the Social Revolutionaries' campaign of terror, and the Okhrana pleaded with Azev to return to work. The opportunity to top up his now considerable fortune proved too much for him to resist.

Once back in Russia, Azev arrived to find Gershuni planning the assassination of the Czar himself. He reported this to the Okhrana, who promptly arrested 28 conspirators. Gershuni, meanwhile, conveniently died. His health had been ruined by his time in Siberia. Coming back to the stresses and strains of life as a violent revolutionary finished him off.

Azev now took the plot into his own hands, warning his fellow revolutionaries that planning and preparing for such a high-level assassination would be immensely expensive. The Social Revolutionaries duly organized a series of fund-raising efforts. Azev siphoned off the money to his own account and continued to pass on the names of revolutionaries to the Okhrana.

Various plans were put forward. A young priest who had joined the revolutionaries volunteered to kill the Czar. A group of bombers said they could blow up the Czar's private train. Then a plan was put forward to assassinate the Czar when he went to Glasgow, in Scotland, to launch a Russian cruiser which was being built in a shipyard there. This particular plot seemed like the best one, and Azev even went to Glasgow to supervise the assassination. But a young sailor who had volunteered to carry out the killing changed his mind at the last minute.

Azev's days with the Social Revolutionaries were numbered. One of their members, a mild-mannered historian named Vladimir Burtzev, had long suspected Azev was a police spy. He carried out his own investigations and discovered that Azev was suspiciously wealthy. When Burtzev contacted a retired Okhrana officer who told him Azev was their top informer, the game was up.

Burtzev put his evidence before another Social Revolutionaries tribunal, which was held in Paris. Azev, still reluctant to give up the source of his rapidly growing fortune, was foolhardy enough to attend. Evidence was once again produced against him, but this time his own alibis and excuses were proved to be false. Azev was asked to return to the tribunal the next day to hear further evidence against him, but he knew his life was now in great danger. The prospect of a wealthy retirement beckoned, and Azev vanished into the back streets of Paris, deserting the revolutionaries he had led so spectacularly and betrayed so heartlessly.

Afterwards

In 1909, Azev fled to Germany clutching a handful of fake passports – a leaving present from the grateful Okhrana. He took with him a German cabaret singer he had met in Russia, named Heddy de Hero.

The couple settled under one of their many fake identities in an elegant quarter of Berlin.

Azev became a member of the Berlin stock exchange and set about investing his money and other peoples' – something he did extremely successfully. For a few years all went well. Azev and Heddy blended into Berlin society perfectly, entertaining new friends in a home that was laden with silver, cut glass and at least one grand piano.

Then in the summer of 1912, on a visit to Frankfurt, Azev was sitting on a park bench when, quite by coincidence, Vladimir Burtzev sat down next to him. After Azev had got over his initial shock, the two men fell into conversation. Azev tried to convince Burtzev he was not a traitor after all, and told him: "If you hadn't reported my relationship with the Okhrana, I would have been able to assassinate the Czar."

But Azev knew Burtzev did not believe him, and would report their meeting directly to his fellow revolutionaries. Soon assassins would be sent to Germany to track him down. He and Heddy were forced to give up their plush Berlin stockbroker life and go into hiding. Two years later they returned to Berlin, but Russia and Germany were now at war. Azev had invested all his money in Russian stocks and shares, and these were now worthless. The fugitives were broke. Heddy remained by his side, but worse was to come. In 1915, Azev was arrested as a suspected terrorist and thrown into prison for two and a half years. When the war between Russia and Germany ended he was released, but his health had been seriously damaged. In April 1918 he went into a hospital with a kidney complaint, and died within a week.

Azev had been one of the most successful double agents in history. He had played both sides against each other and won. But his achievements went unnoticed. He was buried on April 26, 1918, in a Berlin cemetery. Heddy de Hero was his only mourner.

After the Russian Revolution in 1917, Okhrana files were inspected by Russia's new communist masters. Lenin and others had thought of Azev as one of the great revolutionary leaders of the 1900s, and were deeply shocked to learn of his double-dealing treachery.

High living in Lisbon

Most spies are anonymous "little" men who blend into the background, and do their often deadly work unnoticed and unremembered. As William Colby, head of the CIA during the 1970s, once remarked, "the ideal spy is a grey man who has a hard time catching the eye of a waiter in a restaurant."

Not so Dusko Popov – such was the high-living, gambling lifestyle of this handsome ladies' man, that speculation continues to this day as to whether he was the role model for Ian Fleming's famous fictional spy, James Bond.

Much of Popov's life seemed to be straight from the pages of a racy novel. On one evening in 1941, for example, he was standing casually by a roulette table in the smoky grandeur of Portugal's Estoril Casino. A blonde woman next to him slid three chips onto the green baize. The numbers she chose were 22, 18 and 15. She looked up and caught his eye. He nodded. Then she placed a fourth chip on zero. Popov nodded again. The roulette wheel spun and a hush fell over the people gathered at the table as the ball clattered around the slots in the wheel.

Popov didn't really care where it landed. The important activity for him had taken place before the wheel had spun. The woman, who was the personal secretary to the head of German military intelligence in Portugal, was not really gambling. She was arranging a meeting between Popov and her boss. The first number was the day, the second the hour, the third the minute – 18:15 (6:15pm) on the 22nd of that month. The fourth number told Popov where that meeting would be. Following a pre-arranged code, zero meant Lisbon.

As he always did, Popov waited to see where the ball would land. He knew from past experience that the woman was an unlucky player, and this time was no exception. He smiled to himself and left the building, looking around to make sure no one was following him.

Popov lived a complicated life and one that required a quick wit capable of remembering exactly who he was supposed to be, with any of the people he came into contact with. That night he had been meeting the Germans. They had employed him to spy on the British and Americans during World War Two. But Popov was actually a double agent, working for exactly the people the Germans were paying him to spy on. He had to stay on his toes.

He had been born into an aristocratic family in the Yugoslavian port of Dubrovnik, which is now in Croatia. Popov was a textbook playboy. Wealthy enough not to work, he spent his days meandering between Europe's most glamorous hotels and resorts, mixing with some of the wealthiest and most influential people on the continent. But there was more to Popov than nightclubs, casinos and an endless succession of girlfriends. He was bright enough to speak most European languages, he had a taste for adventure, and he had a strong sense of what was right and what was wrong. And as far as Popov was concerned, the Nazis were most definitely wrong. When World War Two broke out in 1939, he was in his element.

It was the Abwehr (German Secret Service) that first approached him. His contact with the organization was an extremely rich German friend named Johnny Jebsen. He and Popov had known each other since their college days together. After one student prank, Jebsen had arranged for Popov's release from police custody, and now he was hinting strongly that Popov could pay him back. Jebsen asked him to provide a list of Yugoslav politicians who would be willing to work with the Nazis, if Germany invaded their country.

It was an ill-judged approach, given Popov's views on the Nazis. Although he agreed to his friend's request, he went immediately to some acquaintances who had contacts with the British secret service. Put in touch with them, he reported what he had been asked to do, and offered to work for them as well. The British knew a sparkling opportunity when they saw one, and were more than pleased to make use of him. He became an agent in the XX (Double Cross) system, run by spymaster John Masterman, and was given the codename "Tricycle."

Now it was Popov's turn to approach Jebsen. He told Jebsen that he had a friend in London who was willing to spy for the Germans. Popov also suggested that he could set himself up in neutral Portugal, posing as a businessman in the capital city, Lisbon. From there he could make regular journeys to London, to collect secret material from his agent there, and maybe even recruit others to spy on the British. The Germans thought that this was a wonderful idea. This was how he ended up arranging his secret meetings via roulette chips in the casino at Lisbon.

The whole scheme, of course, was an elaborate hoax. What Popov really wanted to do was pick up information from the Germans, deliver it to London, then bring back misleading reports for the German secret service.

It was a highly dangerous game, but it worked like a charm. Popov set himself up in Lisbon in 1940 where he made contact with the head of German intelligence there, a man named von Karsthoff. He duly set off to London, returning with a batch of bogus documents from his non-existent spy, all carefully concocted to mislead the German secret service. On one of his trips from London to Lisbon, Popov was accompanied by Ian Fleming, who worked for British Intelligence. (It was this meeting that led people to believe Fleming had based his character James Bond on Popov, an idea Fleming always denied.)

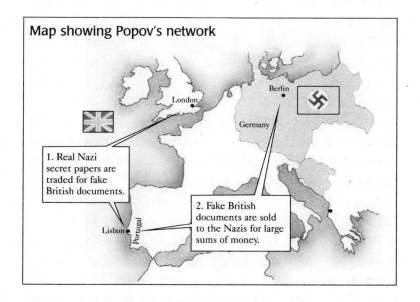

Map showing Popov's network

Berlin

London

Germany

1. Real Nazi secret papers are traded for fake British documents.

2. Fake British documents are sold to the Nazis for large sums of money.

Lisbon

Portugal

When von Karsthoff's bosses in Berlin read the documents he brought back from London, they were delighted. Popov was immediately rewarded with $10,000, which was then a huge sum of money. Popov carried on playing this game for a year and a half, and the Germans lapped up everything he brought them.

But Popov was not quite as clever as he thought he was. His friend Johnny Jebsen had discovered Popov was also working for the British. If Jebsen had revealed this, it could have led to Popov's torture and execution, but Popov was a very fortunate man. Jebsen's friendship with him was stronger than any political or national loyalties, and Jebsen did not betray him. Besides, Popov sensed his friend was becoming as anti-Nazi as he was, although they never discussed this openly.

Jebsen now began to alert Popov whenever his colleagues at the Abwehr made routine checks on Popov's activities. He also passed on to Popov any interesting news that he heard in Berlin. One piece of gossip Jebsen picked up was that Germany's ally Japan was planning to launch surprise air attacks on American Navy bases. The information was rather vague, but astonishing. Many people had suspected that Japan was planning to attack America, and this seemed to confirm that they had every intention of doing so.

These reports seemed even more likely when von Karsthoff summoned Popov to tell him he was to be sent to America to form a spy ring there. At the time Germany and America were not yet at war, but America was a strong supporter of Britain, one of Germany's greatest enemies. Among other tasks, he was to investigate how well prepared America's Navy was for war. Most particularly, he was to visit the Pacific islands of Hawaii to find out as much as he could about the Pearl Harbor Navy base there.

Von Karsthoff also had something interesting to show Popov.

"Look at this," he beamed with obvious pride. "These, Herr Popov, are something never seen before, and quite remarkable."

Then he took out a small box full of tiny black rectangles, each one no bigger than 2mm.

"These are microdots, Herr Popov. You are the first agent to be supplied with them. You have to pick them up with tweezers, and they contain pages and pages of information, which can only be seen under a microscope. A page of a document is photographed and the film is reduced to this minuscule size. You can hide them, of course, very easily – under a stamp of a letter, even under your skin – look, they are no bigger than a freckle."

Popov was impressed, and wondered what the British and Americans would make of this marvellous new technology. Von Karsthoff dismissed him with a hearty slap on the back.

"Once you are in America, Herr Popov, we will send you all the equipment you need to make these microdots," he said.

So it was that Popov flew to America in August 1941, armed with $20,000 (now worth around $400,000) with which to set up his spy ring. The war was gathering pace. Barely two months before, the Germans had invaded the Soviet Union. The Soviet armies had crumbled before them, and now the German army was heading for Moscow.

Such news distressed Popov, as it would anyone who hated the Nazis, but he consoled himself with the thought that his trip was going to cause no end of trouble for the Germans. The news he carried about Pearl Harbor was nothing short of sensational. Also, he was presenting the Americans with a golden opportunity to set up and control a German spy ring on their own doorstep. This they could then monitor closely, and feed with false information to confuse the Germans. And, with the microdots, he was bringing along the very latest piece of Nazi high technology espionage equipment. Surely, the Americans would welcome him to their country with open arms?

But they didn't – Popov's spell in America brought only intense frustration. As soon as he arrived he made contact with the FBI (Federal Bureau of Investigation), a branch of the American government which, among other duties, was concerned with anti-spying activities. They refused to let him recruit any spies. They were immensely suspicious of Popov, and wanted to control any bogus spy ring themselves. They threatened to arrest him if he even tried to go to Hawaii on a bogus spying mission for the Germans. Worst of all, they refused to believe his warnings about a Japanese attack on Pearl Harbor.

"Your information is too precise," they told him. "It spells out exactly where, when, how, and by whom we are to be attacked. If anything, it sounds like a trap."

Most of all it was J. Edgar Hoover, the director of the FBI, who disliked Popov. Hoover was a strange, repressed and prudish man, who took an extremely dim view of what he saw as "personal immorality" in other people. Popov, in his usual way, had launched himself onto the New York social scene in great style, buying a luxury apartment, visiting the most fashionable clubs, and acquiring several very glamorous girlfriends.

The two men met only once, and Hoover made his disapproval all too clear:

"I'm running the cleanest police organization in

the world. Then you come here out of nowhere and within six weeks you install yourself on Park Avenue and start chasing film stars. I'm telling you right now I won't stand for it."

What Hoover really wanted to do was to use Popov as a lure to catch other, real, spies. He could not understand that Popov was too useful a contact to waste in this way.

Popov stayed in the United States for long enough to see his predictions come true, for the Japanese did indeed attack the Americans at Pearl Harbor, on December 7th, 1941. Eventually, the FBI allowed Popov to recruit just one bogus spy. This man then began to transmit false information to Germany. However the FBI would not tell Popov what these messages said.

When the Germans sent a courier carrying Popov's microdot equipment to the United States, Popov had to beg and plead with the FBI not to arrest the man as a spy. This would have completely blown Popov's cover. It was the final straw. He had had quite enough of the Americans and the FBI, and demanded to be sent back to Lisbon.

Popov's British contacts were unhappy about this move, especially as Popov had no idea of the content of the messages the FBI had allowed their bogus spy to transmit. If the Germans questioned him about these messages, they would soon become very suspicious. If they realized Popov was acting as a double-agent, he would be tortured and killed. But Popov insisted on returning to Lisbon. His British secret service contact, Lt. Commander Ewen Montagu, called this "the greatest instance of cold-blooded courage" he ever saw. And Popov got away with it too.

Back in Portugal there were furious exchanges with von Karsthoff. What did Popov have to show for all the money he had been given? Where was his spy ring? However Popov gave just as good as he got, angrily telling von Karsthoff he had not been given nearly enough money to carry out his mission properly.

But there was good news too. Popov's Abwehr friend Johnny Jebsen arrived from Berlin to greet him. For the first time, Jebsen openly admitted that he had turned against the Nazis. During the time that Popov had been in America the Germans had invaded Yugoslavia, and Jebsen now suggested that the two men help to set up an escape route for Yugoslavs who wanted to flee from the Nazis. They intended to take them secretly across the Mediterranean sea to Lisbon, and then from there on to London. This was a very round about route, but by then most of Europe was under the control of Nazi Germany.

The scheme was a great success, and around 150 people were smuggled out. But when one of the escapers went missing between Lisbon and London, Popov and Jebsen feared the Nazis had sent one of their own spies on their escape route, and wondered if they had been betrayed.

On one of his trips to London, Popov discovered that this was exactly what had happened, although he did not know if he and Jebsen had been uncovered personally. His contacts in England begged him not to return to Lisbon, but once again he took a huge risk and went back. He was especially interested in returning because he wanted to recruit his friend Johnny Jebsen to spy for the British.

When Popov arrived back in Lisbon, he went at once to von Karsthoff's office to make his usual report. When he got there he found that von Karsthoff was out, and he was asked to wait. Popov immediately began to suspect that something was wrong. On this occasion he had brought a pistol with him, and he was all set to use it at the first hint of trouble. He waited nervously in the office, staring out of the window. Then he heard von Karsthoff's voice behind him.

"Turn around slowly, Popov, and don't make any sudden moves."

Popov's blood turned to ice. He had been betrayed. He was about to reach for his pistol to shoot his way out when he noticed von Karsthoff's reflection in the window. There was a monkey on his shoulder.

"An agent from Africa gave it to me," von Karsthoff laughed. "He's not tame yet and might bite if he's frightened."

Close escape or not, that incident appeared to be an omen. It seemed as if Popov's luck was finally running out. He did meet with Johnny Jebsen again, and successfully recruited him as a British spy. But in the weeks that followed, there were very clear clues that the Germans were on to him. One afternoon, Popov's car blew up shortly after he parked it on a beach. Then, after a successful evening at a casino, he found his latest girlfriend searching through his belongings. But still he hung on.

Finally, he heard that Johnny Jebsen had been betrayed by a colleague, and arrested. Popov could tempt fate no longer. He caught the first plane he could back to London, where he was to stay for the rest of the war.

Afterwards

Johnny Jebsen died in the hands of the Gestapo, a fate that could very easily have befallen Dusko Popov. After the war, Popov settled in Britain and became a British citizen. He continued living life to the full, as he had always done. He became an international business man, winning and losing a series of fortunes on business interests extending from Europe to South Africa. He published an account of his wartime experiences called *Spy/Counter Spy* in 1974. His second wife, with whom he had four sons, did not know of her husband's wartime exploits until she read his book. Later in life he settled in the South of France, and died there in 1981, aged 70.

The playboy sergeant

It was late 1960. Jack Dunlap, wife by his side, was talking to some new friends in the bar of one of Washington's swankier restaurants.

"I'm just an ordinary guy who got lucky," he said. "There I was pulling $100 a week in the military, with a nice little desk job ferrying around documents. I even worked evenings at a gas station for a dollar an hour to make ends meet. Five kids costs a lot of dough. My wife Diane here doesn't work either – too much to do at home. Then I inherited this plantation in Louisiana from a great uncle. I hardly knew him – how about that! I still keep my old job though – it's important for a man to have a job, don't you think?"

Jack's friends were impressed by his modesty and down-to-earth appreciation of his good fortune. Still, no one would have guessed he was a humble messenger for the US Army. Why, his outfit alone must have cost a couple of weeks pay. And that Cadillac outside – Elvis Presley himself would have been proud to drive it.

But catch Jack on another night, in other company, especially his statuesque, blonde mistress, and he'd have another tale to tell.

"Hey," he'd brag to her quietly, in the smoking room of some exclusive yachting club, "I shouldn't be telling you this, but I'm not who I say I am. My title at the Agency is 'clerk-messenger', but you should see some of the stuff I get to look at, and some of the jobs they ask me to do. . ."

His girlfriend would listen wide-eyed, and pump him for more details.

"I can't tell you anymore, baby," he'd crack. "If you knew what I actually did, I'd have to kill you."

"Boy," he thought, "was she impressed!" Actually, she knew he was just bragging. He seemed too ordinary to be the person he was pretending to be, but she didn't care. Jack had set her up in her own little apartment, and he took her to all sorts of exciting places – speedboat races, exclusive clubs, out in his cabin cruiser. Where he got his money from was none of her business.

The real Jack Dunlap was a sergeant in the US Army. Every working day he checked into Fort Meade – the National Security Agency's labyrinthine headquarters in Washington. The NSA, as it was known, was America's top intelligence-gathering organization. The building itself was vast – its main corridor was the length of three football fields. Its walls contained more electrical wiring than any other building in the world. Its basement housed the most powerful computers then known to man. Its roof sprouted radio antennae which collected information from all over the world. Surrounding it were three rows of electrified barbed-wire fences, patrolled around the clock by armed marines.

Dunlap's job was indeed "clerk-messenger". He had to collect files from one department, then trundle down the corridors with his trolley, to another. Often the material he handled was highly sensitive – "raw" top secret messages on their way to be encoded before they were transmitted to Embassies and undercover agents all over the world. But Dunlap was considered to be a water-tight security risk. He had fought with great bravery in the Korean War and had the medals to prove it. He had been serving in the Army for eight years with no blemish on his record. He did his job with such quiet efficiency and little fuss that even if people recognized his lanky frame they often had trouble putting a name to it.

In 1960 the Cold War between the USA and the Soviet Union was at its peak, and the Soviets were prepared to pay a small fortune to find out what went on in the endless, echoing corridors of the NSA. One night a Soviet agent who had discovered Jack Dunlap's daytime occupation approached him. They fell into conversation, and Jack was in an expansive mood. Yes, agreed the agent, five children were a terrible expense, especially on the kind of money the US Army paid their clerical staff. Still, he suggested, perhaps he could help Jack out financially – quite handsomely – in return for information? The huge sum of $50,000 per year was offered. This was nearly ten times what Jack was currently earning, and he told the agent he could count on him.

Smuggling information out of the NSA was surprisingly easy. Jack slipped documents he was supposed to deliver under his shirt. Then he had them photographed or photocopied by a Soviet agent who worked in Washington. It was a piece of cake. One time he even took his mistress with him, although he didn't tell her he was delivering US secrets to the Russians.

Bizarrely, no one at the NSA seemed particularly concerned about Sergeant Dunlap's lavish new lifestyle. They swallowed his story about the plantation hook, line and sinker. So he drove his flashy new cars to work, and regaled workmates with tales of his new cabin cruiser and speed boat, and nobody thought to check him out more thoroughly. The Agency even gave him days off work for speedboat racing. When he injured his back in a regatta, they sent an ambulance to bring him back to a military hospital.

His friends were awestruck at this VIP treatment. Dunlap played the situation up to the hilt.

"They were afraid the sedatives might make me tell a lot of secrets I know," he confided.

But in March 1964 Dunlap's term of duty with the NSA came to an end and he was due to be posted elsewhere. What was he to do? How would he manage without his extra income? More to the point, how would he explain to his wife, and every one else, that he no longer had it. Dunlap had become used to his luxuries. Life was good and he wanted to keep things the way they were.

As he pondered, he realized there was a way around this problem. Dunlap told his bosses he and his family were too settled in Washington to move, and he would like to remain in his post at the NSA. He offered to resign from the army, if he could rejoin the Agency as a civilian.

As far as they were concerned, Dunlap had worked well and efficiently, and they were happy to let him stay. After all, the NSA did employ plenty of civilians. But there was a snag. Army personnel were considered above suspicion, but civilians had to pass a series of tests, including a session on a lie detector, before they could be taken on. Jack protested to his commanding officer.

"Look, I've been with this organization since 1958. Do I really have to go through this rigmarole?"

"Sorry Sergeant," the officer said. "Rules are rules. If you come back as a civilian, you gotta jump through all the right hoops. Anyway, you're a war hero, you're the right stuff, you won't have any problems."

Dunlap brooded. He started to get anxious. He'd had such an easy ride he wasn't used to dealing with hitches. Then he started to psych himself up, wandering around giving himself a pep talk.

"Hey!" he told himself, "I've been smuggling out those documents for nearly four years. I'm cool – there's not been a sniff of bother in all that time. There's no way superspy Jack Dunlap is going to fail that lie detector test."

But he did.

They sat him down in a little office with a machine that measured his heartbeat, respiration and perspiration. Then they asked him a lot of questions, taking a careful note of how his body responded to each and every one of them.

The test results were damaging. They pointed to a character capable of "petty thievery" and "immoral conduct". The fact that Dunlap was committing high treason rather than stealing office stationery says a little about the limitations of the lie detector, but from that moment on, his life took a turn for the worse.

Dunlap was allowed to keep working as normal, but his poor showing in the lie detector test led to further investigations. NSA agents delved into his financial affairs and soon discovered there was no such thing as his Louisiana plantation. His income was obviously coming from an illicit source.

Nothing was said for two whole months. Dunlap was having sleepless nights wondering what was going on, and what his bosses did and didn't know about what he'd done. He knew things would be very serious if the scale of his treachery became known. Spies had been sent to the electric chair for less. Even if he escaped the death penalty, he would probably spend the rest of his life in a top security prison. Either way, the future looked bleak.

Finally, with no explanation, Dunlap was moved from his job ferrying confidential documents, and given more mundane clerical work to do. He was sharp enough to realize he was now in serious trouble. He rang his Soviet contact, but the man refused to see him.

"Don't call again," he told Dunlap menacingly. "You're on your own now."

Work became a nightmare. When he arrived every morning Dunlap had visions of himself being carted off by burly security guards, and his wife and mistress reading about his betrayal in the newspapers the next day. When were they going to pounce? The strain was becoming unbearable.

In June 1964, Dunlap went to a stock car race with friends, and hinted that he was going to kill himself. Nobody believed him, but the next day they found him barely alive, having taken an overdose of alcohol and sleeping pills.

Another month went by, and nothing happened. The manner of his arrest continued to torment him. Would it be an early morning knock at the door, and a squad of heavily armed soldiers? Or would a silent, sinister man come up to him in the corridor at the NSA and whisper: "Mr. Dunlap, will you come this way please?"

He was beginning to crack.

On July 20, while at work, he tried to shoot himself. But a friend on duty pulled the gun away from him just in time. Dunlap told him he was having "woman trouble", and wanted to end it all.

Two days later he finally succeeded. Driving to a deserted creek in one of his flashiest cars, he wound up the windows and suffocated himself with the car's exhaust fumes. His body was found the next morning.

Afterwards

A month after his death, the NSA finished their investigations. Dunlap was right to assume they'd find him out – they had gathered enough evidence to prove that he was a spy. But officials were still in the dark about precisely what information he had given to America's enemies. They later admitted they never really knew which documents passed through his hands, and had had to assume that everything that went through Dunlap's section was now no longer a secret to the Soviets.

Dunlap's wife did what she could to help. She discovered a large number of government documents in their home, and turned these over to investigators. Some material from Oleg Penkovsky, the Soviet officer who had spied for Britain and America (see "The salesman and the superspy", pages 371-386) passed through Dunlap's hands, although there is no proof he was responsible for Penkovsky's betrayal and arrest. However, he certainly provided the Soviets with useful information on US coding machines and also told them how much the Americans knew about Soviet military strength.

Bizarrely, because the whole episode was so embarrassing, and because the investigation was so vague in its understanding of exactly what Dunlap had done, the NSA kept the whole scandal secret. Dunlap was buried as a serving US Marine in Arlington Cemetery, in Washington. His grave was only a stone's throw away from the spot which was soon to become President J.F. Kennedy's final resting place. In a strange twist of fate, one of America's greatest heroes ended up lying next to one of its most damaging spies.

The Venlo snatch

It was October 21, 1939, and World War Two had just begun. In Zutphen, a town in neutral Holland, rain drummed down on the roof of a large Buick limousine. Behind the wheel Sigismund Best adjusted his monocle and squinted through the window of his car. Suddenly another car drew up. A man jumped out. Best leaned over to open the door and the man climbed in beside him. The Buick roared into life and rolled through the streets, wipers flailing.

Best looked like the typical English gentleman. Tall, with an aristocratic manner, he wore spats and a tweed suit. His hair was carefully oiled; he even wore a monocle. But this was deceptive. Best was in fact half Indian. He was also a spy. He lived in Holland with his Dutch wife, and ran a small business importing bicycles, but really he was a member of Z Branch – an independent group of agents which formed part of Britain's Special Intelligence Service (SIS).

Best's credentials were impressive. He spoke four languages, and during World War One he had run a successful network of spies behind enemy lines. Currently, he was trying to make contact with dissatisfied Germans willing to fight against Hitler and the Nazis. As far as he could tell, things were going very well indeed.

Best had been contacted some weeks earlier by one of his agents, a refugee who had fled from persecution in Germany. The man knew many high ranking officers within the German army and he had assured Best that there was a great deal of resentment against Hitler, resentment which had built up to a strong resistance movement. Best had probed deeper and had been given the name of an officer involved with the resistance movement – Hauptmann Schaemell. This was the man now sitting in the car with him.

Best spoke German well, and the two men drove through the Dutch countryside chatting together in German about classical music. At the town of Arnhem, they picked up two of Best's colleagues, an English officer named Major Stevens, and a Dutch officer named Captain Klop. Although Holland was neutral at the time, Klop was assisting the British. He wanted to keep his nationality a secret, so he was pretending to be Canadian and was using the name Coppens. This was a convincing alias. Klop had spent several years living in Canada, and the country was an ally of Britain's.

Best drove on. Schaemell, he reflected, seemed like a good catch. As they drove, the German reeled off a list of officers who were eager to see Hitler's downfall and named an important general who was prepared to lead the resistance. Schaemell promised to bring the general to their next meeting, which they set for October 30.

What Best didn't know was that the Germans were one step ahead of him. The refugee who had introduced him to Schaemell was in fact a German spy named Franz Fischer. The resistance movement Best was hearing all about did not exist. Schaemell himself didn't exist either. He was really Walter Schellenberg – a 29 year-old ex-lawyer who was now head of German foreign intelligence. Instead of spying for Best, he wanted to annihilate him.

Schellenberg's plan was simple. Over the coming weeks, he intended to lull the British and Dutch agents into a false sense of security, by pretending to be a willing collaborator. Then he would lure them into meetings, which would enable him to penetrate the SIS and find out about their operations.

First, however, Schellenberg had to convince Best that he was genuinely working against the Nazis. When he returned to Holland from Germany on

October 30, he brought with him two army friends. One of the men was silver-haired, with an old-fashioned elegance which made him look as if he might be a disgruntled aristocrat seeking to overthrow the Nazis. It was a plausible disguise – many upper class Germans did regard Hitler as a common upstart.

They crossed the border and drove to Arnhem, where Best had agreed to meet them. But Best was not there. They waited. After three-quarters of an hour, they were about to give up when they saw two figures approaching their car. But these were not the British agents they were expecting. They were Dutch police officers, and

they got into Schellenberg's car and curtly ordered him to drive to the police station.

This was not at all what Schellenberg had been planning. He was meant to be hoodwinking them, and now it looked like they had caught him instead. The head of German foreign intelligence was quite some prize.

There at the station Schellenberg and his army friends were given a thorough going over. Their clothes and luggage were searched from top to bottom, and this was nearly their undoing. In the wash-bag of one of Schellenberg's accomplices, open on the table ready for inspection, was a small packet of aspirins. Unfortunately for the Germans, these were not any old aspirins. They were a type issued to the SS (*Schutzstaffel*), the elite Nazi military corps, and bore the official label *SS Sanitaetschauptamt* (the main medical office of the SS). When Schellenberg spotted the pills, he turned white with alarm.

Thinking quickly, he looked around the room. Fortunately for him, the police officers searching their luggage were preoccupied with another bag. So Schellenberg swiftly snatched the aspirins and swallowed the lot – wrapper and all. The bitter taste was still in his mouth when there was a knock at the door. It was Klop, alias Coppens, Best's fellow agent. Schellenberg could only fear the worst.

But Klop had come to rescue them. He apologized profusely for the trouble they had been put to. It was all an unfortunate misunderstanding, he assured them. But Schellenberg was no fool. He knew exactly what had been going on.

The British and Dutch still suspected them, and this whole exercise had been a test to see if they could expose the Germans. If the police had found anything suspicious, such as the SS aspirins, then they would have been arrested.

Schellenberg himself had an even luckier escape. The paper and silver foil of the aspirin wrapper prevented his stomach from absorbing the drug, which could have seriously damaged his body.

From then on, everything went smoothly for the Germans. They were driven to the SIS headquarters in the Hague, and wined and dined like visiting royalty. The next day, Schellenberg and his friends were given a radio set and a call sign. They were told to keep in contact by radio, and that a future meeting would soon be arranged. They all shook hands and were driven back to the German border.

Over the next few weeks Schellenberg was in daily radio contact with Best's group. Two more meetings were held, and he now felt confident that they had accepted him as completely genuine.

But then a major fly landed in Schellenberg's ointment, and flies didn't come much bigger than Heinrich Himmler, head of the SS. There had been an assassination attempt on Hitler – a bomb had exploded shortly after he had left a Nazi party celebration in Munich. Hitler was convinced the SIS was behind the plot, and wanted Best and his men captured immediately.

Schellenberg protested strongly. This would ruin his carefully thought-out scheme.

"The British are completely fooled," he pleaded. "Just think of all the information I'll be able to wheedle out of them."

But Himmler was curt.

"Now you listen to me. There's no but, there's only the Fuhrer's order, which you will carry out."

So that was that.

With no option, Schellenberg devised a plan. He had already arranged his next meeting with the British – at Venlo, a small town on the Dutch-German frontier. He now contacted Alfred Naujocks of the SS, and arranged for a squad of twelve SS men to accompany him. Schellenberg met the men for a hurried briefing, and they sped off to the border.

Naujocks, a thuggish character, was known as "the man who started World War Two". Two months earlier, he and a hand-picked squad of men dressed as Polish soldiers, had staged a fake raid on a German radio station on the German-Polish border.

This gave the Nazis the opportunity to claim they had been attacked by the Poles, and an excuse to offer their own people, and the world, for invading Poland, which they wanted to turn into a German colony.

Curiously, Naujocks was not impressed with Schellenberg, and later described him as a "namby-pamby, pasty-faced little man." He wondered how he would cope with the unquestionably dangerous business they were about to undertake.

The rendezvous with Best was at two o'clock, at the Café Backus, which was situated in a strange no-man's land between the German and Dutch frontier posts. Schellenberg was very uneasy and ordered a brandy to steady his nerves.

Finally, at 3:20pm, nearly one and a half hours late, Best's Buick came into sight. It turned into an alley by the café. Best and Klop got out, and Stevens stayed in the car. Schellenberg walked over as if to greet them, but as he did so shots rang out and a car roared down the street. It was the SS who had been lurking on the other side of the border. They had driven straight over the barrier firing as they went. It broke all the rules of neutrality – Holland was not at war and German soldiers had no right to cross the frontier.

There was instant chaos. Klop drew a pistol and fired at Schellenberg who flung himself to one side. The SS car pulled up at the end of the alley. There were soldiers hanging from its doors and two machine gunners perched on its front fender. Klop ducked and shifted his aim. He fired, then let loose another shot, narrowly missing Naujocks in the front seat of the car. He jumped out and returned fire from behind the open door, while his men scattered for cover, their guns blazing.

Naujocks ran up to Schellenberg and shouted in his face.

"Get out of this! God knows how you haven't been hit!"

Schellenberg ducked around the corner to avoid the shots and ran head-on into an SS soldier. Unfortunately this man had not been to the briefing and did not recognize Schellenberg. He assumed he was Best, as both men wore a monocle. The soldier grabbed him and stuck a pistol in his face.

"Don't be stupid," said Schellenberg, "put that gun away!"

There was a struggle and the SS man pulled the trigger of his gun. Schellenberg grabbed his hand and felt a bullet skim past his head. At that moment Naujocks ran up and told the soldier he'd got the wrong man – for the second time that day he'd probably saved the "namby-pamby" man's life.

Schellenberg peered around the corner and saw Klop making a break for it. He had been hit and was now trying to get away across the street, the spent shells pumping from his pistol as he fired. But it was no use. A burst of machine gun fire brought him to his knees, and he crumpled into a heap. As he fell, SS men swarmed over to drag Best and Stevens into their car. A couple of them stopped to pick up Klop too, bundling him into their car like a sack of potatoes, but he was already dead. The German cars sped off to their side of the border, with a roar of over-revved engines, burning rubber marks into the asphalt road.

In the moment after they left, a strange silence hung over the scene. Passers-by and border guards emerged from doorways and blockhouses, and stood open-mouthed and motionless. Engine exhaust, burning rubber and the acrid tang of spent bullet cartridges hung in the air. A few pools

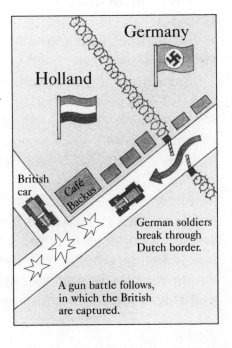

German soldiers break through Dutch border.

A gun battle follows, in which the British are captured.

of red blood stained the road, glistening sickly in the fading autumn afternoon.

The operation had been a huge success for Schellenberg. He had learned much about the methods of the SIS, and had obliterated Z Branch in Holland. A major threat to the Nazis had been put out of operation – and the war was barely two months old.

Afterwards

The Venlo incident was easily the British secret service's most embarrassing blunder of the entire war, and it had huge repercussions. Hitler used the event to justify the German invasion of Holland in 1940, claiming it proved that the Dutch were not really neutral after all. Furthermore, when Germans who were genuinely opposed to Hitler tried to make contact with British intelligence agents later in the war, they were treated with such suspicion that nothing ever came of their approaches.

Following their capture, Best and Stevens were interrogated at length by the Germans, and gave much away. Stevens was even carrying a list of all the British agents in Holland when he fell into the German trap.

Both men were sent to Sachsenhausen concentration camp where they remained for the rest of the war. They were freed when the camp was liberated by American soldiers in April 1945. Stevens died in 1965 and Best in 1978.

Schellenberg rose to become the head of Nazi foreign intelligence. After the war he settled in Italy, and died in 1952. Naujocks survived the war too, and died in 1960.

Behind the mask

Was there ever a spy more cunning than Richard Sorge? Regarded as one of the greatest secret agents of the 20th century, he led a double life from the moment he came into the world. His mother was Russian and his father was German; he was born in Baku, Russia, but raised in Germany.

Sorge was a fiercely patriotic German boy and, when the First World War broke out in 1914, he left his studies and volunteered for the army. He was sent to the Eastern Front where he fought bravely, receiving the Iron Cross (first class) for his efforts. But he also received shrapnel wounds to his legs which would leave him with a limp for the rest of his life.

As he recovered from his injuries back in Berlin, Sorge's view of the world began to change. He had lost faith in his youthful patriotism, but another ideology beckoned. He read the works of communism's leading writer, Karl Marx, and became convinced that this philosophy was the way to world peace and unity. By a curious coincidence, there was a family connection here too – Sorge's great uncle had been Marx's personal secretary.

When he was released from hospital, Sorge returned to his studies. He graduated from the University of Hamburg with a Ph.D. in political science. By now he was a committed communist and he worked hard recruiting students to his political cause. However, the German police suspected he was a communist spy and made plans to arrest him. Acting on a tip off, Sorge fled to Moscow. In 1917, Russia had become the world's first communist state, renaming itself the Soviet Union. Its leaders welcomed such an intelligent and diligent recruit to their cause. They were also charmed and fascinated to know of his family connection with Karl Marx, who had now become a figure of almost religious respect in the country. In Moscow, Sorge was trained as a spy, and taught to speak French, Russian and English. For the rest of his life, he would serve his mother's native country with unswerving loyalty and devotion.

To begin with, Sorge was dispatched on spying missions all around the world. His most successful assignment was a four-year stint in the Chinese port of Shanghai. Here he found work as a freelance journalist for German newspapers – a very convenient cover for someone operating as a spy. The Soviet Union was eager that China become communist, and decided that Shanghai, with its huge foreign population, flourishing industry and world famous criminal community, would be the ideal starting point for a revolution.

Sorge was not a shrinking violet, and being inconspicuous was not part of his nature. He was a tall, fierce-looking man, who liked to drink, and was stridently independent in his dress and manner. He could be loud, rude, obnoxious even. Yet he had great charm too, and many people felt irresistibly drawn to him. Such a person made friends quickly, even in a strange land. Sorge soon had a network of colleagues and acquaintances that he could recruit to his cause. He hand-picked a group of American and Japanese residents in Shanghai, including Hotsumi Ozaki, a Tokyo journalist who would become a life-long friend.

For two years Sorge provided useful, if not earth-shattering, information, and proved he could work with great efficiency. But then Japan invaded and occupied China's northern province of Manchuria, which was on the Soviet Union's south-eastern border. Having an aggressive and effective Japanese army in its backyard caused great consternation in the Soviet Union. Sorge was recalled to Moscow. His commanders let him know they had been very pleased with his work in Shanghai, but now he was to be sent somewhere far more important – Tokyo. His mission was to find out whether Japan intended to invade the Soviet Union.

For a European like Sorge, Japan was one of the most difficult nations in the world in which to spy. The few westerners who lived there were highly conspicuous. They also had to learn a completely unfamiliar foreign language, and come to terms with some very different social customs. (In Japan for example, it is considered the height of bad manners to blow one's nose in public.) As a final obstacle, the Japanese were also highly suspicious of any likely spying activity. It was a tough assignment and one which required a long-term strategy.

Sorge began by inventing a suitable persona for himself. He would become a German journalist, and to do this effectively he had to return to his former home. But in Germany, Adolf Hitler and the Nazi party had recently come to power. They were fanatically anti-communist, and Sorge was sure that the Gestapo (Nazi Secret Police) would know about his days as a student communist in Hamburg.

Courageously, he returned anyway. Luck was with him. Perhaps his records remained untouched in the furthest reaches of some dusty police file? Perhaps a communist spy within the Gestapo had secretly destroyed the incriminating evidence? He never found out why he was not arrested.

Sorge asked editors with whom he had previously worked for references, and created a credible identity for himself as an ardent Nazi journalist, keen to work for the good of Germany and its new Nazi masters. He was so convincing the Abwehr (German secret service) even asked him to do a little spying for them. He quickly obtained a German passport and left for Japan in August 1933.

Sorge knew he would have to stay in Japan for a long time. He spent the first two years there just getting used to this strange new country and its unfamiliar culture. He rented a small house, and immersed himself in Japanese life. He filled his home with Japanese books and art, slept on a low, Japanese bed called a futon, and left his shoes at the front door, in traditional Japanese fashion. To complete his education, he acquired a succession of Japanese girlfriends. While he was doing this, he dispatched a steady stream of newspaper reports that were to establish his reputation as one of Germany's leading foreign correspondents.

Friends in the German newspaper world provided letters of introduction to important people in Tokyo, and soon Sorge was a popular face at social gatherings for Tokyo's small but elite German community. As his confidence in his surroundings grew, he began to make contacts that would be useful for spying.

Sorge was made particularly welcome at the German Embassy, where officials were delighted to meet a fellow countryman who knew so much about the Far East. While Sorge would tell them all he could about China, they would fill him in on the latest stories about Japan and its foreign policy. Significantly, Sorge struck up a close friendship with a military attaché at the Embassy, Lieutenant-Colonel Eugen Ott. So believable was Sorge's loyal Nazi persona that Colonel Ott even allowed Sorge to travel with him on a fact-finding mission to Manchuria.

As a spy Sorge was managing magnificently on his own, but his Soviet masters also wanted him to set up his own spy ring, so he began to recruit suitable members. The first, and most obvious candidate, was Ozaki Hotsumi. His old friend from Shanghai was now back in Tokyo, and still a journalist. Hotsumi did not share Sorge's faith in communism, but he was unsettled by his country's invasion of Manchuria and aggressive intentions towards the rest of China, which he saw as a threat to world peace. Like Sorge, he knew a lot of useful, influential people.

Also in the team was a Yugoslavian communist named Branko Vukelic, who worked as a photographic technician and journalist – both useful spying skills. Then Japanese-American Miyagi Yotoku was recruited. He had recently returned to Tokyo from California, and was an artist who made a small living selling his paintings. Finally, Max Klausen, a fellow German, was added to the team. He had worked with Sorge in Shanghai, and would be their radio operator, transmitting reports straight to the Soviet Union.

As a spy ring, it had its faults. Most of Sorge's fellow conspirators were foreigners. Even Miyagi, who was Japanese by birth, had been brought up as an American. He often found Japanese customs and conduct as baffling as the rest of them. Hotsumi, though, was invaluable. He managed to recruit informants in the highest circles of government. In his work as a journalist he became a special consultant to Prince Konoye, Japan's prime minister. While working with the Prince he was given access to masses of confidential information.

Sorge, in turn, was accepted at the German Embassy almost as one of the staff. They asked him to write reports, and gave him a small office where he worked as an unofficial secretary to the military attaché. In the privacy of this office, he photographed any document that was likely to be of interest to the Soviet Union. His position grew even stronger when his friend Eugen Ott was appointed German Ambassador. On one occasion, Sorge made plans to visit to Hong Kong, where he intended to deliver a batch of secret material to a Soviet agent. When Ott found out he was going, he gave him an equally secret batch of documents to carry safely to the German Embassy there. Sorge could not believe his luck.

But spying is a very dangerous, difficult game. Once in a while, Sorge was careless. Shortly after he returned from Hong Kong, he was invited out for the evening by one of Tokyo's most important Germans – Prince Albert von Urbach. The two men visited several of the city's bars. By two o'clock in the morning, Sorge was seriously drunk and eager to go home. Rashly, he got on a motorcycle he often used to get around Tokyo, and roared off into the night.

Before long, he took a corner too fast, and crashed into a wall near the American Embassy. American security guards hurried over, saw Sorge bleeding and unconscious, and called the German Embassy. First to arrive to collect him was von Urbach himself. Sorge, now recovering consciousness, remembered he had several documents stolen from the German Embassy in his pockets. He muttered: "Tell Klausen to come at once." Fortunately von Urbach did as he was asked. Sorge stuffed the documents into Klausen's hand and passed out again.

The accident left him with some serious head injuries, and thereafter Sorge had difficulty moving some of the muscles in his face. Because of this, his expression would often become fixed, or contorted into an angry scowl – like that, said one friend, of a Japanese mask.

But as he recovered from his accident, Sorge's time as a spy was about to enter its most vital phase. In September 1939, Germany invaded Poland, and the Second World War began. This was particularly significant news for the Japanese government, as they were Germany's allies.

Sorge's masters were desperate for information about Japanese plans. The Soviet Union had signed a pact with Germany a month before the war began, with each side promising not to attack the other. But the Soviets were still deeply suspicious of the Japanese on their Manchurian border. Sorge's reply set them at ease. Japan, he told them, had no interest in the Soviet Union. Its real aim was to conquer China and defeat the Western powers – America, Britain, France and Holland – who had armies and colonies in the Far East.

But Sorge soon picked up other vital information which was deeply disturbing. He discovered that Germany had no intention of keeping its pact with the communists. When the time was right, Hitler planned to invade, and send his armies deep into the heart of the Soviet Union.

Such news was distressing enough, for someone as committed to communism as Sorge, but worse was to come – the authorities in Moscow did not believe him. Horrified, Sorge continued to pass on every snippet of evidence to back up his claim. By May 1941, he had conclusive proof – Germany had massed some 19 divisions on the Soviet border. They intended to invade in a month's time. Sorge even gave Moscow the exact date – June 22. But still, his spymasters, and especially the Soviet leader Joseph Stalin, continued to dismiss his reports as "doubtful and misleading information."

The invasion took place exactly as Sorge predicted. When he heard the news, along with everyone else in the world, from papers and radio reports, he broke down and wept. His Japanese girlfriend Miyake, who did not know he was a spy, found him sobbing in his study. She asked why he was so upset.

Sorge, feeling very vulnerable, was as honest as he could be without giving himself away.

"Because I am lonely. I have no real friends," he said sadly.

"But surely you have Ambassador Ott and other good German friends?" she said.

"Oh no. No, they are not really friends."

His face crumpled and he began to sob some more. Miyake waited expectantly, but Sorge would say no more. She knew him well enough not to inquire further.

But just as he was at his lowest ebb, Sorge was about to provide the most essential information of his career. With the invasion in full flow, German army divisions were pouring into the Soviet Union in great numbers. Soviet troops were fighting desperately against them. But large sections of the Soviet army were still based in Siberia, on the Soviet Union's eastern frontier. This was because Soviet commanders were sure that Japanese soldiers in nearby Manchuria would join their Nazi allies in the invasion of the Soviet Union. Sorge and Hotsumi once again scoured their sources for evidence of plans for such an attack.

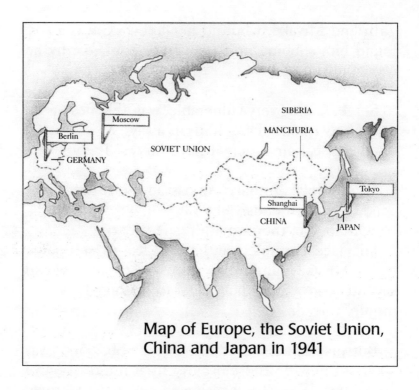

Map of Europe, the Soviet Union, China and Japan in 1941

In early October, Sorge sent a report to Moscow. Japan, he said, was definitely not going to attack the Soviet Union. This was the best news they had had since the German invasion began. Thousands of troops were rushed from Siberia to the west of the country to fight against the Germans. This decision almost certainly saved the Soviets from defeat.

But Sorge also told Moscow that Japan was planning an even more daring move. The Japanese were going to attack the United States navy base at Pearl Harbor. He even had a date, November 6, which turned out to be exactly a month too early.

It was the last signal Sorge ever sent. In the previous month, the Japanese secret police had arrested several Japanese communists, whom they suspected of plotting revolution against the government. One of their suspects blurted out Miyagi Yotoku's name and he was rounded up a week or so later. It was a routine, almost leisurely operation, but it was to yield massive results. Miyagi was arrested and his apartment was searched.

Miyagi was not a robust man. He survived the first round of violent questioning without giving any secrets away, but decided he could take no more. The next day when police sat him down for another interrogation, he threw himself out of a window. Unfortunately for all of Sorge's spy ring, his fall was broken by a tree, and he only broke a leg. The next day, in terrible pain before the beatings even started, he confessed to everything, naming Hotsumi, Klausen and Sorge as accomplices.

For the Japanese secret police, this was a delicate matter. Sorge, the Ambassador's friend, was simply too important to be arrested. German-Japanese relations might be severely damaged, and this, after all, was a crucial time in Japanese history.

Sorge and Klausen were left alone, but Hotsumi was fair game. He was arrested and tortured. He too broke down, implicating Sorge, Klausen and the Yugoslavian, Vukelic.

Sorge was well aware something was going on. He had not been able to contact Miyagi or Hotsumi for several days, and feared the worst. He met Klausen and Vukelic to warn them, but they all decided to stay. Perhaps their previous successes had made them arrogant enough to think they would get away with it this time too, or perhaps they were just resigned to their fate?

Sorge went about his business as usual. He still met Ambassador Ott, he still worked on his newspaper articles, and he still went drinking at night in the bars of Tokyo. But the strain he was under was affecting his mental health, which was betrayed by the state of his house. It was so untidy it looked as if it had been robbed. Stale whisky, carelessly and regularly spilled over the floor, began to make the place smell like a seedy drinking den.

It was after one of Sorge's nights on the town that they came for him. Arriving home in a German Embassy car around five in the morning, he was watched by a squad of Japanese secret policemen. The Embassy car drove off, and a short while later the police broke down the door. Sorge was arrested in his dressing gown, whisky glass in hand. Klausen and Vukelic were picked up that same morning. All three had left sufficient evidence of their spying activities around their homes to make any denial a waste of time.

Japanese and German friends in Tokyo could not believe what had happened. Sorge himself tried to spin a story with his interrogators about being a double agent pretending to spy for the Soviets, while really spying for the Germans. But after six days of torture Sorge confessed. A secret trial of all of Sorge's spy ring followed. Klausen and Vukelic were sentenced to life imprisonment. Sorge and Hotsumi were sentenced to death. This was the first time a Japanese court had passed such a sentence on a European.

After the trial Sorge's life went into limbo. He spent several years at Sugamo Prison, where he passed the time writing a 50,000 word confession. Then, on November 7, 1944, almost three years after the death sentences had been passed, Sorge and Hotsumi were both sent to the gallows. The date was chosen to taunt Moscow. It was the twenty-seventh anniversary of the Russian Revolution.

Afterwards

Sorge was buried in an unmarked grave, but his Japanese girlfriend, Miyake Hanako, tracked down his remains and had him reburied alongside his friend Ozaki Hotsumi. Miyake remained devoted to Sorge, and even had a ring made from gold teeth extracted from his skull.

The Soviets remained strangely silent about Sorge and his successful spying mission for over 20 years. Then, in 1964, he was declared a hero of the Soviet Union. A Moscow street was named after him, and his face was even put on postage stamps. Books and articles were published about his career. Two decades after his death, he was finally recognized as the brilliant spy he undoubtedly was.

The salesman and
the superspy

Spying is a lonely game, and one which requires immense courage and patience. Many a spy has spent long, sleepless nights, wondering when his cover may be blown, and what terrible fate lies in store for him if he is betrayed, or gives himself away. A spy who is sent to uncover the secrets of an enemy country has troubles enough. But a spy who renounces his own country and seeks to work for an alien power faces almost certain torture and death if he is discovered.

Oleg Penkovsky was such a man. He was tall, handsome, and with an aristocratic courtesy and manner quite unusual in the communist Soviet Union. In 1960 he was a Colonel in the GRU – the Soviet Military Intelligence. Such was his rank he could move freely around the Kremlin, Moscow's fortress-like government headquarters, and had access to countless military secrets.

But Penkovsky eyed his world with a secret disdain. His father had been an officer in the Czar's army, and had fought against the communists in the Russian civil war. Perhaps his family's opposition to Russia's new rulers had never really left him. Over the years he had come to hate the regime he served, and regarded Soviet leader Nikita Khrushchev as an oafish peasant.

At this time the world was embroiled in an era known as the Cold War. Although not actually at war, there were tensions between the communist Soviet Union, and western capitalist nations, such as the United States and the United Kingdom, who had become deeply suspicious of each other. Both sides built up their nuclear forces and engaged in a battle of propaganda and threats. Penkovsky was convinced that his country was planning to launch nuclear missiles against its capitalist foes, and the more he brooded, the more he began to wonder what he could do to undermine his masters.

Yet, as a young man, Penkovsky had been a model product of the Soviet system. He attended the prestigious Frunze Military Academy in Moscow, where he had been assigned to the GRU – an organization which accepted only the best recruits. His first spying mission was in Ankara, Turkey, in 1955. His cover was that of military attaché at the Soviet Embassy. Turkey was an ally of the Soviet Union's greatest enemy, the United States. The country shared a border with the southern Soviet

Union, and the Soviets were anxious to find out as much as they could about Turkish military equipment and the US bases that operated there. Penkovsky was a very thorough, reliable agent, who carried out instructions to the letter.

Penkovsky returned to Moscow after a year, for further training. By 1960 he had been promoted to Colonel, although he was passed over for promotion to even higher rank because of his family's anti-communist record. Yet despite this, he was still trusted enough to lead a Soviet trade delegation to London, where, it was hoped, he would be able to set up a Soviet spy ring.

It was during the time when arrangements were being made for this trip that Penkovsky met a man who would have a major impact on his life. His name was Greville Wynne, and he was a British businessman.

Wynne, who represented a British company manufacturing electrical goods, remembered the day he met Penkovsky quite clearly. It was a cold winter afternoon in an upper room at 11 Gorky Street, just off Moscow's Red Square. Wynne had been trying to persuade six Soviet officials to let a group of British businessmen visit the country.

This was no easy task. At the time, relations between the two countries were very strained. Britain was a close ally of the United States. Suspicions raged on both sides. Still, life went on, and if a little trade could be arranged, then that might benefit both countries. Besides, trade, and trade delegations, gave both sides the opportunity to do some spying.

Wynne was not actually a spy, but like all western businessmen who visited communist countries, he was asked to keep his eyes open for anything the British secret service might find useful. Having served as a British intelligence officer during World War Two, Wynne was quite happy to cooperate.

That winter day in Moscow, the meeting seemed to be going well. Wynne had spent five years selling equipment in the Soviet Union and other communist countries in Eastern Europe. He was known to most of the men he was negotiating with here, and he thought they trusted him. By late afternoon, agreement was reached. In the Russian tradition, vodka was brought out to toast the arrangements.

As the men knocked back their drinks, they relaxed, and the conversation became more jovial. But Wynne's attention was drawn to one man he didn't know – he seemed better dressed than the rest of them, and had an air of authority. He drank very little and did not join in the general banter that passed around the table. That man was Oleg Penkovsky.

Perhaps Penkovsky was keeping an aloof distance from his more junior colleagues, but his uneasy manner was also due to the intense anxiety he was feeling. In August that year he had passed a message to the American Embassy in Moscow, offering them his services as a spy. Now four months had passed, and there had been no reaction. What if the KGB – the feared Soviet secret police – had a spy in the Embassy, and Penkovsky's treachery had already been exposed? Actually, the Americans were extremely excited by his offer, but had been unable to find a safe way of getting back in touch with him. Perhaps, thought Penkovsky, Wynne or one of his colleagues would provide an opportunity for him to make contact with the West?

A month later, in December 1960, Wynne and a group of British businessmen arrived in Moscow on the business trip he had arranged at Gorky Street. Penkovsky was their official guide and he was waiting to greet them.

In the time they spent together, Wynne watched Penkovsky closely. He was sure the Russian had something on his mind, but the Colonel did not choose to confide in him. Instead, he approached another British businessman on the trip, who steadfastly refused to take any of the messages Penkovsky offered him.

This wasn't surprising – Westerners on such trips were warned to be careful of such approaches by seemingly friendly Russians, in case they become sucked into some KGB plot and exposed to blackmail. Penkovsky would have to wait some more.

Wynne returned to the Soviet Union again in April 1961 to organize a return trip to Britain for Soviet businessmen. Once again Penkovsky was involved in the negotiations, and gave Wynne a list of names of those who would be going on the trip. His own name was right at the top.

"So you're coming too, Colonel?" said Wynne. His inquiring tone invited further disclosure.

"I am, Mr. Wynne," said the Colonel. Then he looked around to see who else might be listening, and his voice dropped to a low whisper: "But I have to say it is not for pleasure I come to London. I have many things to tell you."

With that, Penkovsky passed the startled Wynne a thick envelope. When he returned to his hotel, Wynne opened the packet. It contained details about Penkovsky and his career, and a number of Soviet military secrets.

Penkovsky had chosen his man well. When they met the next day, Wynne took him to one side.

"I know people you can talk to," Wynne confided. "I'll arrange for you to meet them when you come to London."

A few weeks later Penkovsky arrived in London with his delegation. They were wined and dined by British trade organizations, and enjoyed themselves immensely, shopping and taking in the capital's top tourist spots. Wynne acted as their guide. Then, every evening, after his colleagues had gone to bed, Penkovsky would be taken to a room in the hotel. Here he would be cross-examined by a team of American and British intelligence officers from the CIA and MI6.

They could hardly believe their luck. By the end of the first week Penkovsky had given them a mass of information, from the state of the Soviet Union's missile projects to the contents of the Kremlin phone directory. He was open about his reason for wanting to spy for the West, and convinced them that his main motive was his disillusionment with the Soviet regime. Penkovsky told his interrogators that he felt it was his mission to help maintain world peace. He also said he wanted to become a citizen of Great Britain or the United States, and be accepted as a Colonel in each of their armies.

The British and Americans were all too keen to oblige. In a ceremony set up especially for him, Penkovsky was sworn in as a citizen and colonel in both the United States and British army. Their man was a rare catch. He was a Kremlin insider of high rank. He seemed to be motivated by his conscience, rather than greed. He did ask to be paid for his work, but this was essentially to set himself up for his new life, which he envisaged taking up in the United States when his spying days were over. He did not ask for the normally outrageous sums requested for such information.

Yet, for all his obvious usefulness, both the CIA and MI6 had reservations about him. No one doubted his sincerity, or suspected he was a double agent for the Soviets, but some of his ideas were highly risky, or even ludicrous. He suggested, for instance, that they should plant a number of small atomic bombs in Moscow's military headquarters.

His character also caused concern. Penkovsky obviously saw himself as a hero who could single-handedly change the course of history. Above all, he told them he wanted to be remembered as "the best spy in history". Such vanity did not bode well for a long life.

Penkovsky and his trade delegation returned to Moscow in May 1961, and his spying began in earnest. At Moscow airport his luggage was not searched. After all, he was too important a passenger to be bothered by such indignities. It was just as well. In one case he had hidden a miniature Minox camera and enough film for thousands of shots.

As he snapped his way though the Soviet Union's most sensitive secrets, Penkovsky arranged other trade trips for himself. He returned to London in July and visited Paris in September. On both occasions he met Western secret service officers to drop off his films. Altogether he delivered photographs of some 5,000 top secret documents. He also told his contacts, in fascinating detail, all that he had learned over nearly 25 years of service in the Soviet army and intelligence service. The CIA and MI6 had never known anything like it.

As well as his owns trips abroad, Penkovsky was also regularly visited by Wynne in Moscow. The British businessman acted as a courier, passing film between Penkovsky and the CIA/MI6 team, and bringing fresh rolls for the Minox camera. When Wynne was unavailable Penkovsky was asked to make contact with Janet Chisholm, the wife of a British Embassy official in Moscow. This was a surprisingly safe arrangement. Like all Embassy officials Janet Chisholm's husband was under surveillance by the KGB, but Janet herself was not considered a security risk, and was free to come and go as she wished.

She met Penkovsky at a park in Moscow, taking her three young children along for the trip. Pretending to meet by chance, Penkovsky chatted amiably and naturally with her and the children, and then gave her a bag of fruit candy for them. If any one from the KGB had been watching, it would have looked like a harmless exchange of pleasantries, but the bag contained undeveloped film from the Minox.

This risky game went on over the winter. Penkovsky met Janet Chisholm ten further times, but by the end of January 1962 he realized he was being followed. What he didn't know was that an

American serviceman named Jack Dunlap, who worked for the National Security Agency, the top intelligence-gathering organization in the USA, was playing exactly the same game that he was (see "The playboy sergeant", pages 51-60). Reports from Dunlap to the KGB suggested strongly that Penkovsky was leaking secrets to the Americans.

On Wynne's next trip to Moscow, a very edgy Penkovsky confided that he was sure the KGB were on to him. Wynne passed this information on, and both the CIA and MI6 decided it was time to get Penkovsky out of Moscow. But how would they do it? One plan involved smuggling him out of Moscow airport inside a packing case. There was even talk of having him picked up by a submarine off the Baltic coast. While Western security services dithered, Penkovsky got more and more anxious, especially when he was refused permission to take trips abroad, a sure sign that he was under suspicion.

In July 1962, Wynne flew to Moscow on yet another trade mission. Returning one night to his hotel, he discovered that his suitcase had been searched. The KGB were on to him too. Three days later, he arranged to meet Penkovsky for an evening meal in a restaurant. As he arrived he noticed he was being watched by two men. Just then Penkovsky turned up too, but they could not find an empty table. Penkovsky turned and left, waiting for Wynne outside. The two men had a brief, hurried conversation.

"You are being followed. You must leave tomorrow on the first available plane," said Penkovsky, then vanished.

Wynne turned around to return to his hotel and immediately walked into the two men he had seen watching him earlier. Surprised to find themselves face to face with their quarry, they hurried away. Next morning Wynne went straight to the airport. He felt completely out of his depth. This was no situation for a businessman who had decided to dabble in a little spying. Penkovsky was there too to see him off with a desperate plea.

"Tell my friends that I must come out soon, very soon. I will carry on, but it is very dangerous."

Wynne decided that it would not be safe for him to return to the Soviet Union, but in the autumn of 1962 he took a convoy of mobile exhibition trailers around several trade fairs in communist Eastern Europe. On November 2 he was in Budapest, the capital of Hungary. He spent an enjoyable evening entertaining prospective customers in an expensive restaurant, and then headed back to his trailers. Here, life took a considerable turn for the worse.

Four men stepped out of the shadows. They were all short and thickset, wearing identical dark suits and hats. They looked like a theatrical act, but what they did was far from entertaining. Wynne was grabbed by the arms and hurled into the back seat of a car. He shouted for help but a fist struck hard in his kidney, taking the breath from his body. A metal bar hit his head and a black shroud seemed to fall around him.

When Wynne recovered consciousness he was in a police station. The world seemed to swim around his eyes and he spent the next few days in a drugged stupor. He was taken to the Lubyanka, the KGB's headquarters in Moscow, the most feared prison in the Soviet Union.

Here, the KGB made a determined attempt to break Wynne's spirit. He was given a bare bunk to sleep on with only one blanket. An iron drum stood in the other side of his cell, for use as a toilet. Although it was winter, the guards would sometimes take away his blanket, and it was so cold he would freeze to his iron bed frame.

But all those business lunches, and the many evenings spent entertaining clients, had not softened the former wartime intelligence officer completely. Wynne was made of stern stuff, and he knew exactly what his captors were trying to do.

He repeatedly insisted that he had done nothing wrong, and kept to his cover story, which was that he had been unwittingly duped into helping the British secret service. Despite all his ill treatment, he refused to sign a confession.

The KGB had come for Penkovsky in October 1962, a month before Wynne had been kidnapped. The two men saw each other for the last time at their joint trial in May 1963. The trial was a showpiece of Soviet justice. It was held in an elaborate courtroom where the judge sat beneath a huge, red and gold hammer and sickle – the distinctive emblem of the Soviet Union. Cameras rolled and journalists scribbled, as Penkovsky and Wynne stood in the witness box.

The judge gave his verdict. Wynne was sentenced to eight years imprisonment. As a Soviet citizen and traitor, however, his partner's punishment was to be much worse.

"Oleg Vladimirovich Penkovsky," the judge announced solemnly to the hushed, expectant courtroom, "guilty of treason to the Motherland, to be shot to death and all his personal property to be confiscated."

Whatever terrible tortures Penkovsky's interrogators visited on him in the last days of his life can only be imagined. His actual fate is still something of a mystery. It was whispered that when the KGB had extracted every last shred of useful information from him, they took the Colonel to a basement and fed him slowly, feet first, into an incinerator. Maybe that was just a story meant to frighten any other high-ranking Soviet officer who might be thinking of betraying his country. But maybe it was true. . .

Afterwards

After the trial, Wynne was returned to the dreaded Lubyanka. His treatment there was so harsh that on one occasion he had to be taken to a hospital, suffering from starvation. Then, in April 1964, he was suddenly dragged from his cell and put on a train and then a plane. He had no idea where he was being taken.

At 5:15am in the morning of April 22, 1964, a yellow Mercedes carried Wynne to Checkpoint Heerstrasse, on the eastern side of the border between East and West Berlin. At the same time, a black Mercedes drew up on the western side. Out of it stepped Konon Molody, the Soviet spy known by his alias of Gordon Lonsdale (see "This charming man", pages 289-304). He too had been captured and imprisoned, and he was now being traded for Greville Wynne. The two men walked across the border towards each other, and on to their own freedom.

The British government refused to admit that Wynne had been a spy, and did nothing to help him settle back into his disrupted life. He was treated far better by the Americans, who paid him $213,700, as compensation for his hardships. Unfortunately, he lost most of this money in unsuccessful property developments.

Wynne wrote two accounts of his adventures. Both books (*The Man from Moscow*, published in 1967, and *The Man from Odessa*, published in 1981) are said to be full of inaccuracies. He died in 1990.

Eye of the Morning

Fame and espionage seem an unlikely combination. Who would have thought that beautiful Margaretha Zelle, the Dutch-born dancer who had enchanted all of Europe in the early years of the 20th century, would make a suitable spy? In fact, who would have thought she would be remembered as one of the most famous spies of all time?

At the height of her fame as a dancer, she toured the capitals of Europe, from London to Rome, Vienna to Berlin. In Paris, such was her popularity that police had been called out to control the crowds that flocked to see her. She had a string of famous lovers, including the German Kaiser's son, Crown Prince Wilhelm. But Margaretha's fame was not like fame is now. In the days before television, and newspapers and magazines obsessed with celebrity life, her face faded soon enough in the memory of most men and women in the street.

Margaretha's life was anything but ordinary. Born in 1876 to a wealthy Dutch hat maker and his Javanese wife, she was spoiled as only a privileged, unusually beautiful child can be. But her mother died when she was only 14, and Margaretha was sent off to a convent. At 19, she married a Dutch army officer named Rudolph MacLeod. The couple went to live in Java (now part of Indonesia), which was then a Dutch colony.

Married life was far from easy for Margaretha. MacLeod was a brutal man who drank heavily, and was often unfaithful. He also tried to hoodwink acquaintances by setting them up in compromising situations with his wife, and then blackmailing them.

A son was born to the couple in 1896, followed by a daughter. The son was poisoned by a servant whom MacLeod had mistreated, and died. Shortly after this tragic event Margaretha divorced her husband and returned to Holland with her daughter.

Margaretha, now approaching 30, was alone and penniless, and had no obvious way of making a living. But what she did have was a supple body and a vague memory of some Javanese dances learned during her time in the colony. And she was still stunningly beautiful.

Leaving her daughter with relatives, she set about completely reinventing herself. Margaretha Zelle left for Paris, and arrived there as exotic oriental dancer Mata Hari, which means "Eye of the Morning" in Javanese. She soon found work in a prestigious night club, and became the talk of the city. Margaretha was also an accomplished ballet dancer, and appeared in acclaimed ballet productions. Nine years of celebrity followed, and famous or wealthy lovers who showered her with money and jewels.

But in 1914 World War One began, and Margaretha's merry-go-round life came to an abrupt end. She was in Berlin at the time, and returned home to Holland as soon as she could.

Life was so much drearier in wartime. Margaretha was now almost 40, and for the first time in her life she was bored. After two years of wartime in neutral Holland, stuck at home with nothing to do, she was desperate for excitement.

So she was in a particularly receptive state of mind when an unusual visitor knocked on her door one night in May, 1916. He was Karl Kramer, Press Attaché to the German Consulate in Holland, and he had a particularly unusual request. He sat down with her at the dining table. When he was certain they were alone, he began to speak.

"In all your years of fame," Kramer explained delicately, "you have known some of the most powerful men in Europe. Would you consider returning to Paris now to mingle again with these influential gentlemen? And, while you're doing this, might you be able to keep me informed of anything interesting they might say?"

Margaretha looked curious but non-committal.

Kramer went on, "We could pay you well for this information – say 24,000 francs."

Margaretha allowed herself to show a glimmer of interest.

"Possibly, Herr Kramer, possibly. 24,000 francs might do well enough."

But, inside, Margaretha was absolutely thrilled. She was missing the money and excitement of her previous life quite acutely. What could be more glamorous than being a spy?

Kramer returned to her house a few days later, carrying a small leather case. Inside was 24,000 francs and three small bottles. Two held a pale, transparent liquid, the other a bright, blue-green substance.

Kramer explained, "This, my dear Madame Zelle, is invisible ink. Now watch this very carefully.

First you dampen the sheet of paper with the fluid in the first bottle, then you write down any useful information for me with the liquid in the second bottle. Then you dab the blue-green liquid over the top and let it dry. . ."

Margaretha looked on with great interest. Kramer felt like a magician performing a magic trick.

". . . and then, you can write a more innocent letter over the top, telling me about the ballet you went to last night, or your dear little poodle or whatever. Then, when I get it, I sprinkle yet more chemicals on top, and the message underneath comes through quite clearly."

Kramer almost added, "Make sure you do it right though. If you're caught, you could be shot." But somehow, he felt, this would be an unwelcome dose of reality in Margaretha's world. He did give her a code name, however – she was to be known to him as "H21".

Margaretha returned to Paris only with some difficulty. At this time, the border between France and neutral Holland was being guarded very carefully, and the border police were only letting people with special passes travel between the two countries. But Margaretha showed her worth at once. She knew many important people in France, and several letters from politicians and high-ranking army officers to the French Consulate in Amsterdam soon persuaded officials to provide her with the necessary pass.

Margaretha didn't take her spying career very seriously. To her it was just a game which allowed her to spend 24,000 francs. Some invisible ink reports filtered back to Kramer, but most of the time, Margaretha just enjoyed renewing old acquaintances and visiting the haunts of her glory days. Actually, she was having the time of her life.

But while she didn't take her spying very seriously, the French and British secret services did. They had received reports that she might be a German spy, and were watching her closely. But nothing she did gave them any cause to believe their suspicions were justified.

In Paris, Margaretha met a young Russian officer named Vladimir de Masloff and soon they were passionately in love. Then Vladimir, who was fighting alongside the French, was wounded on the Western Front. Margaretha was desperate to see him, but he had been sent to a hospital near the front, which was forbidden to civilians. Margaretha went at once to the French War Ministry, intent on getting a permit to visit her lover. When she got there she marched through the first door she came to. Before her sat an official at a large, important looking desk, and she began to explain why she had come.

What Margaretha didn't know was that the War Ministry building also housed the French Security Service. By a strange quirk of fate, she found herself sitting opposite Captain Georges Ladoux, head of French counterintelligence – the agency set up to investigate foreign spies.

He knew all about Margaretha Zelle, and was quite aware that she might be a spy. Now here she was, sitting before him, telling him she wanted to visit a forbidden area. It was too good to be true. He played her along, and told her she would get her pass at once. When she had gone he immediately notified two of his agents, telling them to follow her and watch her like a hawk.

Of course, Margaretha had wanted her permit only with the intention of visiting Vladimir. Ladoux's agents had nothing suspicious to report. So, after her return, Ladoux called her into his office. Like Karl Kramer, he too knew that she had friends in very high places, and he tentatively inquired if she might be able to travel to Germany and do a little spying for the French.

As far as Margaretha was concerned, this was all money for nothing. Fate was offering her another wonderful slice of good fortune. But, cool as ever, she looked him straight in the eye and asked him for one million francs.

Ladoux struggled to keep a straight face. That was more than he would pay a dozen of their best agents put together. He was frank with her.

"Madame Zelle," he said, "you are virtually unknown to us. We don't know if we can trust you, and even if we decide we can, I can pay you no more than 25,000 francs for your services."

Margaretha shrugged. It could be worse. Then she made an error so fatal she could have been signing her own death warrant. Eager to show Ladoux she would be value for money, she boasted:

"I know a man who can organize everything for me in Germany. His name is Kramer."

Ladoux knew him too. If Margaretha Zelle was familiar with him, then in all likelihood she was a German spy after all. Clearly, there was more to her than met the eye. He asked her to go back to Holland and await instructions.

Margaretha returned home by sea, but en route her boat was stopped in the English Channel by a

British ship. The British were searching for a dangerous German agent named Clara Benedict, and they had with them a photograph of the woman they were seeking. Unfortunately for Margaretha, she bore a close likeness to Clara, and she was arrested immediately and taken to England.

Two weeks of interrogation followed. After a great deal of shouting and unpleasantness, Margaretha convinced the British that she was the famous Mata Hari, and not Clara Benedict. But even then, she was not released. Her interrogator, Sir Basil Thomas, told her:

"I would be delighted to set you free, but something rather curious has happened. We have been in touch with our people in Holland, and they tell us that Madame Zelle, or Mata Hari, is suspected of being a German agent."

Margaretha's double dealings were catching up with her. She thought wildly, then burst out:

"I am not a German agent. I work for Captain Ladoux in Paris."

Thomas contacted Ladoux at once. "Never heard of her," came the baffling reply. Ladoux obviously did not want to admit to asking Margaretha to spy for the French.

Eventually, the British let Margaretha go. Thomas had her placed on a boat bound for neutral Spain, warning her that she was way out of her depth and playing a very dangerous game. But Spain was the worst place they could have sent her. Madrid was teeming with spies of all nationalities. Once again, Margaretha was penniless, only this time she was in a foreign country. She decided to buckle down and get some serious spying done.

Uncertain of whether to work for the French or the Germans, she decided to spy for both sides – after all, she reasoned, they had been stupid enough to let her do so before. To the French she gave reports of German agents landing by submarine on the coast of Morocco. To the Germans she passed on news of forthcoming attacks by French and British troops.

But all of her information was second hand, and no more than what each side was certain the other side already knew. The French and German secret services were just testing her, almost certain that she was working for both sides. Eventually the Germans lost patience. They had wasted 24,000 francs, and now they had had enough. They deliberately leaked information to the French, to confirm that she had been working for them.

Margaretha was summoned to Paris. No sooner had she arrived than she was immediately arrested and sent to Captain Bouchardon of the French Secret Service to be interviewed at length. He had been expecting a legendary beauty, and was surprised to see Mata Hari looking tired and gaunt.

Tired she may have been, but Margaretha was not going to give up without a fight. As they talked she denied everything, trying frantically to offer explanations of her dealings with the German secret service. She even tried to pass off Kramer's 24,000 franc payment as compensation for some valuable furs she had left in Berlin.

Bouchardon looked at Margaretha Zelle and sighed. He remembered her as a fabulous, exotic dancer in pre-war Paris. How much had changed. Clearly, she was no longer the exotic beauty who had enchanted an entire continent, but she was still a striking woman, and Bouchardon was not immune to her charms.

Everything about Margaretha told Bouchardon that she was a bumbling amateur. Whatever information she had given to the Germans was almost certainly worthless, and she had been working for the French too. In another time they would have let her go home to Holland, with a stern warning never to come back to Paris. But the war was going badly for France. Millions of men had been killed and people were demanding scapegoats. Spies, it was said, were everywhere. An example had to be made. So it was decided that Margaretha was to be tried as a spy – a crime that carried the death penalty.

On July 24, 1917, Margaretha Zelle stood before a closed military court. She was on trial for her life. Her lawyer, an old lover who could not believe that she had been a traitor to France, hoped to call influential friends from her past as character witnesses to defend her. But the tide had turned against her. Nobody wanted to be publicly associated with a woman who was now perceived as a dangerous German spy.

The trial went badly from the start, although Margaretha defended herself bravely. As she had done with Bouchard, she tried to pass off evidence of German payments to her as compensation for lost belongings, or gifts from lovers. It all looked increasingly implausible. Yet equally implausibly, the prosecution described her as "one of the greatest spies of the century", and alleged that she was "responsible for the deaths of tens of thousands of soldiers". Margaretha listened to the accusations unbowed. But when the prosecution also revealed her secret German code name, H21, her resistance and composure collapsed. She began to panic and her whole body started to tremble.

It was all over in less than two days. Margaretha was found guilty of spying against the French and sentenced to death. In deep shock, she could not bring herself to believe her wonderful life had turned out so badly.

"It's not possible, it's not possible," she repeated over and over.

Margaretha watched the summer fade to autumn from her cell window. Appeals were lodged and rejected, and now a date had been set for her execution – October 15. She was to be taken to Vincennes, a chateau on the edge of Paris, and shot by firing squad.

She slept well the night before, and was woken by Captain Bouchardon at 4:00am. In her cell were two nuns, there to keep her company.

"It's not possible," she said again to them. Then, "Don't worry sisters. I know how to die. You'll see a good death."

She had decided she would leave the world as she had lived – with as much splendour as she could manage. She put on an expensive dress, some beautiful shoes, a fine shawl, a hat and long gloves. She seemed quite calm.

"Why do you have this custom of executing people at dawn?" she said to the nuns. "In India and elsewhere it takes place at noon. I'd much rather go to Vincennes about three o'clock, after a good lunch."

And so she continued for the final two hours of her life. She stepped out of the car that took her to Vincennes with as much dignity as she could manage, and walked confidently before the firing squad. She refused a blindfold and would not be tied to the stake set up for her execution.

It was over mercifully quickly. Twelve shots rang out and she slumped to the ground. As the morning mist lifted, the body that had once entranced a continent was loaded into a coffin and taken away.

Afterwards

Mata Hari continues to be an object of great fascination in the world of espionage. Plenty of photographs still exist showing the dancer in her sultry prime, and ensuring that she is still remembered over eighty years after her untimely death. Her stage name has become an all-purpose description for an attractive female spy. The Dutch Mata Hari Foundation, an organization set up to prove her innocence of the charges made against her, still hope that she will one day receive an official pardon.

Her story has been the subject of several films and, until the creation of James Bond, she was the classic symbol of glamorous espionage. Greta Garbo played her in a 1931 film called *Mata Hari*. Like many films, the truth is buried among the drama on the screen, which focuses on her love affair with Vladimir de Masloff. In the film, she sends news to her lover that she is dying in a hospital, rather than about to be shot. Another film of her life was made in 1985, this time starring Sylvia Kristel.

In the late 1990s Margaretha was in the news again, for a very bizarre reason. After her execution her head was preserved in a private museum, but it was stolen, and has so far not been recovered.

The allure of Mata Hari stretches into the 21st century, and recently a computer software package for seeking out hard-to-find Internet information was named after her.

The gentleman's gentleman

Ludwig Moyzisch was not amused. He had been woken from a deep sleep and summoned to the house of the First Secretary to the German Embassy in Ankara, Turkey. In the middle of the night. What could possibly be this important?

It was October, 1943. Europe was deep into World War Two. Neutral Turkey, uncomfortably positioned between Nazi-occupied Europe and Soviet Russia, was teeming with spies. Moyzisch, a member of the German secret service, the SD (Sicherheitsdienst), was one of these spies. He had a cover job as a trade representative at the German Embassy, and he was often expected to do odd, unexpected things at strange times of the day.

Nonetheless, he was even more irritated when he got to the house. The First Secretary had gone to bed, and it was his wife who greeted Moyzisch at the door.

"There's a strange sort of character in there," she said, pointing to the drawing room. "He has something he wants to sell us."

Then she too left for her bed, telling him to be sure to close the door properly when he left.

Moyzisch was seething, and walked briskly into the drawing room. He was determined to sort this visitor out as soon as possible. His eyes searched around the clutter and paraphernalia of the room, and it took a few moments before he noticed a still, pale figure, sitting stock still on a sofa, his face hidden in shadow. Something about this man made Moyzisch stiffen suspiciously. His temper receded, and he concentrated on clearing his head.

The visitor stood up. He was small and squat, with thick black hair and a high forehead. Moyzisch later recalled his face as being "that of a man accustomed to hiding his feelings", but on this occasion his dark, piecing eyes darted around the room, betraying his unease.

The man went over to the door, and suddenly jerked it open, to see if anyone was hiding behind it. Moyzisch's irritation returned. He was a spy, not one of the Marx Brothers, and this was not a silly film. But he kept his silence and let his visitor do the talking.

"I have an offer to make to you," the man began, talking in fluent but heavily accented French. "But first I must ask for your assurance that nothing I say now will go beyond you and your chief. If you betray me, your life will be as worthless as mine. I'll see to it if it's the last thing I do."

With that, he drew his hand across his throat.

Moyzisch looked at the man coldly. Certainly, he could not take a threat like that seriously. But he was a professional spy, and his training told him to wait and see what else this stranger had to say. It was certainly interesting. . .

"I can deliver to you photographs of top secret information – extremely secret information – from the British Embassy. But if you want it, you'll have to pay me a great deal of money. I'll risk my life for you, so I want you to make it worth my while."

Moyzisch spoke for the first time: "And what sort of sum would you be thinking of?"

"I want £20,000 – sterling – in cash."

Moyzisch's mask slipped. He could not resist a sneer.

"That's completely impossible," he replied. "What on earth have you got that would be worth such a huge sum of money?"

In 1943, such an amount was a veritable fortune.

"Well, think about it," said the stranger. "I'll give you three days to decide. Then I'll call you at the German Embassy and identify myself as "Pierre". I shall ask if you have any letters for me. If the answer is yes, I shall come and see you. If no, then you shall never hear from me again. If you're not interested, there are others who certainly will be."

Something about this man made Moyzisch hesitate to dismiss him. He almost certainly meant to take his information to the Soviet Embassy in Ankara if the Germans turned him down, and he certainly did mean business. Moyzisch agreed to this arrangement and the man got up to leave. Just as he got to the door he turned and smiled slyly.

"I'll bet you're dying to know who I am. Well, I'll tell you. I'm the British Ambassador's valet."

Before Moyzisch could say any more the door slammed shut, and the strange little man was gone.

The next morning Moyzisch arranged to see the German ambassador, Franz von Papen. The sum of money this man demanded was so huge they would have to ask permission to give it to him from the German Foreign Secretary, Joachim von Ribbentrop, himself. They were certain he would say no. But a reply came back accepting the arrangement. A special courier was being sent from Berlin with the money.

Moyzisch gave his stranger a code name – Cicero, after a famous Roman orator – and made preparations for his visit. Sure enough, the phone call from "Pierre" came and they arranged to meet at the Embassy at 10:00pm that night.

Moyzisch was well prepared. He arranged for a darkroom, complete with a photographic technician, to be made ready, so he could check the film on the spot. The strange man turned up right on time, and the two of them began a tentative, suspicious exchange. Cicero wanted the money first, and then he would hand over the film. Moyzisch wanted the film to check if it was genuine, then he would hand over the money. They came to a compromise. Moyzisch counted out the £20,000 in front of him, then returned it to the safe and took the film to the darkroom.

The results were spectacular: unquestionably authentic top secret documents, all with recent dates. Cicero got his money, and a further arrangement was reached whereby the Germans would pay him £15,000 for every subsequent delivery. The money was an astronomical amount, but then, the information was simply extraordinary.

The next night Cicero returned again with yet more film. When he left he asked Moyzisch to drive him back to the British Embassy. The German was astonished.

"But why not?" said Cicero, simply. "That's where I live."

More films followed, each revealing documents containing highly sensitive information. The Germans could not believe their luck. Cicero was simply too good to be true, and they suspected he was playing a game of double-bluff with them, supplying fake information to confuse and mislead the German Secret Service.

Moyzisch was instructed to find out all he could about their contact in the British Embassy, and soon built up a picture of Cicero. His actual name was Eleyza Bazna. He was an Albanian who had made his way to Turkey and settled in Ankara. Here he found work as a chauffeur, then a butler, and then as a valet to high ranking diplomats. He had worked for the Yugoslav ambassador and a German diplomat who had fired him for reading his mail. Finally, he had found work at the British Embassy as the valet for a high ranking official.

Bazna was very good at his job. He was servile, efficient, and had a knack of being able to second-guess what his master wanted. He was intelligent too, and spoke several languages fluently. When the position of valet at the residence of the ambassador Sir Hughe Knatchbull-Hugesson came up, Bazna got the job.

What Sir Hughe didn't know was that his new manservant had several interests which were to prove quite counter-productive. One was photography, another was Mara, a maid at the Embassy, and the third was snooping around in Embassy files. When Bazna discovered how easy this was, it became a full time passion.

Bazna found out that his new master was a man of punctilious habits. Everything in Sir Hughe's life was run like clockwork. He liked to bathe morning and evening, play the piano after lunch, and have his meals at exact times of the day. When he went out in his purple Rolls-Royce, he knew exactly when he was leaving and when he would return.

Another of Sir Hughe's habits could not have been more accommodating – he liked to read top secret documents in his residence, and kept them in a safe there.

One evening, while Sir Hughe was having his bath, Bazna slipped into his bedroom, on the excuse of laying out his evening clothes, and made a wax impression of the safe key. He then had a replica key made up by a friend. After that, everything

Sir Hughe kept in his safe was given a thorough read by his manservant.

Such a routine was perfect, and the more Bazna snooped, the more daring he became. On one occasion, after Sir Hughe had taken a sleeping pill, Bazna even read and photographed his secret papers on a bedside table.

And what secrets they were! Plans to launch air attacks from Turkey against Nazi ally Romania ... Details of meetings between the American president Franklin Roosevelt, British Prime Minister Winston Churchill, and Soviet leader Joseph Stalin ... best of all for the Germans, Bazna passed on news of the forthcoming Allied invasion of Europe from England to France. Bazna even gave the Nazis its codename – "Operation Overlord".

But, bizarrely, the Nazis still believed such information was too good to be true. Although they thought Bazna was genuine, they assumed the information he was supplying was fake – deliberately planted by British intelligence for him to find and pass on to the Germans.

Bazna cared little for what the Germans did with his information, and even less for what they thought of it – just as long as the bank notes kept coming in. The money was piling up. He made no great effort to hide it, and kept it under his bedroom carpet.

Not all of his ill-gotten gains were saved for a rainy day. Bazna began to spend extravagantly. A country cottage was rented and equipped with every modern convenience. In another alarming breach of secrecy, Bazna even called it "Villa Cicero" after his German code name, and had a little plaque with this put up above the door. He and girlfriend Mara became regular customers at the ABC Store on Ataturk Boulevard – the most fashionable shop in all of Turkey. Their clothes and jewels would have shamed high society socialites.

Moyzisch became irritated with the way Bazna flaunted his wealth, especially when he began to wear a gold watch. Even Mara, who believed he was working for the Turks, started to chide him.

"People are going to start to wonder about how we can afford such wonderful clothes. You're just a valet after all."

"Don't you worry," he smiled. "They're all too stupid."

But they weren't. Curiously, it was the Turks who first started to take an interest in Bazna. They were neutral in the war. As the conflict dragged on, they began to wonder which side it would best suit their own interests to support. One night, after Bazna had dropped off more film at the German Embassy, and Moyzisch was driving him home, they noticed a large black car was following them. Moyzisch slowed, the car slowed. Moyzisch speeded up, the car speeded up. Desperate to shake them off, Moyzisch hit the accelerator and sped through Ankara's fashionable boulevards at a death-defying 190kmph (120mph).

Later that week, Moyzisch bumped into a Turkish official.

"My dear man," said the Turk, "you really are a most reckless driver. You should take more care – especially at night."

It was a warning, and the first hint that Bazna's spying days were numbered.

More alarming events followed. At the British Embassy a team of security experts arrived to install a security system on the ambassador's secret documents. But Bazna heard Sir Hughe discussing the system with one of these men, and was able to work out a way of bypassing it.

Secrets still continued to flow from the British Embassy to Germany, but Bazna was about to be given away by a spy of far greater daring than he. In the German Foreign Ministry worked Fritz Kolbe, a German who hated the Nazis. Kolbe had direct access to all the material that Cicero was supplying to the Germans in Ankara, and he alerted the Americans. The Americans then told the British that they must have a spy on the loose inside their Embassy.

But still British intelligence could not establish Cicero's identity. His eventual betrayer came from within the German Embassy. Moyzisch had a surly, deeply inefficient secretary named Nellie Kapp. She was blonde, 20 years old, and pouted and sulked her way through the working day. She was so lazy that Moyzisch really wanted to get rid of her – the only reason he didn't was that her father was a high-ranking German diplomat.

But curiously, Nellie, for all her faults, did at least show quite an interest in Moyzisch's work. This was because Nellie was also a spy. She worked for the American Office for Strategic Services (OSS) and had had a key cut to fit Moyzisch's safe. She too photographed everything that passed through it. Before long, she had a very good idea that Cicero was Eleyza Bazna.

❖

By the end of March 1944, Nellie had done her job, and decided it was time to escape. After all, if staff at the German Embassy discovered she had been spying on them, she would be tortured and then shot. She cut her hair, dyed it black, and took a plane out of Turkey.

Meanwhile, the British secret service was still not quite sure Bazna was their man, so they set a trap. One night a British security officer, Sir John Dashwood, settled down in Sir Hughe's office with a glass of whisky. He switched the lights off and waited. Soon enough, the door opened, the light came on, and there stood Bazna, key in hand. The two men looked at each other. Not a word was said. Then Bazna turned and left. It was all over.

Bazna could not be arrested, as he had broken no Turkish law. After a furious row with a spluttering, highly indignant Sir Hughe, he rounded up his possessions, including all the money under his carpet. Then he left the Embassy for good, to lay low in one of Ankara's more exclusive districts.

Moyzisch, meanwhile, was having a very uncomfortable time. His secretary had vanished under extremely suspicious circumstances, and now his best agent had been uncovered. His masters in Berlin were extremely displeased, and had sent him a stream of telegrams demanding his immediate return to Germany. Moyzisch feared for his life. To buy some time, he telegraphed back that he was ill, and could not travel. Shortly afterward, he received a phone call at his home.

"I'm calling on behalf of the British," said a mysterious voice. "If you go back to Germany you will be shot. Come over to us and save your life."

It was a terrible dilemma to be in, and Moyzisch was reluctant to betray his country. He was a loyal Nazi who had joined the party before Hitler came to power. Even now, he still believed in the Nazi's evil cause. But, fortunately for him, he never had to make the decision. Shortly after, the Allies did indeed invade France, as Cicero had predicted, and the war turned very definitely against Germany. The Turks took this as a cue to join the Allies. All German diplomats, including Moyzisch, were arrested and detained for the rest of the war.

Afterwards

Bazna was extremely pleased with himself. He was still alive, and he was fabulously rich. He took himself, and £300,000, off to Portugal, and then to South America. But here the world turned sour. Bankers turned up at a luxury villa Bazna had rented, and told him that all the banknotes he had placed with them were counterfeit.

Bazna took the news well. He laughed out loud at the Germans' deception. They had decided his information was useless, and they were not going to pay real money for it. But what followed was far from funny, at least for him. Bazna was arrested, and sent to prison for passing forged banknotes. When he was released he headed for Germany, and asked the then West German government to compensate him for his lost "earnings". Unsurprisingly, his request was not successful. He died, lonely and poverty stricken, in Istanbul in 1971.

Ludwig Moyzisch did rather better after the war. He gave evidence at the Nuremberg trials of Nazi war criminals and then returned to civilian life in Austria. Here he took up his bogus embassy alias for real – becoming an export manager for a textile firm. He wrote a book, *Operation Cicero*, about his spying activities, which was later made into a film called *Five Fingers*, starring James Mason.

Love conquers all, or does it?

It all seemed too good to be true. On August 12, 1961, Bogdan Stashinsky, the Soviet Union's greatest Cold War assassin, arrived at West Berlin's police headquarters and gave himself up. That evening, Stashinsky was grilled by an astonished group of high-ranking intelligence officers. The story he had to tell was not a pretty one.

Stashinsky was born in the Ukraine in 1931, when it was part of the Soviet Union. Many Ukrainians wanted independence and were in revolt against Soviet rule. Among them were members of Stashinsky's own family. Bogdan was different. He was a committed communist and to show his dedication he betrayed his relatives.

The authorities were impressed, and Stashinsky was soon recruited to the KGB, the Soviet Union's intelligence service. After two years training, he was given a variety of undercover jobs, hunting down anti-Communists in Soviet-occupied Eastern Europe. The KGB watched the progress of their young recruit with interest. He was good enough to be assigned the riskiest of jobs. In 1957 he was given a mission worthy of his talents – the assassination of Ukrainian resistance leader, Lev Rebet.

The KGB called Rebet the "Sly Fox" and he was a formidable opponent. Little was known about him. All Stashinsky had to go on was that he ran his resistance organization from Munich, an area of Germany that was outside the control of the Soviet Union. His secret headquarters were in a building known as "the bunker". He was a powerful man, quick on his feet, who wore glasses and hid his shaven head under a beret. He ran his organization with an iron fist. Anyone Rebet suspected of being a Soviet spy was shot without hesitation.

Unperturbed, Stashinsky flew into Munich and set to work. He began to stalk known meeting places of Ukrainian exiles, and within a few days he was certain he had identified Rebet. Now all he had to do was kill him.

The weapon Stashinsky intended to use was a newly developed gas gun. It was a light metal tube which fired a poisonous spray which would kill within 90 seconds. The spray left no trace, and if used effectively, would give the impression that its victim had suffered a heart attack. The poisonous gas was so dangerous that Stashinsky had to take an antidote pill before he fired the gun, in case he caught a whiff of it.

It worked like a dream. Stashinsky caught up with Rebet on the stairway of an office block. He walked past him, hiding the gun in a bag of sausages, and squirted him with one swift movement. Rebet staggered back, and fell down the stairs. By the time his body was found, Stashinsky had slipped quietly away.

Stashinsky was hailed as a hero and rewarded with a special KGB banquet. A year later, the Soviet authorities decided another Ukrainian exile in Munich needed to be assassinated. His name was Stefan Bandera, and Stashinsky was the obvious man for the job.

One autumn day Bandera returned to his apartment, loaded down with groceries. As he fumbled with his door lock, a stranger approached. It was Stashinsky. He smiled and asked Bandera if his door key worked. Bandera looked puzzled, but saw the gas gun too late to react. Stashinsky fired it straight into his face, then calmly walked away. But this assassination was not so smooth.

Bandera staggered off to get help, and died on the way to hospital. The West German police were in no doubt that he had been murdered.

Discreetly or not, Stashinsky had done his job. Again, he was hailed as a hero, and given the KGB's highest award for bravery, the Order of the Red Banner. But just as his career was going so well, Stashinsky ruined it. While on assignment in Soviet-controlled East Berlin, he fell in love with a 21-year-old German hairdresser named Inge Pohl.

The KGB were appalled. They thought a love match from within the KGB would be far more suitable for their star assassin. But Stashinsky had made up his mind. The couple were married and he brought his new bride to live with him in Moscow.

Falling in love seemed to have mellowed Stashinsky. He confessed all to Inge and told her his work now sickened him. She was appalled and encouraged her husband to give up his grisly profession. She also told him she hated living in Moscow, and openly suggested the two of them defect to West Germany.

Alas, the KGB were watching Stashinsky and his new wife very closely – so closely, in fact, that they had bugged the couple's apartment, and were opening their mail. When Stashinsky found this out he was furious. The row he had with his commanding officer ended his career.

Inge, now pregnant, returned to her parents in East Berlin. Stashinsky was refused permission to follow, and told he must remain in the Soviet Union for the next seven years. A child was born, but died six months later. In these tragic circumstances the KGB allowed Stashinsky to visit his wife in Berlin, and attend the funeral.

It was too good an opportunity to miss. During the visit both Stashinsky and Inge slipped away. Using false papers they entered West Berlin, where Stashinsky gave himself up to the police. Here he confessed to the murders of Rebet and Bandera, and a high profile trial followed. In 1962 he was sentenced to 13 years in prison. But the spy who had given up his job for love was in for a shock. Inge Pohl divorced him in 1964.

Afterwards

Stashinsky was released from prison after serving only four years of his sentence. He vanished soon afterwards. It is thought he was taken to the United States where he could assume a new identity, far away from the KGB assassins who surely be sent to hunt him down. There is speculation that his ex-wife also joined him in the USA, and that their divorce was just a ruse.

Also from Usborne True Stories

TRUE ESCAPE STORIES

Paul Dowswell

Finally, the night had come to take a trip to the roof. Morris spent the day beforehand trying to curb his restlessness. What if the way up to the roof was blocked? What if the ventilator motor had been replaced after all? All their painstaking work would be wasted. The 12 year sentence stretched out before him. Then another awful thought occurred. The holes in the wall would be discovered eventually, and that would mean even more years added on to his sentence.

As well as locked doors, high walls and barbed wire, many escaping prisoners also face savage dogs and armed guards who shoot to kill. From Alcatraz to Devil's Island, read the extraordinary tales of people who risked their lives for their freedom.

Also from Usborne True Stories

TRUE
POLAR
ADVENTURES
Paul Dowswell

By day, they pushed on through towering seas, while men not rowing bailed furiously to keep their open boats afloat. By night, they clambered aboard passing ice floes, to shiver in their tents. But one night there was a loud crack, and the ice split through the middle of a tent. Ernest Holness, one of the *Endurance's* strokers, fell through. He floundered in the freezing sea, trapped in his soaking sleeping bag, stunned almost to paralysis by the shock of the icy water.

Guarded by frozen seas and vast fields of snow, the North and South poles are among the world's most mysterious places. But these bleak environments are no place for humans, as the explorers who set out to unearth their secrets have found to their cost.

Shortlisted for the Blue Peter Book Awards 2003

TRUE EVEREST ADVENTURES

Paul Dowswell

Tejbir collapsed soon afterwards, telling Finch and Bruce he had no strength to go on. Defeated, he returned to the tent. Then as Finch and Bruce climbed higher, a terrible wind blew up, making progress extremely slow. At 8,320m (27,300ft) disaster struck. Finch, who was leading the climb, suddenly heard Bruce call out in alarm: "I'm getting no oxygen!" Finch turned to see his companion wavering and about to topple off the mountain.

Everest has fascinated climbers ever since it was first discovered 150 years ago. Since then, over a thousand of them have stood triumphant on its summit. But the frozen bodies that litter its slopes tell another tale of tragedy, misfortune and reckless ambition.

Also from Usborne True Stories

TRUE STORIES OF

CRIME &
DETECTION

GILL HARVEY

On a wind-blasted, stormy night in August
1998, the people who lived next to Hyde
cemetary got the fright of their lives...
a caretaker at the retirement home
overlooking the cemetary saw something
that made his blood run cold.
"There are people with shovels in the
graveyard," he wispered into his telephone,
"and they're digging around the tombs.
Send for the police."
He almost dropped the receiver when he
heard the reply: "But that is the police, sir."

Are the real criminals and detectives anything like the
ones you read about in novels or see on the television?
You can find out in these ten exciting stories. Serial
murderers, art forgers, kidnappers, robbers, runaways
and forensic scientists are all here, as well as cases
of real-life horror that will chill you to the bone.